WAR CRIMES TRIALS AND OTHER ESSAYS

Carlos Whitlock Porter

WAR CRIMES TRIALS AND OTHER ESSAYS
By Carlos Whitlock Porter

ISBN 978-1-593-64054-5

Liberty Bell Publications
PO Box 890
York, SC 29745

http://www.cwporter.com

Table of Contents

ANATOMY OF A NUREMBERG LIAR

In my book *Not Guilty at Nuremberg* I wrote: "Telford Taylor was incapable of repeating the simplest statement truthfully. (See *IMT* XX, 626, the statements of General Manstein, compared with Taylor's 'quotation' from Manstein (*IMT* XXII, 276)."

The following are "quotations" from Taylor (*Anatomy of the Nuremberg Trials*, Back Bay Books, Little Brown & Co., paperback, by arrangement with Alfred A. Knopf, Inc. 1992), compared with actual quotations from the Nuremberg Trial transcript (*IMT*).

There were 13 Nuremberg Trials. Taylor's book is about the first one only. Even the title is a fraud. It is accurate with regard to the first trial only insofar as Taylor describes the sexual promiscuity and party atmosphere which pervaded the entire prosecution staff, including himself, but with the exception of the Russians.

MANSTEIN ACCORDING TO TAYLOR

"We are not concerned here with the ordinary German conscript who made up the bulk of the Wehrmacht. We are concerned entirely with professional soldiers, and with the most zealous, ambitious, and able German officers in the business. Most of them chose a military career because it was in their blood; as Manstein put it, 'they considered the glory of war as something great.' They slaved at it and were devoted to their profession, and if they reached the status of commander-in-chief, they were, like Manstein, proud that an army had been entrusted to them." (*IMT* XXII, 276)

And again: "For some of the generals, war was ingrained. Manstein 'considered the glory of war as something great.' " (*Anatomy*, p. 531)

WHAT MANSTEIN ACTUALLY SAID

"VON MANSTEIN: I have been a soldier for 40 years. I come from a family of soldiers and I have grown up with military conceptions.

"The example from among my nearest relatives which I had before me was Hindenburg. We young officers naturally considered the

5

glory of war as something great, and I do not wish to deny that I was proud when during this war an army was entrusted to me. But our ideal, and that applies to my comrades too, did not lie in the conduct of war, but in the education of our youth to be honorable men and decent soldiers. Under our orders these youths went to their death by the million.

"And if I may say something personal: My eldest son died as a lieutenant in the infantry, when he was 19; two of my brothers-in-law, who grew up in my house, died as young officers; my best comrades in this war, my young adjutant and my young chauffeur, were killed. Nearly all the sons of my brothers and sisters were killed. That we, the old soldiers, should have led into war for a criminal purpose that youth of ours which was so dear to us, would far exceed any wickedness of which man could be thought capable. It is possible that a man without a family and without tradition, who is obsessed with fanatical belief in a higher mission, may go beyond the limits of human law, but we, the old soldiers, purely from a human point of view, would not have been able to do so. We could not lead our youth into crime." (*IMT* XX, 626)

RIBBENTROP ACCORDING TO TAYLOR

"Joachim von Ribbentrop's statement was angry and stupid, but it is hard to see what he could have said to better his position. 'I am held responsible', said he, 'for the conduct of a foreign policy which was determined by another'. True, but not enough to mitigate the willing support of Hitler's policies from the annexation of Austria to the eventual collapse of the Thousand Year Reich. Ribbentrop purported to 'deplore the atrocious crimes which became known to me here', but was silent about his full participation in the deportation of Jews from France and the other German occupied countries to the extermination camps in Eastern Europe. With a final snarl, Ribbentrop declared: 'The only thing of which I consider myself guilty before my people – and before this Tribunal – is that my aspirations in foreign policy remained without success.' To which the listener can only reply: 'Thank God!' " (*Anatomy*, p. 537)

[Note: The quotation given three lines above is incorrect: it should read: "*not* before this Tribunal".]

WHAT RIBBENTROP ACTUALLY SAID

"This Trial was to be conducted for the purpose of discovering the historical truth. From the point of view of German foreign policy I can only say:

"This Trial will go down in history as a model example of how, while appealing to hitherto unknown legal formulas and the spirit of fairness, one can evade the cardinal problems of 25 years of the gravest human history.

"If the roots of our trouble lie in the Treaty of Versailles – and they do lie there – was it really to the purpose to prevent a discussion about a treaty which the intelligent men even among its authors had characterized as the source of future trouble, while the wisest were already predicting from which of the faults of Versailles a new world war would arise?

"I have devoted more than twenty years of my life to the elimination of this evil, with the result that foreign statesmen who know about this today write in their affidavits that they did not believe me. They ought to have written that in the interests of their own country they were not prepared to believe me. I am held responsible for the conduct of a foreign policy which was determined by another. I knew only this much of it, that it never concerned itself with plans of a world domination, but rather, for example, with the elimination of the consequences of Versailles and with the food problems of the German people.

"If I deny that this German foreign policy planned and prepared for a war of aggression, that is not an excuse on my part. The truth of this is proved by the strength that we developed in the course of the second World War and the fact how weak we were at the beginning of this war.

"History will believe us when I say that we would have prepared a war of aggression immeasurably better if we had actually intended one. What we intended was to look after our elementary necessities of life, in the same way that England looked after her own interests in order to make one-fifth of the world subject to her, and in the same way that the United States brought an entire continent and Russia brought the largest inland territory of the world under their hegemony. The only difference between the policies of these countries as compared with ours is that we demanded parcels of land such as Danzig and the Corridor which were taken from us against all rights, whereas the other powers are accustomed to thinking only in terms of continents.

"Before the establishment of the Charter of this Tribunal, even the signatory powers of the London Agreement must have had different views about international law and policy than they have today. When I went to see Marshal Stalin in Moscow in 1939, he did not discuss with me the possibility of a peaceful settlement of the German-Polish conflict within the framework of the Kellogg-Briand Pact; but rather he hinted that if in addition to half of Poland and the Baltic countries he did not receive Lithuania and the harbor of Libau, I might as well return home.

"In 1939 the waging of war was obviously not yet regarded as an international crime against peace, otherwise I could not explain Stalin's telegram at the conclusion of the Polish campaign, which read, I quote:

" 'The friendship of Germany and the Soviet Union, based on the blood which they have shed together, has every prospect of being a firm and lasting one.'

"Here I should like to emphasize and stress the fact that even I ardently desired this friendship at that time. Of this friendship there remains today only the primary problem for Europe and the world: Will Asia dominate Europe, or will the Western Powers be able to stem or even push back the influence of the Soviets at the Elbe, at the Adriatic coast, and at the Dardanelles?

"In other words, practically speaking: Great Britain and the United States today face the same dilemma as Germany faced at the time when I was carrying on negotiations with Russia. For my country's sake I hope with all my heart that they may be more successful in their results.

"Now what has actually been proved in this Trial about the criminal character of German foreign policy? That out of more than 300 Defense documents which were submitted 150 were rejected without cogent reasons. That the files of the enemy, and even of the Germans, were inaccessible to the Defense. That Churchill's friendly hint to me that if Germany became too strong she would be destroyed, is declared irrelevant in judging the motives of German foreign policy before this forum. A revolution does not become more comprehensible if it is considered from the point of view of a conspiracy.

"Fate made me one of the exponents of this revolution. I deplore the atrocious crimes which became known to me here and which besmirch this revolution. But I cannot measure all of them according to puritanical standards, and the less so since I have seen that even the enemy, in spite of their total victory, was neither able nor willing to prevent atrocities of the most extensive kind.

"One can regard the theory of the conspiracy as one will, but from the point of view of the critical observer it is only a makeshift solution. Anybody who has held a decisive position in the Third Reich knows that it simply represents a historical falsehood, and the author of the Charter of this Tribunal has only proved with his invention from what background he derived his thinking.

"I might just as well assert that the signatory powers of this Charter had formed a conspiracy for the suppression of the primary needs of a highly developed, capable, and courageous nation. When I look back upon my actions and my desires, then I can conclude only this: The only thing of which I consider myself guilty before my people – not before this Tribunal – is that my aspirations in foreign policy remained without success." (*IMT* XXII, 373-375)

HESS ACCORDING TO TAYLOR

"But after reading for twenty minutes or more, Hess lapsed into incoherent repetition, for example:

" 'However, at that time the world was confronted with an insoluble riddle, the same riddle which confronts it today with regard to the happenings in the German concentration camps. At that time the English people were confronted with an incomprehensible riddle, the same riddle which today confronts the German people with regard to the happenings in the German concentration camps.'

"That last sentence was then repeated, substituting 'South African' concentration camps, and then again, substituting 'Reich Cabinet' for 'English people.' " (*Anatomy*, p. 536)

WHAT HESS ACTUALLY SAID

"It is a historical fact that a monument was erected for 26,370 Boer women and children who died in British concentration camps, and who for the most part died of hunger. Many Englishmen at that time, among others, Lloyd George, protested strongly against these happenings in British concentration camps, and likewise an English eye witness, Miss Emily Hopfords [Correct name: Emily Hobhouse. This error may be due to an incorrect stenographic notation. Many of Hobhouse's books are available at reasonable prices from Amazon. – C.P.].

"However, at that time the world was confronted with an insoluble riddle, the same riddle which confronts it today with regard to the happenings in the German concentration camps.

"At that time the English people were confronted with an incomprehensible riddle, the same riddle which today confronts the German people with regard to the happenings in the German concentration camps. Indeed, at that time, the British Government itself was confronted with a riddle regarding the happenings in the South African concentration camps, with the same riddle which today confronts the members of the Reich Cabinet and the other defendants, here and in other trials, regarding the happenings in the German concentration camps." (*IMT* XXII, 371)

And finally, once again:

MANSTEIN ACCORDING TO TAYLOR

"I then offered in evidence the new document of November 20, 1941, signed by Manstein, which reads in part:
" 'Since 22 June the German people have been engaged in a life-and-death struggle against the Bolshevist system.
" 'This struggle is not being carried on against the Soviet armed forces alone in the established form laid down by European rules of warfare... [Note deletions.]
" 'The Jewish-Bolshevist system must be exterminated once and for all. Never again must it encroach upon our European living space.
" 'The German soldier has therefore not only the task of crushing the military potential of this system. He comes also as the bearer of a racial concept and as the avenger of all the cruelties which have been perpetrated on him and on the German people... [Note deletions.]
" 'The soldier must appreciate the necessity for the harsh punishment of Jewry, the spiritual bearer of the Bolshevist terror. This is also necessary in order to nip in the bud all uprisings, which are mostly plotted by Jews.'
"Manstein feebly insisted that he could not remember the document, but admitted that he had signed it. His credibility was shattered..." (*Anatomy*, p. 520)

[Note: The passage continues with much bragging about Taylor's immense cleverness.]

WHAT MANSTEIN ACTUALLY SAID

"COL. TAYLOR: ...I will now ask that the witness be shown a new Document 4064-PS, USA-927.

[Note: The document is a mimeograph with a mimeographed signature. There was never the slightest pretense that it bore Manstein's original signature or that Manstein recognized it as such.]

"Will you look at this order, Witness, and tell us if this is not a document issued out of your headquarters and signed with your facsimile signature, on 20 November 1941? It is already in the record.

"VON MANSTEIN: I must first read the document thoroughly. I do not recollect this order.

"COL. TAYLOR: Is that your signature?

"VON MANSTEIN: It looks like it, but I must first of all read the order to see whether I gave it or not.

"COL. TAYLOR: The document, as indicated at the top of the page, states 'XXX. Corps Ref. IC.' That is the intelligence office, is it not?

"VON MANSTEIN: Yes, that is the name of the office that dealt with enemy intelligence and countering enemy espionage. It has nothing to do with Secret Service as such.

"COL. TAYLOR: And just below there is a stamp of the 72nd Division, 27 November 1941, Diary Number IC, and at the left it appears to have been issued by Army High Command XI at army headquarters, 20 November 1941. Secret. I quote:

" 'Since 22 June the German people have been engaged in a life-and-death struggle against the Bolshevist system.

" 'This struggle is not being carried on against the Soviet Armed Forces alone in the established form laid down by European rules of warfare.

" 'Behind the front too, the fighting continues. Partisan snipers dressed as civilians attack single soldiers and small units and try to disrupt our supplies by sabotage with mines and infernal machines. Bolshevists left behind keep the population freed from Bolshevism in a state of unrest by means of terror and attempt thereby to sabotage the political and economic pacification of the country. Harvests and factories are destroyed and the city population in particular is thereby ruthlessly delivered to starvation.

" 'Jewry constitutes the middleman between the enemy in the rear and the remainder of the Red Armed Forces which is still fighting, and the Red leadership. More strongly than in Europe it holds all the key positions in the political leadership and administration, controls commerce and trades, and further forms the nucleus for all unrest and possible uprisings.

" 'The Jewish-Bolshevist system must be exterminated ["ausgerottet werden" – C.P.] once and for all. Never again must it encroach upon our European living space.

" 'The German soldier has therefore not only the task of crushing the military potential of this system. He comes also as the bearer of a racial concept and as the avenger of all the cruelties which have been perpetrated on him and on the German people.

" 'The fight behind the lines is not yet being taken seriously enough. Active co-operation of all soldiers must be demanded in the disarming of the population, the control and arrest of all roving soldiers and civilians, and the removal of Bolshevist symbols.

" 'Every instance of sabotage must be punished immediately with the severest measures and all signs thereof must be reported.

" 'The food situation at home makes it essential that the troops should as far as possible be fed off the land and that furthermore the largest possible stocks should be placed at the disposal of the homeland. Particularly in enemy cities a large part of the population will have to go hungry. Nevertheless nothing which the homeland has sacrificed itself to contribute may, out of a misguided sense of humanity, be given to prisoners or to the population unless they are in the service of the German Wehrmacht.

" 'The soldier must appreciate the necessity for the harsh punishment of Jewry, the spiritual bearer of the Bolshevist terror. This is also necessary in order to nip in the bud all uprisings which are mostly plotted by Jews.

" 'It is the task of leaders of all grades to keep constantly alive the meaning of the present struggle. Support for the Bolshevist fight behind the front by way of thoughtlessness must be prevented.

" 'The non-Bolshevist Ukrainians, Russians, and Tartars are expected to acknowledge the New Order. The nonparticipation of numerous alleged anti-Soviet elements must give place to a definite decision in favor of active co-operation against Bolshevism. Where it does not exist it must be forced by suitable measures.

" 'Voluntary co-operation in the reconstruction of occupied territory is an absolute necessity for the achievement of our economic and political aims.

" 'It demands as a primary condition the just treatment of all non-Bolshevist sections of the population, some of whom have for years fought heroically against Bolshevism.

" 'The ruling of this country demands from us results, strictness with ourselves, and submergence of the individual. The bearing of every soldier is constantly under observation. It can make enemy propaganda ineffective or give it a springboard. If the soldier in the country takes from the peasant the last cow, the breeding sow, the last chicken, or the seed, then no restoration of the economy can be achieved.

" 'In all measures it is not the momentary success which is decisive. All measures must, therefore, be judged by their lasting effectiveness.

" 'Respect for religious customs, particularly those of Mohammedan Tartars, must be demanded.

" 'In pursuance of these concepts and other measures to be carried out by the later administration, such as the enlightenment of the population by propaganda, encouragement of personal initiative, for instance by rewards, significance must be given to extensive collaboration of the population for combating the partisans and to the development of the local Auxiliary Police.

" 'For the achievement of this object the following must be demanded:

" 'Active co-operation of soldiers in the fight against the enemy in the rear; no soldier to go about alone at night; all motor vehicles to be equipped with adequate armament; a self-assured, but not overbearing attitude on the part of all soldiers; restraint towards prisoners and the other sex; no waste of food.

" 'Severest action to be taken: against despotism and self-seeking; against lawlessness and lack of discipline; against every transgression of the honor of a soldier.'

"And it appears that it is to be distributed right down to the regiments and independent battalions.

"Did you not issue that order as a result of the suggestion which came to you together with the Reichenau order? The resemblance between the two is, to say the least, striking and the date is about the same.

"VON MANSTEIN: I must say that this order escapes my memory entirely. According to the signature and particularly what is contained in the last part, I must assume that the order is genuine and has been issued by me. Whether it was given on the strength of the Reichenau order or not I cannot possibly tell you now. But I do want to point out to you that if it says here that the system must be exterminated, then that is extermination of the Bolshevik system, but not the extermination of human beings.

"I must further point out to you that nowhere is there mention of collaboration with the SD, a collaboration which, because of the lack of knowledge we had of the doings of the SD, was out of the question in this area. I must point out to you the demands which I made of my soldiers – namely, that they must not take the last cow away from the farmers, that they must respect religious customs, that they must respect the other sex and that, on the other hand, they naturally must not be careless of the danger of partisans, as unfortunately the German soldier always was. I point out to you that any wilfulness and any self-seeking is expressly prohibited, also any barbarism, any lack of discipline, and most of all any breach of the honor of a soldier.

"COL. TAYLOR: You were asked about the General Reichenau order before the Commissioner, were you not? You were asked, and I read on page... I will have to find the page, Your Honor. I have a typed copy here, Your Honor, without the final page reference.

"Were you questioned before the Commissioner as follows:

" 'You know the order of General Reichenau in which he stated that there should be no consideration shown to the civilian population? Did you see the order, and did it have any influence whatever on your attitude and that of your troops to the civilian population?'

"And you answered:

" 'We were informed of this order upon the suggestion of the Führer, but none of the other leaders were of the same opinion as Reichenau, and it was never carried out, especially in my area.'

"You had not forgotten the Reichenau order, had you?

"VON MANSTEIN: I had quite forgotten the Reichenau order until it appeared amongst the documents here, and I have no recollection especially of this order of mine. After all, that is not surprising, because that is a number of years ago, and during these years I have signed hundreds, if not thousands, of orders, and I cannot possibly remember every detail.

"COL. TAYLOR: Did you sign a lot of orders like this one? Is that why you have such difficulty remembering it?

"VON MANSTEIN: No, I certainly have not signed a lot of orders like this one, but I have signed a lot of other orders. Above all, I had to write and read a large number of reports and if I forgot this order, a fact which I admit, it is not surprising. I only know that this order, at any rate, as opposed to the Reichenau order, very strongly emphasizes the demands which I made for decent behavior on the part of my soldiers. That, after all, is the important point.

"COL. TAYLOR: You remember the Reichenau order, and you remember that it was suggested that you pass it down, and the only thing you have forgotten is that you did?

"VON MANSTEIN: No, I said that I remembered the Reichenau order only when I came here, when it was shown to me among other documents and when I was before the Commission; also that, try as I may, I did not recollect giving that order. If I had done so, I would most certainly have mentioned it, because the first part of the order is absolutely contrary to my conceptions.

"COL. TAYLOR: You think that you wrote the second part and not the first?

"VON MANSTEIN: I did not write the order at all myself. Very probably the order was shown to me in draft and then I signed it. If the first part mentions the fight against the system and the extermination of the system as well as the fight against the Jews as the supporters of the partisan movement, in the last analysis it had its proper justification. But all that has nothing to do with the fact that Jews were to be exterminated. They were to be excluded, and the system was to be removed. That is the point that matters.

"COL. TAYLOR: I think you told the Tribunal a few minutes ago that you did not even know that Jews were likely to be opposed to the new administration. It looks as if you very definitely wrote that for the attention of your soldiers, doesn't it?

"VON MANSTEIN: No, I did not know that, and this order that Jews were to be exterminated cannot possibly recall it to my memory because it does not mention a word that the Jews were to be exterminated. It merely says that the system is to be exterminated.

"COL. TAYLOR: I call your attention to the paragraph:

" 'The soldier must appreciate the necessity for harsh punishment of Jewry, the spiritual supporters of the Bolshevist terror. This is also necessary in order to nip in the bud all uprisings, which are mostly plotted by Jews.'

"Now, I ask you, Witness, the Einsatzkommandos could not have liquidated Jews without the soldiers knowing something about it, could they? Is that true?

"VON MANSTEIN: That is perfectly possible, because as Ohlendorf has described it, the shootings of the Jews were camouflaged as 'resettlement.' The Jews were taken to desolate places and were shot and buried there, so that it is quite certain that the commanding authorities had no knowledge of that. Naturally, it is possible that some soldier or other, quite by accident, may have seen such an execution, and there is in fact evidence of it. I remember in the Russian indictment the description by an engineer who was present during such a shooting, I believe in the Ukraine in the vicinity of Zhitomir or Rovno, and described it in most horrible terms.

[Note: Manstein is referring to Document PS-2992, an affidavit by Hermann Friedrich Gräbe, read aloud in court. Gräbe never appeared personally to testify.]

"One can only ask why that man did not report it to the command post. The answer is that the fear of the SS was such that this man, instead of reporting this dirty business, kept it to himself and now comes out with it. At that time – it was not in my area, but somewhere else – had he gone to some high military command post and described these events, then I am convinced that the commander in question would have intervened; and then, of course, we would also have heard of it. But the fact is that we did not hear about it.

"COL. TAYLOR: One more question on this subject, Your Honor.

"*[Turning to the witness.]*

"Witness, isn't it true that this order is very carefully drawn so that the troops would understand and, shall we say, sympathize with what the Einsatzkommandos were doing in the way of mass extermination of Jews?

"VON MANSTEIN: You mean my order?

"COL. TAYLOR: Yes.

"VON MANSTEIN: No. There can be no question that I at any time urged my troops, even between the lines, to co-operate in such methods. How could I have concluded by stressing the soldier's honor?

"COL. TAYLOR: My Lord, the Prosecution has no further questions of this witness.

"THE PRESIDENT: We will adjourn now." (*IMT* XX, 641-646)

[Note: That Manstein got much the better of the prosecution is apparent when one reads the testimony as a whole, including the direct examination, not reproduced here.]

KALTENBRUNNER ACCORDING TO TAYLOR

"Kaltenbrunner now testified that he had no correspondence with the burgomaster of Vienna...

[Note: This is untrue. Kaltenbrunner admitted that they were close friends and corresponded frequently.]

"Amen then read to him a letter signed by hand 'Yours Kaltenbrunner'... Amen abandoned all pretense of questioning: 'Is it not a fact that you are simply lying about your signature on this letter in the same way that you are lying to the Tribunal about almost everything else you have given testimony about?' Kaltenbrunner lost control and shouted 'for a whole year I have been submitted to this insult of being called a liar.' He spoke incoherently, saying that his mother 'who died in 1943 was called a whore and many other things were hurled at me.' Lawrence told Kaltenbrunner to try to restrain himself..." (*Anatomy*, pp. 361-362)

WHAT KALTENBRUNNER ACTUALLY SAID

"KALTENBRUNNER: Mr. Prosecutor, for a whole year I have had to submit to this insult of being called a liar. For a whole year I have been interrogated hundreds of times both here and in London, and I have been insulted in this way and even much worse. My mother, who died in 1943, was called a whore, and many other similar things were hurled at me. This term is not new to me but I should like to state that in a matter of this kind I certainly would not tell an untruth, when I claim to be believed by this Tribunal in far more important matters.

"COL. AMEN: I am suggesting, Defendant, that when your testimony is so directly contrary to that of 20 or 30 other witnesses and even more documents, it is almost an incredible thing you should be telling the truth and that every witness and every document should be false. Do you not agree to that proposition?

"KALTENBRUNNER: No. I cannot admit that because I have had the feeling each time a document has been submitted to me today, that it could at first glance be immediately refuted by me in its most vital points. I ask, and I hope that the Tribunal will allow me, to refer to single points and to come into closer contact with individual witnesses, so that I may defend myself to the last. Throughout the preliminary interrogations your colleague has always adopted the attitude unjustly that I was refuting and opposing insignificant points. The conception of expeditious trial proceedings has been unknown to me in this form. Had he talked to me in broad lines about the ways to find out the real truth, I believe he would have sooner arrived at considerably larger and more important issues. I am perhaps the only defendant who, on receiving the Indictment and being asked, 'Are you ready to make any further statements to the Prosecution,' stated 'Immediately,' and I signed it – please produce the signature – 'from today on after receiving the Indictment I am at the disposal of the Prosecution for any information.' Is it not so? Please confirm it. That gentleman *[pointing to an interpreter]* interrogated me. I have always been ready, that is, during the last 5 months, to give information on any question, but I have not been asked any more." (*IMT* XI, 348-349)

[Note: Is this incoherent? The document, 3803-PS, is Kaltenbrunner's "letter" to the Mayor of Vienna, SS-Brigadeführer Blaschke, dated 30 June 1944. The letter was then forwarded to the Tribunal accompanied by a "cover letter" from the succeeding Mayor, Körner (no first name given), dated 11 March 1946. Typeset versions of both letters are reproduced in Volume XXXIII 167-169 of the *IMT* document volumes. Having examined photocopies of the originals of both letters very carefully with a magnifying glass, I am absolutely certain that they were both produced on the same typewriter. If this is so, Kaltenbrunner's "letter" would be one of the rare forgeries of an "original document" bearing an "original signature". Since Kaltenbrunner's "letter" purports to be an "original document", it seems strange that its credibility should have to be shored up by a "letter" from the person claiming to have "found" it, particularly when thousands of unsigned "copies" of other documents (such as the Einsatzgruppen reports) were accepted into evidence with nothing more than a rubber stamp and signature from a Soviet army officer or official. One gets the impression the prosecution felt very uneasy about this document for some reason best known to themselves. It should be noted that we do not even know for certain who "Körner" was, or whether he actually wrote the cover letter involved.

In a real trial, Körner would appear as a witness, identify the document, and then submit to cross-examination as to the circumstances under which he found the document. The cover letter was probably produced to evade the possibility that the defence might demand his appearance as a witness, a right to which they would theoretically have been entitled had he signed an affidavit.]

[Note: Kaltenbrunner's "letter" contains a false geographical term:
"VON SCHIRACH: I do not know of the correspondence between the Codefendant Kaltenbrunner and the mayor of Vienna. To my knowledge Camp Strasshof is not within Gau Vienna at all. It is in an altogether different Gau. The designation, 'Vienna-Strasshof,' is, therefore, an error. The border runs in between the two." (*IMT* XIV, 416)]

18

PAUL SCHMIDT ACCORDING TO TAYLOR

"[Ribbentrop] told Admiral Miklos Horthy, Regent of Hungary, that 'Jews must either be exterminated or taken to concentration camps.'

"... Far worse for his defence was his last witness, Paul Otto Schmidt, who had interpreted at many of Hitler's conferences with foreigners and was bright and well informed. His direct testimony gave Ribbentrop no real help..." (*Anatomy*, p. 352)

WHAT PAUL SCHMIDT ACTUALLY SAID

"SCHMIDT: During this conference there had been a certain difficulty, when Hitler insisted that Horthy should proceed more energetically in the Jewish question, and Horthy answered with some heat, 'But what am I supposed to do? Shall I perhaps beat the Jews to death?'

[Note: The verb is "totschlagen", "to kill". "Totschlag" in law means "manslaughter" or "second-degree murder".]

"Whereupon there was rather a lull, and the Foreign Minister then turned to Horthy and said, 'Yes, there are only two possibilities – either that, or to intern the Jews.' Afterwards he said to me – and this was rather exceptional – that Hitler's demands in this connection might have gone a bit too far." (*IMT* X, 203-204)

[Note: In view of the fact that he considers Schmidt to be a credible witness, Taylor is indulging in something of a half-truth here.]

AUSCHWITZ ACCORDING TO TAYLOR

"Reading de Menthon's (de Menthon was one of the French prosecutors) many passages on Nazi war crimes forty years later reveals a jarring omission of reference to Jews and the Holocaust. In part this is due to the division of evidence, on a West-East basis, between the French and Soviet delegations... Auschwitz is mentioned, but only to observe that many of its inmates were 'sterilized', and that 'the most beautiful women were set apart, artificially sterilized, and then gassed.' " (*Anatomy*, p. 296)

[Note: This bizarre hallucination is a perfect example of the atmosphere of lunacy which pervaded the entire Nuremberg Trial. What is the point of sterilizing people if you are going to gas them afterwards? But the original text is even stupider than Taylor's "quotation", as we shall soon see.]

WHAT THE NUREMBERG TRIAL TRANSCRIPT ACTUALLY SAYS

"At Auschwitz the most beautiful women were set apart, artificially *fertilized*, and then gassed." (*IMT* V, 403)

[Note: This is not a misprint in English. The same passage in the German transcript reads, on page 454, "In Auschwitz wurden die schönsten Frauen abgesondert, künstlich befruchtet [fertilized] und sodann vergast."

Apparently the original was a bit thick – even for Taylor – so he simply faked the quotation. The point is that Taylor cannot be trusted.]

SAUCKEL ACCORDING TO TAYLOR

"Determined to make this jerry-built system work, on January 6, 1943, Sauckel summoned some 800 officials to a meeting in Weimar and told them:

" 'Where the voluntary method fails (and experience shows that it fails [es versagt] everywhere) compulsory service takes its place...

" 'We are going to discard the last remnant of our soft talk about humanitarian ideals. Every additional gun which we procure brings us a moment closer to victory. It is bitter to tear people from their homes, from their children. But we did not want the war. The German child who loses his father at the front, the German wife who mourns her husband killed in battle, suffers far more. Let us disclaim every sentiment now... [Note deletion.]

" 'This is the iron law for the Allocation of Labour for 1943. In a few weeks from now there must no longer be any occupied territory in which compulsory service for Germany is not the most natural thing in the world.' " (*Anatomy*, p. 430)

[Note: Not only is this quotation taken drastically out of context, but Taylor has even gotten the order of paragraphs mixed up! The third paragraph above is actually the second sentence! This is typical of Taylor's sloppiness.

The following is my translation of the entire document, omitting the introduction only.]

WHAT SAUCKEL ACTUALLY SAID

"...1. Where voluntary recruitment fails (and experience shows that it is failing everywhere), compulsory service takes its place. That is now the Iron Law of the year 1943 in the labour service: in a few weeks, there should be no occupied territory in which compulsory service for Germany is not the most natural thing in the world. We will slough off the last dregs of our humanitarian daydreaming. Every additional cannon which we manufacture brings us one minute closer to victory! It is bitter to tear people away from their homes, from their children. But we didn't want the war! The German child who loses his father at the front, the German woman who bewails her fallen husband, suffers much more deeply. Let us renounce all false sentimentality here.

"2. Even though I wish to come to terms with the severity of the war, I nevertheless request that under no circumstances may the German nation, the name of the Führer, my own name, or even your names, be exposed to shame. What we must do, will be done. But it will be done so that, with all severity – and I will punish pitilessly where necessary – account is taken of the principles of German correctness. We are not a perverse, bestially-inclined nation whose highest joy is to torment prisoners. With us, everything is done according to regulations, but with chivalry. This chivalry has been proven a thousand times by German soldiers. We are also guided by the recognition here that, in the long run, efficiency in production can only be demanded from foreign workers if they are satisfied with their lot. I will not tolerate men being mistreated. You must compel people to do their duty, you must cart them away under certain circumstances, but you must not commit a fault, you must not torment and play tricks; rather, I hereby make you personally responsible for ensuring the greatest possible comfort for our foreign labour recruits during their transport and in their accommodation, for the purpose of bringing healthy workers to Germany, people who are able to go to work immediately.

"3. As recruitment commissioners in foreign countries, you must under no circumstances whatsoever promise things which are not possible according to the applicable guidelines and regulations, or not practicable due to the war situation. It is much better to go up to persons liable for labour service and tell them 'You must do this, and, in return, you will have the rights of workers working in Germany'. Anyone who works in Germany has a right to life in Germany, even if he is Bolshevik. We will watch strictly to ensure that no shame falls upon the German name in so doing. You may demand every sort of protection from me in your service territory, but not for any crimes. The name of our nation is holy. For the first time in German history, you must represent the principles of German labour for the Reich. Be conscious of this at all times.

"4. For your part, you must tell the truth about labour service in Germany at all times. You of the labour service are an advance troop of German National Socialist propaganda in foreign countries. You must learn to represent our German standpoint, the standpoint of our Führer, our people, and the Reich, in foreign countries. I wish to make you responsible, in addition to your official and professional duties, for being propagandists of the National Socialist life and faith. You must create validity and respect for the true facts.

"5. You must also spread the word in foreign countries that anyone who works properly in Germany will enjoy the best protection for his life and health. This promise must make the rounds in the occupied territories. The sick rate in the camps of Soviet workers working in Germany is less than two percent. That is unequalled! The reason for this is that the Soviet workers are cleanly and hygienically housed, and decently nourished. Carry this out, regardless of all lies. You can and must represent the concept in foreign countries that there has never been a labour service like the one in Germany!

"6. We must also spread the word, as a further promise, that everyone who works in Germany is helping to bring Europe closer to peace, and to eliminate the misery caused by Roosevelt, Churchill, and Stalin from the world. All soldiers and all offices must cooperate in keeping this promise. Anyone who works in Germany is protecting his life, and is working to eliminate mass misery from the world.

"7. Every recruiter is obliged to take care that the recruited workers bring as much food, clothing, and, possibly, bedding, along with them as possible in any way. All useful things must be packed and brought along. We do not have these things in abundance in Germany at the present time.

"8. In no case may sick people, or people who are unable to work, be taken along to work – or children who are unable to work.

"9. The transports must be carefully prepared and cautiously carried out.

"The German labour service, I emphasize once again, must be the best life insurance for foreign peoples. This is how our propaganda should work. That which was not yet good enough, should be improved; that which was better, will be made more perfect by us. I demand this of you, not for ourselves, but for the Führer, for his soldiers, and for our beloved German people." (Defence document Sauckel-82, *IMT* XLI, 226-228, my translation from German.)

FIELD MARSHAL MILCH ACCORDING TO TAYLOR

"Milch floundered from forgetting to lying and ended with a flat denial that he had ever had prisoners of war shot, in the face of his own report:
[Note: It is not his own report. It is a "quotation" from a "photocopy" of unsigned "minutes" of the Central Planning Board that he had ordered the hanging of Russian officers who had tried to escape.]
" 'I wanted them to be hanged in the factory for the others to see.' Milch left the witness chair utterly discredited." (*Anatomy*, p. 324)

WHAT MILCH ACTUALLY SAID

"MR. JUSTICE JACKSON: ... Now, I am still quoting you and I want you to find the entry.
" 'In one case, two Russian officers took off with an airplane but crashed. I ordered that these two men be hanged at once. They were hanged or shot yesterday. I left that to the SS. I wanted them to be hanged in the factory for the others to see.'
"Do you find that?
"MILCH: I have found it, and I can only say I have never had anybody hanged nor have I even given such an order. I could not possibly have said such a thing. I had nothing to do with this question. Neither do I know of any instance where two Russian officers tried to escape by plane." (*IMT* IX, 114)

[Note: Somehow the story rings a bit differently with the added ingredient of the stolen airplane.]

And again:

"MR. JUSTICE JACKSON: It is as follows:
" 'Milch: We have demanded that in the anti-aircraft artillery a certain percentage of personnel should consist of Russians. Fifty

thousand in all should be brought in. Thirty thousand are already employed as gunners. This is an amusing thing ["eine witzige Sache" – C.P.], that Russians must work the guns...'

"What was amusing about making the Russian prisoners of war work the guns?

"MILCH: The words 'We have demanded' do not mean the Central Planning Board, but that Hitler made this demand.

"MR. JUSTICE JACKSON: 'We' means Hitler?

"MILCH: Yes, the German Government. And I myself find it strange that prisoners of war should be made to shoot at planes of their allies. We did not like it because it meant that these men could no longer work for us. We were opposed to their being used in the anti-aircraft artillery.

"MR. JUSTICE JACKSON: You said: 'This is an amusing thing that the Russians must work the guns.'

"What was amusing about it?

"MILCH: What is meant by amusing ["witzig" – C.P.]? ... peculiar, strange. I cannot say, however, whether this word was actually used. I have not seen the minutes.

"MR. JUSTICE JACKSON: Now, I call your attention to the rest of your contribution.

" '...20,000 are still needed. Yesterday I received a letter from the Army High Command, stating: We cannot release any more men, we have not enough ourselves. Thus there is no prospect for us.'

"Whom does 'for us' refer to, if not to your industry requirements?

"MILCH: I consider these minutes incorrect, it has never been discussed in this manner, it must be wrong. I cannot accept the minutes as they stand. To clarify this matter I may say that the proposal was to take people out of the armaments industry and put them into anti-aircraft defense. We who were concerned with armaments did not want to release these men and were opposed to it. That was the idea of the whole thing, and the OKH declared that they did not have enough people.

"MR. JUSTICE JACKSON: I understand the sense of this to be that you applied for certain workmen for the armaments industry and that the Army High Command refused to give you the men, saying that they are already employed making guns and on other work. Now, is that the sense of that, or is it not?

"MILCH: No, not quite.

"MR. JUSTICE JACKSON: Now, just tell me what the sense of it is.

"MILCH: As far as I remember, the armaments industry was to release 50,000 Russian prisoners of war to the Air Force for anti-aircraft defense, and the armaments industry could not spare these people." (*IMT* IX, 103-105)

Note: The Germans were not bound by any treaty with the Russians. Using Russian prisoners to build emplacements or carry munitions would be entirely logical. But to imagine that they could possess the motivation or skills to man anti-aircraft guns and shoot down Allied aircraft is not just "peculiar", it is insane.

The document in question here, R-124, is an unsigned "photocopy" of extracts of stenographic notes, almost certainly retyped and mimeographed by the prosecution, i.e., probably not photocopied from the originals. They are partially reproduced at XXXVIII, 336-362 of the Nuremberg Trial document volumes. This is a very well-known document, containing many sentences commonly quoted against Milch and Sauckel.

R-124 is a typical Nuremberg trial document on several points: it is an unsigned "photocopy", the authenticity and accuracy of which cannot be verified; it contains many statements which appear plausible, and others which appear to make little or no sense; and, most importantly, taken as a whole and translated into English, it does not really prove what the Nuremberg prosecutors thought it did.

Thus, the accusation is made that the Germans "enslaved" millions of people because there was a desperate labour shortage, and, simultaneously, that they "exterminated" millions of people who were perfectly able to work! This doesn't make sense. It seems only natural that nations which consider it an "amusing thing" to burn millions of people to death with phosphorous, jellied gasoline, and atomic bombs – the United States and Britain – should wax indignant over crimes committed by others. Perhaps it was the Germans who brought the slaves to America.

Finite space hardly permits full discussion of Taylor's multitudinous manipulations, distortions, deletions, misrepresentations, oversimplifications, moral pretentiousness, hypocrisy, half-truths, falsehoods, Phariseeism, superficiality, sanctimoniousness and lies.

Gas bag Taylor blowing himself up to mammoth proportions.

NATIONAL ARCHIVE HEAD
FAKES CAPTIONS TO NATIONAL
HOLOCAUST POSTER EXHIBIT

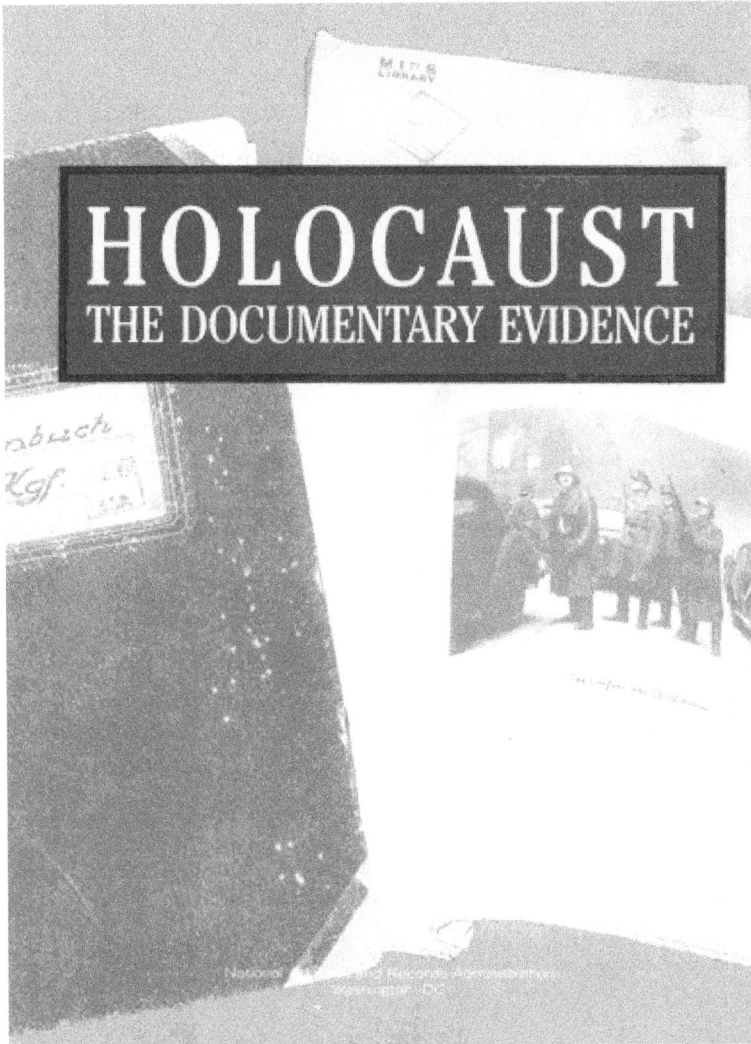

A Review of *Holocaust: The Documentary Evidence*

Documents compiled, translated, and captioned by Robert Wolfe for a poster exhibit in 1990, with introduction by Henry J. Gwiazda II. Astonishingly, the book's original language is listed as "German". Lies have long legs. The present review is based on the 1990 edition, which may or may not differ slightly from the 1993 edition available today.

The intended propaganda impact of this production should not be underestimated.

"In 1978, following the broadcast of the television miniseries 'Holocaust' [a human soap opera and admitted work of fiction. – C.P.] the National Archives prepared an exhibition entitled 'Holocaust: The Documentary Evidence', Robert Wolfe, currently Assistant Director, Center for Captured German and Related Documents, selected the items in the exhibit from captured German records and the World War II war crimes records in the Archives. In 1990, he revised this material for a poster series of the same title. In commemoration of the anniversary of U.S. participation in World War II, the National Archives Office of Public Programs is making the material available as a booklet." [From the introduction by Henry J. Gwiazda. – C.P.] The poster exhibit consists, we are told, of "21 original documents – including German-language texts, transcripts, and photographs... reproduced along with brief captions that explain the significance of each... The flexible exhibit can be installed easily in almost any space... The user may choose to display all 17 posters or to hang a small selection of them. The package has been designed to enable schools, libraries, historical societies, and other groups to adapt the material to their own audiences, educational goals, and budgets. The posters, which are printed on heavy paper and packaged in a sturdy cardboard mailing tube, may be dry-mounted, matted, or framed for exhibition.

Plan Your Own Exhibit or Educational Program Now – Order Today.

During the 12 years of the Third Reich – between Nazi assumption of power in Germany on January 30, 1933 and unconditional surrender on V-E day, May 8, 1945 – the Jews of Germany and Nazi-occupied Europe were subjected to discrimination, loss of citizenship and property, exile, and near extermination. [Like the Palestinians. – C.P.]

So that the world will never forget, Days of Remembrance

[Which really ought to be called "Days of Forgetfulness". – C.P.] are observed each spring in locations around the world." [From inside back cover blurb. – C.P.]

What is most astonishing about it all is that Robert Wolfe obviously cannot read German. How do these people get these jobs? What is certain is the National Archives do have people who CAN read German, and these people – whoever they are – are prepared to lie – and lie brazenly – in the face of all the evidence, which is right there in black and white in front of them.

For example: Page 20: letter from Reinhard Heydrich to Hermann Göring dated November 11, 1938:

THE DOCUMENT ACCORDING TO ROBERT WOLFE: "On November 9, 1938, Nazi-instigated and -condoned anti-Semitic violence broke out throughout Germany", followed by a partial translation: "In numerous cities looting of Jewish shops and businesses has occurred... The reported figures: 815 shops destroyed, 29 department stores set afire or otherwise destroyed, 171 dwellings set on fire or destroyed, give... only part of the real destruction..." [Caption:] "Report: Action Against the Jews..."

WHAT THE DOCUMENT ACTUALLY SAYS:

"The Chief of the Security Police II B 4 – 5716/3638 g
Please indicate above reference and date in your answer.
Berlin SW 11, 11 November 1938
Prinz Albrecht Strasse 8.
Telephone: A 2 Flora 0040
[Stamp:] SECRET
[Stamp:] EXPRESS LETTER
To Minister-President General Field Marshal Göring.
For the attention of Ministerial Director Dr. Gritzbach,
Berlin W8, Leipziger Strasse 3.

Regarding: Action against the Jews

The reports received from state police offices so far give the following overall picture as of 11.11.1938.
Looting of Jewish shops and businesses has occurred in numerous cities. Severe measures were taken to prevent further looting in all cases. In addition, 174 persons were arrested. ["Es wurde, um

weitere Plünderungen zu vermeiden, in allen Fällen scharf durchgegriffen. Wegen Plünderns wurden dabei 174 Personen festgenommen."]

The extent of the destruction of Jewish businesses and dwellings cannot yet be expressed in figures. The figures in the reports are as follows: 815 businesses destroyed, 29 department stores set on fire of otherwise destroyed, 171 dwelling houses set on fire or destroyed, but, insofar as this does not involve arson ["soweit es sich nicht um Brandlegungen handelt"] [i.e., deliberate arson on the part of the Jews. – C.P.] it represents only part of the actual destruction. Due to the urgency of the reporting, the reports have thus far only been restricted to general statements, such as 'many', or 'most businesses destroyed'. The indicated figures should therefore be multiplied several times. 191 synagogues were set on fire, another 76 were completely demolished. In addition, 11 community centres, cemetery chapels, and the like were set on fire and another 3 were completely destroyed. Approximately 20,000 Jews were arrested, in addition to 7 Aryans and 3 foreigners. There were 36 fatalities; serious injuries were also reported. The dead and/or injured are Jews. One Jew is still missing. Among the dead Jews were one Polish national, in addition to 2 Polish nationals among the injured. [Handwritten signature:] Heydrich."

COMMENT: Wolfe's translation ghost-writer forgot to translate the second and third sentences in the second paragraph: The document provides no proof that the violence was Nazi-instigated and/or condoned. Would the Jews really burn their own property, presumably to collect the insurance? Or have I misunderstood something? Of course, there's no proof of that, either.

[Note: There is no proof of it, but it is a reasonable supposition, and personally I believe it. Their property is known to have been very heavily insured, which is why Göring levied a heavy fine on the Jewish community to compensate the insurance companies. How else could the Jews collect the market value of their property? Who is going to pay the full market price for property owned by people known to be desperate to emigrate? The Jews had everything to gain in this situation, while the National Socialists had nothing to gain and everything to lose, and they knew it: this is why looters and arsonists were arrested, as shown by this document.]

Page 22: Transcribed telegram proving that the Jewish community, represented by Jewish councils, cooperated with the National Socialists in occupied Poland on September 21, 1939. Wolfe appears to believe that use of the word "Endziel" (final objective) indicates the existence of a plan to exterminate the Jews as early as September 21, 1939. This is contradicted by his own claim on page 27, according to which the plan was only drawn up at Wannsee on January 20, 1942. The document on p. 22 is a retouched carbon copy without letterhead, stamp, or signature, and contains no mention of extermination. It is not worth translating.

Page 25: Document 1553-PS, invoice for deliveries of Zyklon:

THE DOCUMENT ACCORDING TO ROBERT WOLFE: "This invoice of the Deutsche Gesellschaft für Schaedlingsbekämpfung – [German Association for Pest Control, DEGESCH] – records the shipment of 390 canisters of Zyklon B cyanide gas to be used 'for disinfection and extermination'..."

WHAT THE DOCUMENT ACTUALLY SAYS:

"[DEGESCH LETTERHEAD]
To Obersturmführer Kurt Gerstein,
(1) Berlin,
Leipzigerstrasse 31/32.

Invoice no. [blank] [!]
Frankfurt am Main, 31 May 1944.

On 31 May, we sent the following shipment by ordinary freight, from Dessau, accompanied by an army consignment brief from the army garrison administration of Dessau, to Auschwitz concentration camp, Department of Disinfestation and Epidemic Disease Prevention, Station Auschwitz:
    ZYKLON B, hydrocyanic acid, without irritant
    DGS 50185/97 = 13 cases [each case] containing 30 cans = 390 cans × 500 g per can × 195 kg × unit price 5 DM kg = 975 DM.
    Gross [weight]: 832.00 kg,
    Tare: 276.25 kg,
    Net [weight]: 555.75 kg.
    The labels bear the inscription 'Warning: No Irritant.' "

COMMENT: The word "extermination" does not appear in the document. The term is "Abteilung Entwesung und Seuchenabwehr"

(Department of Disinfestation and Epidemic Disease Prevention).

[NOTE: Due to the fact that "Seuchenabwehr" is a compound word, Wolfe can lie with virtual impunity, because if you look it up in a dictionary, it won't be there. You have to look up "Seuche" [epidemic] (without "n"), then look up "Abwehr" [defense], then combine the two, presumably with some knowledge of German grammar.]

Page 24: Letter from Bishop Hilfrich of Limburg dated August 31, 1941, protesting against euthanasia.

THE DOCUMENT ACCORDING TO ROBERT WOLFE: "...Bishop Hilfrich complained that even children at play chattered knowingly about the smokey [sic] chimney and sickly smell and that implausible [!] death certificates had been received..."

WHAT THE DOCUMENT ACTUALLY SAYS:

"Bishop of Limburg, Limburg/Lahn, 13 August 1941.
To the Reichsminister of Justice [no address]
[Reception stamp: Reich Ministry of Justice, 16 August 1941.]

With reference to the memorandum filed by the President of the Fuldau Council of Bishops, Cardinal Dr. Bertram ["m" crossed out, many illegible handwritten markings. – C.P.] (sub-paragraph IV, pp. 6/7), I consider it my duty to provide the following as a concrete illustration of the destruction of so-called 'useless lives'.

Approximately 8 km from the little town of Hadamar, on a hill immediately above the town, is an installation which, having earlier served for a variety of purposes, most recently as a clinic and sanatorium, has been converted or set up as a site in which, according to general belief ["nach allegemeiner Überzeugung"], the above mentioned euthanasia [programme] has been deliberately carried on for months, approximately since February 1941. The fact is known beyond the governmental district of Wiesbaden, because death certificates have been sent to the locations of residence in question from a registry office in Hadamar-Mönchberg (The installation is called Mönchberg because it was a Franciscan cloister until the secularization of 1803.)

Buses carrying large numbers of such victims arrive in Hadamar several times a week . School children in the area are familiar with these vehicles, and say, 'Here come the murder boxes.' After the arrival of such vehicles, the citizens of Hadamar observe the smoke rising from the chimney and are constantly tormented by thoughts of the poor victims, all the more so when they are annoyed by revolting odours depending on the direction of the wind." [First page only.]

COMMENT: The word "implausible" does not appear in the document. Euthanasia was openly practiced and admitted, and was stopped after protests like this one. Crematory ovens do not smell or emit smoke. The document is covered with handwritten markings which to me are illegible and appears to be a first draft, but it bears a reception stamp. The letter suggests a form of legal procedure which might prove highly expeditious: if you want to know whether anyone is guilty of murder, just ask all the local school children! The letter must have been answered. Where is the answer?

Page 24: Letter from Hitler dated September 1, 1939, authorizing euthanasia:

THE DOCUMENT ACCORDING TO ROBERT WOLFE: "...Hitler's order authorizing certain doctors to kill persons deemed incurably ill...", the implication apparently being that the Nazis themselves declared people incurably ill, and then killed them

WHAT THE DOCUMENT ACTUALLY SAYS: "ADOLF HITLER 1 Sept. 1939 Reichsleiter Bouhler and Dr. Brandt are assigned with responsibility for broadening the powers of certain doctors, to be indicated by name, so that persons deemed incurably ill according to the standards of human judgement may be granted a merciful death subject to the most critical evaluation of their condition."

COMMENT: According to a recent radio broadcast, 40% of all deaths of terminally ill persons in Holland today are by euthanasia. Of course, that is all right, because the Dutch are "anti-fascists".

Page 26: Gas van document 501-PS, the "gas van letter" allegedly sent by Untersturmführer [SS Second Lieutenant] Becker to Obersturmbannführer [SS Lieutenant Colonel] Rauff dated May 16, 1942.

THE DOCUMENT ACCORDING TO ROBERT WOLFE: "...This report states: 'I disguised the wagons as house trailers by painting... windows like those often seen on farmhouses in the countryside.' "

WHAT THE DOCUMENT ACTUALLY SAYS:

"Army postal service 32 704.
Kiev, 16.5.1942.
[Stamp: Secret Reich Matter (Geheime Reichssache)]
To: SS Obersturmbannführer Rauff.
    Berlin, Prinz Albrecht Strasse 8.

Repairs on the vehicles in group D and C are finished. While the vehicles in the first series can be used even if the weather conditions are not too bad, the vehicles in the second series (Saurer) get completely bogged down in rainy weather. For example, if it rains for even half an hour, the vehicle cannot be used because it simply skids. It can only be used in dry weather. The question arises of whether the vehicles can only be used in a stationary position at the execution location. The vehicle must first be driven to the location, which is only possible in good weather. The execution location, however, is usually located 10-15 km away from the roads, and is therefore only accessible with difficulty due to its location, and in damp or rainy weather it is not accessible at all. If the execution victims are driven or transported to the execution location, they immediately notice what is going on and get agitated, which ought to be avoided insofar as possible. There is only one other possibility, that is, to pick them up at collection stations and drive away with them.

I have had the vehicles in Group D disguised as caravans by installing one window [Document 501-PS] on each side of the smaller vehicle, and two windows on each side of the larger vehicle, like the ones often seen on farmhouses in the countryside. The vehicles have become so well known that not only the authorities, but the civilian population as well, refer to the vehicles as 'murder vehicles', as soon as these motor vehicles come in sight. In my opinion, it cannot be kept secret for long even if disguised.

The Sauer vehicles which I transported from Simferopol to Taganrog suffered damage to the brakes en route. At the SK in Mariupol it was found that the sleeve on the oil air-pressure brake was broken in several places. Through persuasion and bribery at the HKP, it was possible to turn out a mould permitting the casting of two sleeves. When I..." [First page only.]

COMMENT: The word "painting" does not appear in the document. The verb is "anbringen", to install or affix. I have always wondered how the pressure buildup would be handled in a vehicle of this kind;

now we know: the gassing victims, or gassing overpressure, simply broke the windows, and that took care of the overpressure! Apparently the idea of "windows" on a "gas van" was a bit thick even for Robert Wolfe's ghost-translator, so the gerund in English was simply altered to "painting"! The Jewish victims were allegedly fooled by a feat of artistic *trompe-l'œil* trickery which presumably also caused the cabin of the truck to become invisible, much as half the house disappeared behind a bookcase in the Diary of Anne Frank.

This must be one of the most ridiculous documents in the history of the world. On May 16, 1942, the highly mechanized and mobile German army had been fighting in Russia for 11 months, including one entire Russian winter, but their fiendishly clever 'murder vans" got stuck in the mud if it rained even half an hour!

The document is signed by an Untersturmführer only. Since thousands of German documents were captured, couldn't we have something from an Obersturmbannführer at least?

This one document is more or less the only proof we have of the existence of any "gas vans" at all. Of course, in the real world, nothing takes place in a vacuum, and nothing can be accomplished with only one document. For example, if an invading army needed to find documentary proof that I have worked as a translator in Belgium, it would find, not one document, but literally tens of thousands: order forms, invoices, payment vouchers, bank statements, credit slips, receipts, complaints, corrections, loan agreements, reminders, lawyer's letters, court judgements, threats of seizure and distraint against people who don't pay, tax, accounting and social security records, debits, credits, deductions, accounts with suppliers, agreements relating to the purchase, delivery, and repair of supplies and equipment, registered mail receipts, delivery vouchers for texts, documentary materials, and supplies, all in duplicate or triplicate, not only in Belgium, but in foreign countries as well.

I would estimate that in 10 years of translation work I must have generated at least 40,000 documents, 75% of which I have never even seen, quite apart from the translations themselves. Yet we are supposed to believe that the Germans killed millions of people in "gas chambers" and "gas vans" on the basis of one or two documents, usually copies, signed, if we are lucky, by a subordinate! The booklet and poster exhibit contains not one single document relating to gas chambers or even crematory ovens – not one.

Page 27: The Wannsee Conference document, January 20, 1942.

THE DOCUMENT ACCORDING TO ROBERT WOLFE: "At an interagency meeting chaired by Reinhard Heydrich, officials of several Nazi government agencies and representatives of the SS and police formalized the 'final solution of the Jewish question', already in full operation [!] since the German invasion of the Soviet Union in late June 1941..."

WHAT THE DOCUMENT ACTUALLY SAYS: Page 2 of the document very clearly states: "preparation for the Final Solution". The significance of this is that it proves that Wolfe absolutely cannot read German. The document contains no mention of extermination. This is the copy with the typewritten SS-rune (there are at least two different versions of the document).

Page 28: The Mauthausen "Death Books". Placing the cause of death in quotation marks in the caption – "angina", "heart attack", "kidney insufficiency" – does not prove that these people were murdered. There were two witnesses from Mauthausen at Nuremberg. The first, Lampe (*IMT* VI, 206-217, German text), described all sorts of atrocities but did not mention a gas chamber, while the second, Boix, two witnesses later, mentioned "gas chambers" repeatedly, in the plural (*IMT* VI 300, 307, German text). Nobody noticed the contradiction; nobody asked Boix where they were, how many there were, or how they functioned. The gas chambers are like Heaven; you are supposed to believe in them, but you are not supposed to ask where they are. They work in a mysterious way their wonders to perform. Glory Glory Hololujah.

On page 29, Wolfe mentions the "presumably oral Commissar Order". The order was in writing (see Documents PS-2542, PS-3718, USSR-151, C-50, USSR-351, OKW(A) 301-376, OKW(A) 301(d), etc.). That it was never put into effect was admitted even by General Paulus, who testified as a prosecution witness at Nuremberg for the Soviets, straight out of a Russian prison camp (*IMT* VII 330, German text), as well as by many other witnesses

Page 30 is an Einsatzgruppen report. That these documents are forgeries is apparent from the fact that they mention Katyn as a German crime (*NMT* IV 112, Einsatzgruppen, "green series"). Wolfe continues to ignore John Ball's research relating to Babi Yar just as he ignores Ball's research with relation to Auschwitz.

Page 31: Letter and report, with photo of test subject having died during a fatal medical experiment, written by Dr. Sigmund Rascher to Reichsführer Heinrich Himmler, dated April 5, 1942.

THE DOCUMENT ACCORDING TO ROBERT WOLFE: "...The subject died. Himmler noted in green pencil: 'sehr interessant' [very interesting]."

WHAT THE DOCUMENT ACTUALLY SAYS:

"Dr. Sigmund Rascher,
Munich, 5 April 1942

Reichsführer, I enclose an intermediate report on the under-pressure chamber experiments conducted in Dachau concentration camp so far. May I most respectfully request that the report be kept secret. SS Reich Doctor Professor Gravitz inspected the experimental arrangements a few days ago. Since time was short, it was not possible to conduct a demonstration experiment for him. SS Obersturmbannführer Sievers took one day of his time to inspect some of the most interesting standard experiments, and will perhaps soon make a report on them. I believe that you would find these experiments extraordinarily interesting! Wouldn't it be possible to conduct a few demonstration experiments for you during one of your visits to southern Germany? If the experimental results obtained so far continue to be confirmed in future, they will result in entirely new scientific discoveries, simultaneously leading to absolutely new concepts in aviation. In view of the intended efforts of Dr. Sievers, I hope that the Air Force will place no further obstacles in my way. I am very much indebted to Obersturmbannführer Sievers for showing great interest in my work. I would like to thank you most sincerely for the realization of my proposal to conduct experiments of this type in the concentration camp.

With the sincerest wishes for your well-being,
I remain,
Yours faithfully,
Heil Hitler!
[Handwritten:] With thanks, Dr. Rascher.

[Page 2]

First Intermediate Report on Under-Pressure Experiment in Dachau Concentration Camp.

The objective was to determine whether the theoretically determined values on survival time in a low-oxygen, low-pressure atmosphere were in accordance with the results obtained in practical experiments. It has been stated that an aviator who parachutes at an altitude of 12 kilometers suffers extremely serious [bodily] harm, and probably even death, from lack of oxygen. Practical experiments on this topic were always interrupted after 53 seconds due to the appearance, both in the present and in the past, of extremely serious altitude sickness.

2. Experiments relating to survival time for a human being above the normal respiratory threshold (4.5-6 kilometers) were never conducted at all, since it was found that the test subject would necessarily suffer certain death. The experiments conducted by myself and Dr. Romberg showed that: Death did not result from lack of oxygen or low atmospheric pressure during experimental parachute jumping at either 12 or 13 kilometers altitude. A total of 15 extreme experiments of this type were conducted, in which none of the test subjects died. Extremely severe altitude sickness appeared, accompanied by unconsciousness, but with complete capacity for action when an altitude of approximately 7 kilometers was reached. The electrocardiograms performed naturally revealed certain irregularities during the experiment, but the curves returned to normal by the end of the experiment, and showed absolutely no pathological changes even over the following days. The extent to which bodily attrition might appear in the case of constantly repeated experiments will only become apparent upon concluding the series of experiments. Extreme, fatal, experiments were conducted on specially assigned test subjects, since this type of control, which is extraordinarily important in practice, would otherwise be impossible." [Second page of report only.]

COMMENT: I have never understood the accusations made against Dr. Rascher, and have no idea how much truth or falsehood they may contain (except for the ridiculous "body heat experiments", in which I do not believe); I am therefore not in a position to discuss them. The document nevertheless appears to imply that very few test subjects actually died. All nations, including the United States, have carried out medical experiments resulting in death, the Americans even while the Nuremberg Trial was still continuing. The difference is that the Germans used criminals in concentration camps, while the Americans used foreign laborers who were too ignorant to understand the consent forms they signed for a few dollars. Dr. Rascher was shot by the SS.

How many German aviators really had to bail out at altitudes of 12 kilometers (about 5 miles)? Wouldn't it have been simpler to equip high-altitude aviators with a breathing apparatus, which they probably wore anyway?

Page 32: The "brutal suppression of the Jewish uprising in the Warsaw Ghetto". I am sorry. To me, the Holocaust means gassing millions of people in gas chamber and gas vans, shooting or starving them by the millions, killing them with all sorts of sadistic tortures, etc. etc. It does not just mean hanging or shooting a few people, or putting them in concentration camps. So how do pictures of the Warsaw Ghetto "prove the Holocaust"? Would the Americans have tolerated a full-scale armed uprising in 1943 by Japanese-Americans at Tule Lake or any other American concentration camp?

Page 33: Arbitrarily labeled and/or doctored aerial photographs of Auschwitz, ignoring John Ball's research.

Page 34: "Statistical Report, Final Solution of the Jewish Question in Europe" by Dr. Richard Korherr, pages 9 and 16.

THE DOCUMENT ACCORDING TO ROBERT WOLFE: "...The last half-page of the report, shown here, says in part, 'In sum, European Jewry since 1933... will soon have lost half its substance,' through murder *and* immigration [sic]". (The word "and", for some mysterious reason, appears in italics in the text by Robert Wolfe.)

WHAT THE DOCUMENT ACTUALLY SAYS: Only two sentences are reproduced from page 16: "The flow of Jewish population movements from the European countries outside the German [sphere of] influence is of a largely unknown magnitude. As a whole, European Jewry will soon have lost half its effective strength since 1933, that is, in the first decade of the German National Socialist show of strength."

COMMENT: Is Robert Wolfe really so ignorant as to be unaware of the difference between immigration and emigration? How do these people get these jobs? One can interpret this document any way one likes, but it contains no mention of murder.

On the contrary: the words "Evacuation" or "Emigration", including the various verb forms, are used *15 times*!

Page 35: Two pages from Himmler's "secret speech". Surprisingly,

"Ausrottung" here is translated, correctly in my view, as "Extirpation", rather than "Extermination". The reason why this is correct is because "Extirpation", like "Ausrottung", can be used figuratively or literally, while "Extermination" can only be used more or less literally, i.e., one can extirpate an influence or an idea, but one cannot exterminate it. In German, "Ausrottung" applies to both, and is in fact used figuratively in this same speech. The quote in the right-hand column of Wolfe's text does not match the page reproduced above – further indication, although not proof, that Wolfe simply cannot read German. It should be noted that there are 21 documents, but only 17 posters, i.e., not even one page per document has actually been reproduced. The typescript is 116 pages long, bears no signatures, stamps, or handwritten markings, and contains not one single sharp S (ß), a standard letter in the German alphabet.

Page 36: Photographs of a motley crew of more or less obscure individuals alleged to be "Holocaust survivors": an American congressman, a Hungarian actress, a certifiably insane writer photographed in the company of a reptilian-looking businessman, and the inventor of the hydrogen bomb! Are these the Michelangelos, the Leonardos, the Bachs, the Dantes, the Mozarts, the Dürers, the Shakespeares, of the Jewish people? If this is the best the Jews can come up with, I feel truly sorry for them, and I mean that. (See page 42 of this book.)

Finally, first things last, the crudity and stupidity of the introduction by Henry J. Gwiazda II (apparently an African obsessed with the evils of "racism" in general, and "white racism" in particular) are such as to devote 5 full centimeters (on page 7) to a quotation from Document L-3, Graphics of Document L-3, a forgery which was never even accepted into evidence at Nuremberg, 250 copies of which were nevertheless distributed to the press as an authentic document. (*IMT* II 286-293). Why not reproduce this document as a poster, including the FBI laboratory stamp? How about a poster exhibit on African, Zionist, or "democratic" atrocities?

Page 6: "...The sheer numbers suggest one reason why the Nazis developed the crematorium to dispose of their victims."

COMMENT: Crematoria were developed by the British in the late 1880s, one of the first modern cremations being that of the body of a horse, without any smoke or odor, "sickly" or otherwise.

Page 7: "...It was as part of this program at mental institutions that the gas chamber and crematorium were developed."

COMMENT: Gas chambers, of course, as everyone knows, were developed by the Americans in the early 1920s.

Page 15: Another photograph with an arbitrarily concocted caption. (See page 43 of this book.) Everything in the background has been blown up by the Americans, but the inmates in the foreground have, of course, all been "murdered" by the Germans. Could we have a bit of proof of that? Or is that too much to ask? So in the end, we are back where we started. If Robert Wolfe and the National Archives possess any "proof of a Holocaust", they can publish it and prove it.

(Note: The city of Nordhausen was bombed by the Americans on April 4, 1945, hitting the Bölcke Kaserne of the concentration camp by mistake, killing thousands of inmates. These are the dead inmates shown in the photograph.)

Belzec, and Treblinka (pp. 27 and 35). More than 1.3 million died in open-air shootings, and hundreds of thousands perished from deliberate privation such as starvation. At least 1 million Slavs are estimated to have died in the death camps, but most of the 9 million to 10 million killed were shot or hanged in thousands of mass and individual executions or were deliberately starved or worked to death (pp. 30 and 31). The total deaths in the Nazis' *racial* war are estimated at 14 million to 16 million, or possibly 1 in 2 deaths of the 30 million Europeans estimated to have died during World War II.[26]

THE MYTH OF "KADAVERGEHORSAM" ("CORPSE-LIKE OBEDIENCE")

More on the Linguistic Illiteracy of War Crimes Prosecutors and Men Like Robert Wolfe

Except for lower-level interrogators, interpreters and translators, the men who tried representatives of the German nation for "war crimes" at Nuremberg and elsewhere had no knowledge of the German language, a shortcoming so serious that Sir David Maxwell-Fyfe even had to ask one of the witnesses at Nuremberg how to pronounce the name of a relatively well-known Austrian chateau and resort, Schloss Fuschl, on Lake Fuschl, near Salzburg.

To remedy this deficiency, at least in the their own eyes, these same men constantly larded their perorations and political speeches in court with a sprinkling of German words which they had no doubt learned parrot-like for the purpose (probably fewer than five words in total). One of these words was "Kulturträger" ("culture-bearer"), a great favourite of the Soviets, who inserted it ironically in many of their "anti-fascist" atrocity stories. Among the Anglo-Saxon prosecutors, the all-time favourite, still commonly found in "anti-fascist" literature today, is the word "Kadavergehorsam".

The term "Kadavergehorsam", allegedly a German word, was utilized to "prove" that wooden, unthinking, "corpse-like" obedience is a characteristic of the German nation, or, more specifically, National Socialists and "Prussian militarists" generally.

As usual, of course, the very word itself is a fraud. "Kadavergehorsam" is simply a translation from Latin of a Jesuit motto originating with St. Ignacio de Loyola, usually, if not always, taken out of context. The Latin phrase is "Perinde ac cadaver." ("Like a corpse".)

As an accusation against Prussian militarists and National Socialists, this is already a bit thick. Even in Latin, it is probably one of the most famous "quotations out-of-context" in all literature.

The phrase was made famous by Houston Stewart Chamberlain in *The Foundations of the 19th Century*, in an alleged attempt to argue that the principle of "corpse-like obedience" is of Basque origin, and is therefore non-Aryan.

(NOTE: Chamberlain seems to be using the word "Aryan" here as a linguistic term, and not a racial term, thus adding to the confusion. – C.P.)

Maxwell-Fyfe and Jackson, shyster lawyers and linguistic illiterates.

The quotation according to Chamberlain is as follows: "As if it were a corpse which lets itself be turned on any side and never resists the hand laid upon it, or like the staff of an old man which everywhere helps him who holds it, no matter how and where he wishes to employ it." ("Perinde ac si cadaver essent, quod quoquoversus ferri, et quacunque ratione tractare se sinit: vel similiter atque senis baculus, qui obicumque et quacumque in re velit eo uti, qui cum manu tenet, ei inservit.") Chamberlain continues: "I think it would be impossible to make the contrast to all Aryan thought and feeling more clear than it is in these words: on the one hand sunny, proud, mad delight in creating, men who fearlessly grasp the right hand of the God to whom they pray;

on the other a corpse, upon which the 'destruction of all independent judgment' is impressed as the first rule in life and for which 'cowering slavish fear' is the basis of all religion." (p. 243)

The great Basque writer, Pío Baroja, hardly a friend of the Jesuits, or even Catholics or Christians generally, says, "This statement is tendentious and false. First, Loyola did not say that one had to obey like a corpse. He said, 'Perinde ac cadaver in omnibus ubi peccatum non cerneretur' (to obey like a corpse in all matters in which one does not fall into sin). Loyola could not have translated this into Basque without using words of Latin origin. It was not, therefore, of Basque origin." (From *Los Jesuitas*, in *Vitrina Pintoresca*, a collection of essays published in 1935; p. 739, Vol. V, *Obras Completas*, Biblioteca Nueva, Madrid.)

If Baroja is correct, the phrase plainly implies that obedience to a sinful order is not required. Since the person receiving the order is the only one who can, and must, for the sake of his own soul, determine whether or not an order is "sinful" (or "illegal"), this could be interpreted to mean that, ultimately, there is no duty of absolute obedience at all, which, taken to the other extreme, is more or less unworkable – i.e., pure Nuremberg, a principle invented solely for export.

Of course, that is undoubtedly not the meaning either. So that, as so often, the phrase itself becomes more or less meaningless depending on how it is interpreted. And this is taken as "proving" the "corpse-obedience" of German patriots interpreted by people who cannot read German!

Obviously, to form a correct interpretation of the principle as applied by the Jesuits, would require a complete knowledge of Jesuit literature, i.e., the full context (probably Loyola's *Letter on Obedience*). In this sense, Baroja was probably right.

"Loyola distinctly excepts the case where obedience in itself would be sinful: 'In all things *except sin* I ought to do the will of my superior and not my own.' ...

"From this it is clear that only in *doubtful* cases concerning sin should an inferior try to submit his judgement to that of his superior, who *ex officio* is held to be not only one who would not order what is sinful, but also a competent judge who knows and understands, better than the inferior, the nature and aspect of the command. As Jesuit obedience is based on the law of God, it is clearly impossible that he [the subordinate] should be bound to obey in what is directly opposed to divine service." (*1911 Encyclopaedia Britannica*, "Jesuits", Vol. 15, p. 338.)

The Jesuits have probably been the victim of more forgeries and quotations out of context than any group of people in history except the National Socialists, whom they in certain respects rather resemble. The most famous of these forgeries is probably the *Monita Secreta*, published in 1612.

In any case, the term "Kadavergehorsam" has no place in a trial of modern Germans.

This is simply one more example of the fraudulence of all Nuremberg proceedings. If a "trial" were required, it could have been held in Switzerland, a German-speaking, neutral country, under existing law, eliminating the need for interpreters and translators almost entirely.

Another favourite trick was to make political speeches quoting Goethe and Shakespeare (and God knows what all else for thousands of pages). How does one prove someone guilty of murder in the 20th century by quoting MacBeth or Richard III? Then, when the defense came up with some real evidence, like 312,022 notarized affidavits for the "criminal organizations", sworn according to COURT-ORDERED AMERICAN PROCEDURES, they were told that the court "didn't have time" to translate and read them! So much for justice.

Appendix

The defense evidence for the "criminal organizations" consists of the testimony of 102 witnesses and 312,022 notarized affidavits (XXII 176 [200]).

The term "criminal" was never defined (XXII 310 [354]; see also XXII 129-135[148-155]).

Nor was it defined when these organizations became "criminal" (XXII 240 [272-273]).

The Nazi Party itself was criminal dating back to 1920 (XXII 251 [285]) or then again maybe only 1938 (XXII 113 [130]) or maybe even not at all (II 105 [123]).

The 312,022 notarized affidavits were presented to a "commission", and evidence before this "commission" does not appear in the transcript of the Nuremberg Trial. The National Archives in Washington do not possess a copy of the commission transcript, had never heard of it when I asked, and did not know what it is.

Of the 312,022 affidavits, only a few dozen were ever translated into English, so the Tribunal could not read them (XXI 287, 397-398 [319, 439]). The President of the Tribunal, Sir Geoffrey Lawrence, understood no German; neither did Robert Jackson.

Due to a last-minute rule change (XXI 437-438, 441, 586-587 [483-485, 488,645-646]) many more affidavits were rejected on technical grounds (XX 446-448 [487-489]).

The "commission" prepared "summaries" which were presented to the Tribunal (x-thousand affidavits alleging humane treatment of prisoners, etc). These summaries were not considered to be in evidence. The Tribunal promised to read the 312,022 affidavits before arriving at their verdict (XXI 175 [198]); 14 days later it was announced that the 312,022 affidavits were not true (XXII 176-178 [200-203]).

Then a single affidavit from the prosecution (Document D-973) was deemed to have "rebutted" 136,000 affidavits from the defense (XXI 588, 437, 366 [647, 483-484, 404]).

The 102 witnesses were forced to appear and testify before the "commission" before appearing before the Tribunal. Then, 29 of these witnesses (XXI 586 [645]), or 22 of these witnesses (XXII 413 [468]) were allowed to appear before the Tribunal, but their testimony was not permitted to be "cumulative", that is, repetitive of their testimony before the "commission" (XXI 298, 318, 361 [331, 352, 398-399]).

Then, six affidavits from the prosecution were deemed to have "rebutted" the testimony of the 102 witnesses (XXI 153 [175], XXII 221[251]).

One of these affidavits was in Polish, so the defense could not read it (XX 408 [446]). Another was signed by a Jew named Szloma Gol who claimed to have dug up and cremated 80,000 bodies, including that of his own brother (XXI 157 [179], XXII 220 [250]).

(In the British transcript he has only dug up 67,000 bodies). The prosecution had already rested its case when this occurred (XX 389-393, 464 [426-430, 506]; XXI 586-592 [645-651]). The prosecution then claimed in its final summation that 300,000 affidavits had been presented to the Tribunal and had been considered during the trial, giving the impression that these are prosecution documents (XXII 239 [272]).

In fact, the prosecution got through the entire trial with no more than a few really important affidavits of their own. (See, for example, XXI 437 [483], where eight or nine affidavits were presented for the prosecution against three hundred thousand for the defense; see also XXI 200 [225]; 477-478 [528-529]; 585-586 [643-645]; 615 [686-687]).

In the various concentration camp trials, such as the Trial of Martin Gottfried Weiss, a simpler expedient was agreed upon: mere employment in the camp, even if only for a few weeks, was deemed to constitute "constructive knowledge" of the "Common Plan". "Common Plan", of course, was not defined. It was not necessary to allege specific acts of mistreatment, or to show that anyone had died as a result of mistreatment. (36 of the 40 defendants were sentenced to death.)

The transcript of the Nuremberg commission is in the Hague, and fills half of one fireproof floor-to-ceiling vault. The testimony of each witness was typed with a pagination beginning with page 1, then re-typed, with consecutive pagination running to many thousands of pages.

The first drafts and clean copy are in folders, together, stapled, on very brittle paper, with rusty staples. It is absolutely certain that, at least at the Hague, no one has ever read this material.

THE *AMISTAD* –
ANOTHER "CHIEF SEATTLE" HOAX?

An introduction to the historical value of old law books. No one would judge an automobile accident in 1910 according to a highway code written in 2008, yet that is the method used by "historians" discussing "war crimes trials" with highly inventive and selective hindsight.

* * *

With the rise of Political Correctness, marginal (and deservedly forgotten) phenomena are routinely disinterred (or invented) and assigned a transcendental significance and prominence which they never remotely possessed (for example: black, gay, and/or bisexual cowboys; lesbians among the pioneers, etc. etc. *ad nauseam ad infinitum)*.

In the 1980s, for example, everybody was talking about "Chief Seattle"; but in the 1950s and 60s, nobody ever heard of him. The reason, of course, was that "Seattle", in his modern form, was invented in 1971 by a white man in California ("Ted Speaks").

More recently, in connection with other matters, I acquired a fair-sized collection of standard texts on international law, published between 1866 and 1948. To my surprise, I found that they contained no mention whatsoever of the *Amistad*. None. Nor had I ever heard of this incident when I was growing up.

The principal slave trading cases mentioned in most texts on international law are the *Antelope*, the *Louis*, the *Jeune Eugenie*, the *Amedie*, the *Amelia*, the *Africa*, the *Fortuna*, and the *Diana*. The *Amistad*, so far as I know, is never mentioned. John Quincy Adams is mentioned solely in connection with the Monroe Doctrine, and his role in the negotiation of various international treaties in 1822 and 1842; never, so far as I know, in connection with the *Amistad*.

Cases on International Law by Chas. G. Fenwick, National Case Book Series, Chicago Callaghan and Company, 1935, contains an Index of Cases on p. xvii. Cases involving ships beginning with the letter A include the *Adula*, the *Alabama*, the *Amelia*, the *Anna*, the *Anne*, the *Annette*, the *Antelope*, the *Appam*, etc. There is no mention of the

Amistad. Slavery is discussed on pp. 7-10 and pp. 369-274.

The *Antelope* case, quoted on pp. 7-10, lays the blame for the existence of slavery squarely where it belongs: on the Africans. The decision, written by Chief Justice John Marshall, says, more or less, that slavery is legal in Africa because the Africans want it that way, and that we have no right to force our legal and moral standards upon them. The only thing we can do is forbid our own nationals from engaging in the slave trade. We have no right to enforce our laws on the citizens of other countries.

Slaves belonging to the citizens of nations permitting the slave trade must therefore be returned to their owners, because of the "absolute equality of nations".

The decision reads, in part:

"THE *ANTELOPE*, THE VICE-CONSULS OF SPAIN AND PORTUGAL, LIBELLANTS.

"United States, Supreme Court, 1825.
"*10 Wheaton*, 66 [6 L. ed. 268]

"...The Consuls of Spain and Portugal, respectively, demand these Africans as slaves, who have, in the regular course of legitimate commerce, been acquired as property by the subjects of their respective sovereigns, and claim their restitution under the laws of the United States.

"...this court must not yield to feelings which might seduce it from the path of duty, and must obey the mandate of the law.

"That the course of opinion on the slave trade should be unsettled, ought to excite no surprise. The Christian and civilized nations of the world, with whom we have most intercourse, have all been engaged in it. However abhorrent this traffic may be to a mind whose original feelings are not blunted by familiarity with the practice, it has been sanctioned in modern times by the laws of all nations who possess distant colonies, each of whom has engaged in it as a common commercial business which no other could rightfully interrupt. It has claimed all the sanction which could be derived from long usage and general acquiescence. That trade could not be considered as contrary to the law of nations which was authorized and protected by the laws of all commercial nations, the right to carry on which was claimed by each, and allowed by each.

"... The question of whether the slave trade is prohibited by the law of nations has been seriously propounded, and both the affirmative and negative of the proposition have been maintained with equal earnestness. That it is contrary to the law of nature will scarcely be denied. That every man has an equal right to the fruits of his own labour, is generally admitted; and that no other person can rightfully deprive him of those fruits, and appropriate them against his will, seems to be the necessary result of this admission. But from the earliest times war has existed, and war confers rights in which all have acquiesced. Among the most enlightened nations of antiquity, one of these was that the victor might enslave the vanquished. This, which was the usage of all, could not be pronounced repugnant to the law of nations, which is certainly to be tried by the test of general usage. That which has received the assent of all, must be the law of all.

"Slavery, then, has its origin in force, but as the world has agreed that it is a legitimate result of force, the state of things which is thus produced by general consent, cannot be pronounced unlawful.

"Throughout Christendom, this harsh rule has been exploded, and war is no longer considered as giving a right to enslave captives. But this triumph of humanity has not been universal. The parties to the modern law of nations do not propagate their principles by force, and Africa has not yet adopted them. Through the whole extent of that immense continent, so far as we know its history, it is still the law of nations that prisoners are slaves. Can those who have themselves renounced this law, be permitted to participate in its effects by purchasing the beings who are its victims?

"Whatever might be the answer of a moralist to this question, a jurist must search for its legal solution in those principles of action which are sanctioned by the usage, the national acts, and the general assent, of that portion of the world of which he considers himself a part, and to whose law the appeal is made. If we resort to this standard of the test of international law, the question, as has already been observed, must be decided in favour of the legality of the trade. Both Europe and America embarked in it; and for nearly two centuries, it was carried on without opposition and without censure. A jurist could not say that a practice thus supported was illegal, and that those engaged in it might be punished, either personally, or by deprivation of property.

"In this commerce, thus sanctioned by universal assent, every nation has an equal right to engage. How is this right to be lost? Each may renounce it for its own people; but can this renunciation affect others?

"No principle of general law is more universally acknowledged, than the perfect equality of nations. Russia and Geneva have equal rights. It results from this equality, that no one can rightfully impose a rule on another. Each legislates for itself, but its legislation can operate on itself alone. A right, then, which is vested in all by the consent of all, can divested only by consent; and this trade, in which all have participated, must remain lawful to those who cannot be induced to relinquish it. As no nation can prescribe for others, none can make a law of nations; and this traffic remains lawful to those whose governments have not forbidden it."

The *Louis* decision of 1817, quoted on p. 374 of the same book [Fenwick, 1935], says, flatly:

"It is pressed as a difficulty, what is to be done, if a French ship laden with slaves for a French port is brought in: I answer, without hesitation, restore the possession which has been unlawfully divested: rescind the illegal act done by your own subject; and leave the foreigner to the justice of his own country..." (Great Britain, High Court of Admiralty, 1817, 2 Dodson, 210.)

The *Jeune Eugenie* decision of 1822, mentioned beginning on p. 1 of the same book [Fenwick, 1935], concluded that slavery was illegal under the laws of France – a highly dubious assertion, contradicted below, in a lengthy footnote by Richard Henry Dana continuing onto p. 177 of *Wheaton*, 1866 edition, with footnotes by Richard Henry Dana – and ordered the slaves in question, not freed, but turned over to the King of France.

Since slavery was not, in fact, illegal under the laws of France at all, it is highly unlikely that the slaves in question were ever freed. By contrast, the slaves on the *Amistad* were allegedly transported to Sierra Leone at the expense of the United States government, and freed, regardless of Spanish law, the rights or claims of Spanish slave owners, and the "*absolute equality of nations*" – at time when slavery was still legal in the United States! Such a Supreme Court decision would not only have overruled the *Antelope* decision, but would have been absolutely revolutionary in its implications, and would necessarily have been perceived as a direct threat to slaveholding interests in the United States. Nobody noticed. I do not see how this is possible.

Henry Wheaton's Elements of International Law, 1866 edition, number 19 in *The Classics of International Law* by Clarendon Press, Oxford, England, with notes by Richard Henry Dana, is an extremely complex and complete classical work of international law, with numerous, exceedingly lengthy footnotes, in small print, often occupying an entire page; indeed, 20% of the book is given over to footnotes. The 1936 commemorative edition (photographically reproduced from the original) is edited, with notes, by George Grafton Wilson, with a preface by James Brown Scott, General Editor. Both men were internationally known authorities on international law, authors and editors of many textbooks on the subject.

The introductory essay, *Henry Wheaton and International Law*, by George Grafton Wilson, says, in part,

"The period of the middle of the nineteenth century afforded new material for Dana's notes. The Monroe Doctrine had been somewhat tested and Dana gives it a long note and takes up the related matter of intervention in Mexico under the convention of 1861 to which France, Great Britain, and Spain were parties. The questions of slavery, recognition of belligerency, contraband, blockade, continuous voyage, convoy, the Trent Affair, and other questions arising during the American Civil War, 1861-5, offer Dana much new material for notes, and many of these topics receive elaborate treatment. The same is true of matters arising during the period 1840 to 1860 and involving naturalization, extradition, and recent practice in civil and criminal legislation... Dana's notes constitute about one-fifth of the volume called the eighth edition..."

The Subject Index states: Adams, J.Q.: responsibility for the germ of the Monroe Doctrine, 82 n.; argument of, on fisheries, 287; on "free ships, free goods", 485 et seq. There is no mention whatsoever of Adams in connection with the *Amistad*.

The Table of Cases, starting on p. xxxiii, mentions, under the letter A, the following ships, among others: the *Abby*, the *Abigail*, the *Acteon*, the *Actif*, the *Adeline*, the *Admiral*, the *Adventure*, the *Africa*, the *Alabama*, the *Alerta*, the *Alexander*, the *Alexandra*, the *Alfred*, the *Amedie*, the *Amistad de Rues* (an unrelated case having nothing to do with the slave trade), the *Amy Warwick*, the *Anna*, the *Anna Catharina*, the *Anne*, the *Antelope*, the *Antonia Johanna*, the *Apollo*, the *Ariadne*, the *Arrogante Barcelones*, the *Arthur*, the *Atrea*, the *Atalanta*, the *Athol*, and the *Aurora*.

There is no mention of the *Amistad*.

(Note: In the following, the terms "prize law", and "prize courts" refer to the wartime crime of blockade running or the recognized legal seizure of enemy vessels and maritime cargoes during wartime.)

The following passages are taken from footnote 86 starting on page 175:

"The *Amedie* and subsequent cases: A careful examination leads to the belief that the case of the *Amedie*, and those following it, have been misunderstood by the author [i.e., Wheaton], as well as by others. The proceeding [the *Amedie*], from beginning to end, was one of prize of war solely; and her condemnation had nothing to do with her being engaged in the slave trade... The explanation of the fact, that this case has so almost universally been cited as one of condemnation of a foreign vessel for being engaged in the slave trade, may be found in the peculiarity of the rules which govern courts of prize... The *Africa* (Acton, ii, i), the *Nancy* (*Ib.*, 2), [1] and the *Anne* (*Ib.*, 6), were all likewise prize causes; and the capture and condemnation in each were *jure belli*, and not for being engaged in the slave trade...

"The *Fortuna* (Dodson, i. 81). This was exclusively a prize cause. The vessel was captured and condemned as a prize of war... the *Diana* (Dodson, i. 95)... the vessel was held to be Swedish, engaged in the slave trade to a Swedish island; and the court decided that the law of Sweden permitted the trade. The claim was, therefore, one that the court could entertain, within the rule of the *Amedie*. The court treated the case as one of civil forfeiture only; and, no ground for that appearing, the property was restored.

"The *Louis* (Dodson, ii. 210). This is the case which is treated by Mr. Wheaton and most others as having overruled The *Amedie*. It was a civil cause for forfeiture, and has no relation to prize law or its presumptions or rules. The grounds taken by the counsel for the captors were, that the vessel was French, and engaged in the slave trade, which was prohibited by French law, and, as argued, by the law of nations; and, further, that the crew had resisted the boarding and search by the king's ship, and killed some of the crew, and were therefore guilty of piracy, and out of the protection of the law of nations.

"The court held, that the boarding and search, by the king's cruiser, of a vessel in time of peace, and not on suspicion of piracy *jure gentium*, but of being engaged in the slave trade, were unjustifiable, and consequently that resistance to them was not piratical; and that the slave trade was not piracy *jure gentium*, nor prohibited by the law of France [p. 177, *Wheaton*, 1866 edition, with footnotes by Richard Henry Dana, see above]. Therefore it was clear that the vessel not only could not be decreed forfeited by any British tribunal, but was illegally seized and brought before the court. The original taking was illegal.

"In the *Amedie*, the visit, search, capture, and bringing in were in the exercise of belligerent right. In the *Louis*, they were in time of peace, and solely for the purpose of suppressing the slave trade. In the *Amedie*, the proceedings were in prize, before a prize court, and governed by the law and rules of prize. In the *Louis*, they were civil, and governed by the law and rules of civil forfeiture. In the *Amedie*, the condemnation was as prize of war. In the *Louis*, if the vessel had been condemned, it could have been only for being engaged in the slave trade. In the *Amedie*, the capture and bringing in were justifiable, and the court had clear jurisdiction. In the *Louis*, the capture and bringing in were unjustifiable. And the general duty of the court was to restore, if a proper claimant appeared. In the *Amedie*, the burden on the claimant was to show legal title and a right to receive the property. In the *Louis*, the burden was on the seizor to show cause for [211] forfeiture. In the *Amedie*, the claim was rejected because the slave trade, though not universally illegal or piracy *jure gentium*, was illegal by the law of the claimant's country. In the *Louis*, the claim was sustained, because the slave trade was neither illegal by the law of nations, nor by the law of the claimant's country [i.e., France].

"It may be, and probably is, true, that British cruisers made use of the belligerent right of search to deliver slaves, and took advantage of the severe and summary rules of war tribunals to secure the condemnation of their prizes, but this is only saying that they made an undue use of opportunities which the criminality of their antagonists put in their power, and does not touch the law decided.

"The result is, that the precedents, from the *Amedie* to the *Louis*, will be found consistent with each other, and with the rules of prize courts, and with the law of nations as to the slave trade."

The Index, under "Slave trade": reads: "piracy and, 165; 169ff n.; treaties for abolition of, 169; prohibited by various nations, 169, 170 n.; the Treaty of Paris of 1814, 168, 170 n.; course of the United States as to the right of search, 170 n.; the Quintuple Treaty of 1814, conceding the right of search, 170 n.; the Ashburton Treaty, 170 n.; treaty between the United States and Great Britain, 1862, conceding a limited right of search, 170 n.; case of the *Amedie*, 171, 175 n.; case of the *Fortuna*, 172, 176 n.; case of the *Diana*, 173, 176 n.; case of the *Antelope*, 177, 178; juridical aspects of, 179 n;. opinion of statesmen and jurists on, 180 n.; conventions and practice of nations in regard to, 182 n."

Under "Slaves", the Index states: "on brig *Creole*, in British port, 139 n.; extradition of, 157; emancipation of, in United States Civil War, 369, n.; status of captured, during civil war, 370."

The *Amistad* is not mentioned.

The Sources of Modern International Law, by George A. Finch, published by the Carnegie Endowment for International Peace, 1937, mentions the *Antelope* on pp. 26-28. The *Amistad* is not mentioned.

Fenwick's *International Law*, 3rd edition, Appleton-Century-Crofts, Inc. 1948, mentions the *Louis* and the *Antelope* on pp. 327-8.

The *Amistad* is not mentioned.

International Law, W.E. Hall, 7th edition, Oxford, 1917. No mention.

A Handbook on International Law, T.J. Lawrence, 11 edition, 1938. No mention.

International Law, Oppenheim-Lauterpacht, 5th edition, Longman and Green, 1935. No mention.

Wheaton's International Law, A. Barriedale Keith, vol. 2, War, Stevens & Sons, 1944. No mention.

Handbook on International Law, George Grafton Wilson (see above), 3rd edition, Hornbook Series, West Publishing Co., 1939, mentions the *Antelope* on p. 74, note. 3, and p. 344, note. 1. There is no mention of the *Amistad*.

QUESTION: Slavery and the slave trade, like piracy, are classic topics of international law. Is it conceivable – can one imagine for an instant – that a "landmark case", argued before the "Supreme Court of the United States", by a "former President of the United States", and also involving – or so we are told – an incumbent President, Martin A. Van Buren, as well as John C. Calhoun, and many other famous people; a case overturning, or at least modifying, the *Antelope* case – even the nationality of the slave owners is identical – could be ignored in Richard Henry Dana's extremely detailed notes, in a classic text on international law, written in the United States, in 1866, only 25 years later? Is it conceivable that a "landmark" case at international law could be ignored by all succeeding works on the subject, so far as I know, for over one hundred years, only to become, in retrospect, one hundred and fifty years later, one of the most sensational events of the nineteenth century? If the *Amistad* was not deemed worthy of mention in 1911, or in the 1930s, why should the same case be of earth-shaking importance in the 1990s?

One of the cases cited by Dana, and mentioned in all texts on international law, the *Anna* (although not always mentioned by name) involved the question of whether the banks of the Mississippi, and therefore the national territory and three-mile limit, began at *terra firma*, or at the outer reaches of some insignificant mud banks. "... a question arose as to what was to be deemed the shore, since there are a number of little mud islands, composed of earth and trees, drifted down by the river, which form a kind of portico to the main land. It was contended that these were not to be considered as any part of the American territory – that they were a sort of 'no man's land' not of consistency enough to support the purposes of life, uninhabited, and resorted to only for shooting and taking birds' nests. It was argued that the line of territory was to have been taken only from the Balize, which is a fort raised on made-land by the former Spanish possessors. But the learned judge was of a different opinion..." (*Wheaton/Dana*, pp. 215-6.). The *Anna* case was, and is, considered to be of crucial importance to international law. But not the *Amistad*.

The *Amistad*, therefore, far from being a "landmark" case, was, quite literally a "non-event" until the 1990s.

Nor is the case mentioned in David L. Hoggan's *Das blinde Jahrhundert* (*The Blind Century*), although he discusses slavery and abolition at some considerable length. He mentions the Nat Turner Rebellion once, and John Quincy Adams repeatedly, but never the *Amistad*. *Das blinde Jahrhundert* is a typical Hoggan production, crammed full of obscure and astonishing information on nearly every topic under the sun, 600 pages long, with a 50-odd-page annotated bibliography and hundreds of annotated and highly complicated footnotes and references, etc. etc., but no mention of the *Amistad*. (He does mention the *Virginius*, a famous case in maritime international law, involving, once again, Spain, Cuba and the United States; but not the *Amistad*.) The only reference I have ever seen to the case in a lifetime of reading is in Hugh Thomas's *History of the Trans-Atlantic Slave Trade*, which was not published until 1997.

By my count, approximately 25 books have been written on the *Amistad*: one in 1840, one in 1941, one in 1942, two in 1953, and about 20 since the beginning of the "Civil Rights" Movement, 4 or 5 of them by Jews, including 4 or 5 admitted works of fiction, screenplays, or novels "based on the screenplay" of the film, produced by Zionist Steven Spielberg.

In actual fact, according to the records, the *Amistad* was a totally obscure and insignificant decision which changed nothing, and in no way threatened, condemned or advanced slavery in the United States; for that reason, it was hardly noticed for 150 years. Slavery was legal in Cuba until 1886 but the African slave trade was prohibited. Therefore the Africans involved did not have to be returned to their owners, but could be returned to Africa, where they reverted to savagery and where the lives of the missionaries sent to look after them became quite dangerous. Typical lawyer stuff, a technicality.

According to the index of *The 1966 Collier's Encyclopedia*, the *Amistad* is mentioned once, in two sentences only, in this 24-volume standard reference work – not in any of the articles on slavery or abolition, or in any of the biographical articles or articles on the United States, but in the article on the "American Missionary Association", which it describes as "precipitated into action by a slave mutiny on the *Amistad* off the coast of Cuba in 1839. The Amistad Committee carried the case successfully through the United States Supreme Court, and sent the liberated slaves to a Connecticut school before expatriating and assisting them in opening the first antislavery mission in Africa." Period. Nor does it tell us that Joseph Sinko (aka Cinque) set himself up as a slave trader after he got back to Africa.

Whatever happened on the *Amistad* in 1839 and/or later, no one thought it worth mentioning for over one hundred years – including the legal writers and specialists, experts on the subject. In view of the intrinsic interest of the case both legally and historically, this seems very strange. Perhaps the moral of the story is that an incident which might arguably be said to illustrate the essential humanitarianism of Christian white Americans, both North and South, will be ignored – or at least kept within reasonable proportions – until it can be blown up into earth-shaking proportions in a "Hate Whitey" screen epic produced by a Hoaxoco$t con-artist.

I am waiting for a Hollywood screen epic depicting the Africans slaughtering whole families of missionaries; necklacing, mutilating and torturing each other, raping nurses, nuns, and children; wrecking everything the white humanitarians were ever idiot enough to give them for centuries; and/or Zionists murdering, maiming and crippling the children of Gaza while lecturing the rest of us on "hatred" and "tolerance". Whatever "hatred" is, Jews are the world's foremost practitioners and experts. While I am waiting – since it will be forever – give me *Ewige Jude*.

"ANTI-SEMITISM" IN THE
ENCYCLOPAEDIA BRITANNICA

Introduction to another Valuable Source
of Unusual Information

A truism of liberalism is that the truth may be approximated through a comparison of opinion. In the *Encyclopaedia Britannica*, for example, all articles dealing directly with Jewish matters are written by Jews and Rabbis, dripping with self-pity and self-praise. Articles on peripheral subjects, however, tell a different story.

* * *

From the *1911 Encyclopaedia Britannica*

RUSSIA: "The Semitic race is represented by upwards of 5,000,000 Jews... The rapidity with which they peopled certain towns (e.g., Odessa) and whole provinces was really prodigious. The law of Russia prohibits them from entering Great Russia, only the wealthiest and best educated enjoying this privilege; nevertheless they are met with everywhere, even in the Urals. Their chief abodes, however, continue to be Poland... Organized as they are into a kind of community for mutual protection and mutual help, they soon become masters of the trade wherever they penetrate. In the villages, they are mostly innkeepers, intermediaries in trade, and pawnbrokers..." (vol. XXIII, p. 855)

"The numerous outbreaks against the Jews are directed, not against their creed, but against them as keen business men and extortionate money-lenders..." (p. 885)

"The wealth of Russia consisting mainly of raw produce, the trade of the country turns chiefly on the purchase of this for export... this traffic is in the hands of a great number of middlemen – in the West, Jews, and elsewhere Russians – to whom the peasants are for the most part in debt..." (p. 890)

"In the rest of the country they had not been allowed to reside in the villages, because their habits of keeping vodka shops and lending money at usurious interest were found to demoralize the peasantry..." (p. 906)

RUMANIA: "Their improvidence soon got them into the hands of Jewish money-lenders, who, fortunately for the peasants, were by law unable to become proprietors of the soil..." (vol. XXIII, p. 828)

"The bitter feeling against them in Rumania is not so much due to religious fanaticism as to the fear that if given political and other rights they will gradually possess themselves of the whole soil... in many places they have a monopoly of the wine and spirit shops, and retail trade generally; and as they are always willing to advance money on usury, and are more intelligent and better educated than the ordinary peasant, there is little doubt that in a country where the large landowners are proverbially extravagant, and the peasant proprietors needy, the soil would soon fall into the hand of the Jews were it not for the stringent laws which prevent them from owning land outside the towns. When in addition it is considered that the Moldavian Jews, who are mostly of Polish and Russian origin, speak a foreign language, wear a distinguishing dress and keep themselves aloof from their neighbours, the antipathy in which they are held by the Rumanians generally may be understood." (p. 829)

HUNGARY: "The Jews... monopolize a large portion of trade, are with the Germans the chief employers of labour, and control not only the finances but to a great extent the government and the press of the country. Owing to the improvidence of the Hungarian landowners and the poverty of the peasants, the soil of the country is gradually passing into their hands." (vol. XIII, p. 897)

GERMANY: "Nearly all the bankers and stockbrokers in Germany were Jews. Many of the leaders of the liberal parties, e.g., Bamberger and Lasker, were of Jewish origin; the doctrines of Liberalism were supported by papers owned and edited by Jews; hence the wish to restore more fully the avowed Christian character of the state, coinciding with the attack on the influence of finance, which owed so much to the Liberal economic doctrines, easily degenerated into attacks on the Jews." (vol. XI, p. 888)

* * *

From the *1922 Encyclopaedia Britannica*

POLAND: "THE JEWISH QUESTION: One of the most important questions to be considered by the new Polish State is that of the Jews.

Numerically they form roughly one seventh of the population. In Warsaw a third of the population are Jews; in many provincial towns four out of every five inhabitants are Jews, and in some nine out of ten, and of these the vast majority are Eastern Jews who in language, religion, and customs differ from the population. Their language is Yiddish, a Middle-High-German dialect; for the purposes of writing, Hebrew characters are used. Their dress is peculiar to themselves and their 'unclean habits and low standards of conduct' are neither European nor modern. The Western Jew is the more civilized type which is generally found in Western Europe, speaking the language and conforming to the habits of Western civilization. The Eastern Jew is essentially a business or commercial man, but rarely a producer. He is usually a middleman or intermediary. In towns the majority of the shops are owned by Jews, but they are a race apart, hated and despised by the rest of the population, devoted to their religion, which is a primitive type of Judaism. The Jews have been settled in Poland between 800 and 1,000 years so that they can hardly be considered 'strangers' in the land; in fact the Slavs cannot be considered very much more native than they. It was not, however, until about 20 years ago that the present quarrel between the Jews and the Poles began. The Tsarist Government drove the Jews out of Russia but gave them exceptional advantages in Poland. These Litvaks (as they were called) openly professed themselves the partisans of Russia and founded the Jewish press which set to work openly to fight against Polish autonomy. The Poles attacked the Jews before the war by means of a national boycott, the only means by which one subject race could attack another. During and after the war the hostility to the Jews was increased by the fact that in the German occupation the Jew was a willing tool of the invader and by the close connection between the Jews and Bolshevism. The hostility to the Jews was marked in 1918 and 1919 by excesses in which some 200-300 have in fact been killed, but which have been enormously exaggerated by the Jewish press...
Capt. Peter Wright, in his very valuable and interesting report states (Cmd 674, 1920, pp. 17-36) that the great majority of the poor Jews are of the Eastern type and extreme Orthodoxy (Chassidim). They form an immense mass of squalid and helpless poverty and Capt. Wright's only recommendation is that the richer Jews should study the condition of the poor Jews, who either trade as small middlemen, as hawkers or touts... They are driven to all sorts of illicit and fraudulent practices as in England, in the East End of London... too large a proportion of convictions for such offenses can be laid to their account. They are unfit for the modern economic world for want of education and for

Western society because of their habits and want of cleanliness. They are devoted to their strange old religion but as they grow richer their piety, as the Chief Rabbi told Capt. Wright, is destroyed by wealth and they take too little interest in their poorer brethren. No one who knows Poland can be surprised at the Polish attitude or the desire of the Poles to be rid of this corrupting influence." (vol. XXXII, p. 123)

HUNGARY: "The Jewish question has become important in Hungary... As they grew rich through trade, the ghetto became too small for them. As they owned no land, they were not tied to the soil and streamed into the cities, where they found more opportunities of making money and adding to their wealth. Above all Budapest, as the centre of commerce and industry and the seat of the banks, had a strong attraction for them. Three distinct classes of the Jews grew up: the Orthodox, who wished to remain Jews with all the habits and customs of the ghetto; those who in most respects relinquished their position of religious isolation and strove after assimilation... and thirdly the cosmopolitan Jews, the revolutionaries, who were the enemies of all national feeling and represented materialistic internationalism. It was the part played by this third class of Jews... which has made the Jewish question acute in Hungary. As Hungary has no true middle class, they exercised great influence on the intellectual life of the country..." (vol. XXXI, p. 408)

"Instead of the national heroes, Marx, Engels & Lenin were glorified... In boys and girls schools, the pupils received enlightened instruction in the processes of generation, birth, etc., with disastrous results to the juvenile morality." (vol. XXXI, p. 416)

"The leaders of the Social Democrats and Bourgeois Radicals were, almost without exception, of Jewish origin. This was also the case with the most prominent members of Government of the Republic..; these were the men who had made it impossible to resist the invasion of Hungary by force of arms..." (vol. XXXI, p. 415)

"Since most of the ruling politicians and People's Commissars... belonged to the younger generation of Jews anti-Communist feeling in the country assumed more and more the character of anti-Semitism." (vol. XXXI, p. 417)

"One consequence of the Bolshevist rule was the still more intense development of anti-Semitic feeling. Since the leaders of the Communists were chiefly recruited among the younger Jewish intellectual circles, the National Assembly in order to prevent the creation of a Jewish intellectual proletariat, in Sept. 1920, proclaimed 'Numerus Clausus' for the universities. Under this clause, Jews could only be admitted to the universities in proportion to their percentage of the population." (vol. XXXI, p. 418)

ANGOLA: "Southern Angola in 1909-11, was regarded as a probable choice by the Jewish Territorial Association as a field for colonization, and Portugal enacted land laws with a view to that contingency. But Angola was rejected as a home for the Jews." (vol. XXX, p. 139)

* * *

From the *1928 Encyclopaedia Britannica*

JEWS: "The Jewish population of the world on the outbreak of the War in 1914 may be estimated at about 14,900,000... The Jews whole-heartedly supported the revolution... Among the Bolshevik leaders and their satellites were a certain number of Jews... At the same time, the American Jews began to play a part of growing importance in the Zionist movement and were concerned in the negotiations leading up to the Balfour Declaration of which President Wilson was a consistent and influential advocate." (vol. II, p. 605)

"In both Russia and Hungary a prominent part in the Bolshevik movement was played by men who, though long disassociated from the Jewish community, were nevertheless of Jewish birth." (vol. II, p. 606)

HUNGARY: "The people's commissars and practically all the leading persons were Jews, a fact which explains the anti-Jewish feeling which later prevailed in Hungary..." (vol. II, p. 393)

ZIONISM: "Not long after the outbreak of the war, Dr. Weizmann and his friends were brought in touch with a number of influential public men... What the Zionists proposed was, in effect, that Great Britain should make it part of the policy to provide in the peace settlement for the establishment in Palestine of a national home for the Jews... By the beginning of 1916, the British Government had come to the conclusion that there were other and more practical reasons for taking Zionism seriously... The hour of decision was approaching in the United States, where there was a Jewish population of over 3,000,000... A declaration in favour of Zionism would help to rally Jewish opinion throughout the world to the side of the Allies... President Wilson had personally intervened to make it clear that he would welcome a British pronouncement in favour of Zionism... in 1922 resolutions associating the United States with the policy embodied in the Declaration were unanimously adopted by both Houses of Congress. At the insistence of

Great Britain a Zionist delegation was given a hearing by the Peace Conference in Paris on Feb. 27, 1919..." (vol. III, p. 1139)

"The Arabs did not take kindly to the Balfour Declaration, which they did not altogether unnaturally misconstrue... there were anti-Jewish demonstrations in Jerusalem in 1920..." (vol. III, p. 1140)

BAVARIA: "Meanwhile, the Nationalist leagues had gained in strength and now began to defy the Governments orders. The most powerful of them were the National Socialists, an extreme militaristic, nationalist, and, above all, anti-Semite body, nominally democratic in tendency, but actually largely used by the rich to break strikes and attack Socialism. This body was raised from obscurity by one Hitler, a good demagogue but no politician... Hitler and other leaders were sent to prison or lunatic asylums." (vol. I, p. 342)

* * *

There is a saying in French: the more things change, the more they are the same. The Jew is eternal.

WAR CRIMES TRIALS

Approximately 10,000 "War Crimes Trials" have been held since 1945. Trials of Japanese military personnel ended in 1949, yet "war crimes trials" of Germans and Eastern Europeans continue to date.

Almost invariably, the charge is "violation of the laws and customs of war", derived, in turn, from international conventions signed at the Hague in 1899 and 1907.

That these trials have little or no basis in law is clear from the wording of the treaties which are said to have been violated.

Let us take a typical example, the Hague Declaration (IV, 3) of 1899 on the Use of Expanding Bullets, dated July 29, 1899.

The Convention states,

"The Contracting Parties agree to abstain from the use of bullets which expand or flatten easily in the human body, such as bullets with a hard envelope which does not entirely cover the core, or is pierced with incisions.

"The present Declaration is only binding for the Contracting Powers in the case of a war between two or more of them.

"It shall cease to be binding from the time when, in a war between the contracting Powers, one of the belligerents is joined by a non-contracting Power."

[IMPORTANT NOTE: This is called an "all-participation clause".]

The United States never ratified this convention, which, thus, never became "international law" in any war involving the United States. This was because American troops were busy using expanding bullets against Filipinos whom they had just "liberated" from the Spanish.

American refusal to ratify this convention meant not only that the United States was free to continue using expanding (or dum-dum) bullets legally in all wars, but from the moment the United States entered any conflict, all other belligerents were free to use them as well.

[NOTE: Dum-dum bullets, first manufactured by the British at Dum Dum, India, are of advantage only in jungle warfare against primitive tribes, where the danger is of sudden rushes of large numbers at close quarters. They are not used in European warfare because they are inaccurate and tend to foul guns. If they offered an advantage, they would be used regardless of any treaty.]

There are fourteen Hague Conventions, almost all of which contain similar clauses, and for this reason have had little or no application since 1907.

The Fifth Hague Convention Respecting the Rights and Duties of Neutral Powers and Persons in Case of War on Land of 18 October 1907, for example, states:

Art. 20: "The provisions of the present Convention do not apply except between Contracting Powers, and then only if all the belligerents are parties to the Convention".

This Convention was never ratified by Great Britain, and never applied after August 4, 1914.

Art. 1: "The territory of neutral Powers is inviolable." Nevertheless, the British and Americans never tired of quoting this clause against the German and Japanese despite their own violations of the neutrality of Iceland, Greenland, Persia, Iraq, Portuguese Timor, and the planned violation of Scandinavian neutrality.

The Third Hague Convention Respecting the Opening of Hostilities, article 1, states:

"The contracting powers recognize that hostilities between themselves must not commence without previous and explicit warning, in the form either of a reasoned declaration of war or an ultimatum with conditional declaration of war."

The problem here is that the "warning" may be as little as one minute, and no verbal formula is required. Poland received two ultimatums and was the first to mobilize. America received a formal declaration 25 minutes late, of which it had actual knowledge 10 days beforehand.

However, the basis of nearly all "war crimes trials" has been the Fourth Hague Convention Respecting the Laws and Customs of War on Land. In the words of Telford Taylor, Chief Counsel and Representative of the United States for the Prosecution of War Crimes at Nuremberg:

"An Annex to the Convention, consisting of 56 articles, sets forth various requirements and limitations with respect to the conduct of hostilities, the treatment of prisoners of war, and the exercise of authority over the occupied territory of a hostile state."

This, then, is the Convention which the Germans and Japanese were alleged to have violated in 10,000 trials.

What does the Convention say exactly?

Art. 2: "The provisions... of the present Convention do not apply except between contracting Powers, and then only if all the belligerents are parties to the Convention."

This condition has remained unfulfilled since August 1, 1914. Non-signatories during WWII included Italy, Greece, and the national states of Yugoslavia. Communist Russia repudiated all Czarist agreements and never made any pretence of obeying the Hague or Geneva Conventions.

Art. 3: "A belligerent party which violates the provisions of the said Regulations shall, if the case demands, be liable to pay compensation."

– This is self-explanatory. No trials were contemplated.

THE ANNEX TO THE 4th HAGUE CONVENTION

The Annex to the Convention was the real basis for nearly all of these 10,000 trials. This is the Convention which defines "war crimes" and "war criminals"...

Articles 1 and 2 prohibit guerrilla warfare, stating that belligerents must be "commanded by a person responsible for his subordinates... have a fixed distinctive emblem recognizable at a distance... carry arms openly... and conduct their operations in accordance with the laws and customs of war."

– The European and Asian resistance movements were ILLEGAL.

Article 43 requires collaboration with occupation governments. "The authority of the legitimate power having in fact passed into the hands of the occupant, the latter shall take all the measures in his power to restore, and ensure, as far as possible, public order and safety, while respecting, unless absolutely prevented, the laws in force in the country."

– The "collaborators" shot, hanged, or imprisoned after WWII were acting in compliance with international law.

Article 23 (3) prohibits weapons calculated to cause unnecessary suffering. Napalm, phosphorous, jellied gasoline, etc. are ILLEGAL.

Articles 25, 27 and 56 prohibit bombardment "by whatever means" of undefended cities, cultural monuments, etc...

– The fire bombings of Dresden and civilian areas of Hamburg, Tokyo, Hiroshima, Nagasaki, etc. were ILLEGAL.

Article 6 states that belligerents may utilize the labor of prisoners of war, officers excepted, for the public service, for private persons or their own account. German and Japanese "slave policy" was perfectly legal insofar as it applied to members of resistance groups or lower-ranking military personnel.

Article 8: "Prisoners of war are subject to the laws, regulations and orders in force of the State in whose power they are. Any act of insubordination justifies the adoption towards them of such measures of severity as may be considered necessary."

– So much for the "mistreatment of prisoners" which formed the basis of so many war crimes trials.

Article 46: "Private property cannot be confiscated."

– The post-WWII expulsions and confiscations were ILLEGAL. The provisions of the Versailles Treaty which confiscated the private property of all German citizens resident outside Germany, including missionaries on South Sea islands, who were expelled and sent home penniless, were ILLEGAL.

Art. 5: "Prisoners... cannot be confined except as an indispensable measure of safety, and only while the circumstances which necessitate the measure continue to exist," and

Art. 20: "After the conclusion of peace, the repatriation of prisoners shall be carried out as quickly as possible."

– The prolonged detention of German and Japanese prisoners by the British, French, Russians and Americans for years after the war was ILLEGAL.

Art. 7: "Prisoners of war shall be treated as regards board, lodging, and clothing on the same footing as the troops of the Government who captured them."

The conditions of detention in "Eisenhower's death camps" were ILLEGAL whatever the death rate. (See *Other Losses* by James Bacque).

Art. 32: "A person is regarded as a parlementaire who has been authorized by one of the belligerents to enter into communications with the other... he has a right to inviolability."

– The detention of Rudolph Hess was ILLEGAL.

Finally, article 23 (h) prohibits declaring "abolished, suspended, or inadmissible in a court of law the rights and actions of the nationals of the hostile party."

If these treaties have any application at all (which is doubtful), the real war criminals were the Americans, the British, the French, and the Russians.

The illegalities of "war crimes" proceedings include the admissibility of oral and written hearsay; the introduction of the concept of "conspiracy" into international law (unknown prior to 1945); the total lack of any pre-trial inquest or forensic evidence; and trial before a court itself composed of actual "war criminals".

To return to the writings of Telford Taylor:

"The issues surrounding the war crimes trials are numerous and complex; discussion and criticism of what was done should be welcomed by all who hope for a continuing development of international law... but what should have been done instead is a problem generally ignored by those who condemn what was done in fact."

The alternative is a fair trial before an impartial court under existing procedures and proper rules of evidence.

ANSWER TO YALE F. EDEIKEN

The following is a "refutation" of my article "War Crimes Trials" (pp. 66-70 of this book) by Mr. Yale F. Edeiken, a practitioner before the Bar of Pennsylvania.

My comments are in square brackets. I apologize for the repetition: I have found that certain subtle but very important points are overlooked unless repeatedly stressed.

* * *

THE FORENSIC SINS OF CARLOS PORTER
by Yale F. Edeiken

[COMMENT: Note the constant introduction of quasi-religious terminology and neologisms: "sin", "denier", etc. – C.P.]

(fo ren sic adj. 1. of, characteristic of, or suitable for a law court, public debate, or formal argumentation.)

Among the staple texts of those who deny the Holocaust are the writings of Carlos Porter. One of his articles "War Crimes Trials" can be found on the CODOH website. It claims to discuss the 1907 Annex to the Hague Convention [COMMENT: There are 14 Hague Conventions; see below. – C.P.] dealing with the laws of war, and this essay is so highly regarded in the denier community that it has been cited by deniers as authoritative on the subject of the Hague Convention. A close examination of Porter's work, however, demonstrates that it is inaccurate both as to the text of the Convention and the conclusions that are derived from the distorted citations. This analysis will deal with both of those issues.

It is only fair to judge an author's work by his intentions. In this case Porter informs us exactly what those intentions are:

"This, then, is the Convention which the Germans and Japanese were alleged to have violated in 10,000 trials. What does the Convention say exactly?"

The purpose of Porter's article, therefore, was not to present edited paraphrases but the text, exact and complete

[COMMENT: There are 14 Hague Conventions (actually 17

including those drawn up in 1899), forming a stack of A5 photocopies approximately 1 inch thick. Was it my intention to reproduce the full text of Hague IV in 2 pages? If so, why did I number my paragraphs 2, 3, and then 1, 2, 43? – C.P.]

He fails miserably. Porter's deletions and paraphrases not only contradict his stated purpose but many substantially alter the meaning of the provisions. It is doubly dishonest in that Porter presents little more than his paraphrases followed by an announcement of what he states they mean. Supporting evidence is virtually non-existent and, in its absence, all a reader has to rely upon is Porter's version of the text.

[COMMENT: I have read this material and provided a concise summary of the arguments derived therefrom, as presented in the defense summations of war crime trials generally and Nuremberg, Tokyo, and the Trial of Martin Gottfried Weiss in particular (those with which I am most familiar). If an exception be made for Rudolf Hess, the merest glance at a few hundred or a thousand pages of defense summation in any of these trials will reveal, not only the arguments enumerated by myself, but many others, backed up in turn by dozens of references to recognized authorities in international law: Fenwick, Wheaton, Wharton, Woolsey, Grotius, Smith, Higgins, Hyde, Hill, Hall, Hackman, Hull, Miller, Twiss, Phillimore, Wilson, Maurice, Wigmore, Hudson + Fuller, Flory, Lawrence, Winfield, Glueck, Blackstone, Oppenheim-Lauterpacht, Bellot, Moore, Scott, Nippold, Singer, Roemer; Gallaudet, Main, Finch, Dickinson, Brierley, Black, Cobbet, Feilchenfeld, etc. These are the arguments which have been presented, whether Mr. Edeiken likes it or not. I have also read thousands of pages of prosecution summation, and they do a much better job of it than Mr. Edeiken. For Mr. Edeiken to pretend that his points of view are the only ones possible, is nothing short of ludicrous. The difference is that where I present a concise, succinct summary in 2 pages, Mr. Edeiken requires 17 pages simply to cause confusion. He found two mistakes: a very short paraphrase represented as a direct quote, the only error being the use of quotation marks (article 3 of the body of Hague IV); and a misspelling. – C.P.]

The problems with the text of the 1907 Convention

[COMMENT: There are 14 Hague Conventions, as noted above. – C.P.]

are only the beginning of the problems with "War Crimes Trials." Porter's laconic conclusions are dependent on his edited readings of the text and his factual assumptions. Many of Porter's unsupported allegations are simply not correct. The second part of this article, therefore, is an analysis of some of Porter's contentions. It is by no means complete; there are clear errors such as Porter's interpretation of Article 43 that are not included. As many of Porter's errors are similar in nature, explaining all of them would be repetitious.

The examples provided do represent an analysis of Porter's shoddy and misleading techniques. Porter's "War Crimes Trials" is, in fact, poorly written, poorly reasoned and inaccurate at various points. The theme of "War Crimes Trials" is embodied in Porter's unsubstantiated accusations.

* * *

Porter's problems with facts begin with the first part of the article where he discusses the applicability of the Convention.

[COMMENT: Which Convention? Mr. Edeiken starts out, it should be noted, by confusing the 1899 Convention on the Use of Expanding Bullets with the 1907 Fourth Hague Convention on Land Warfare. – C.P.]

He states, for example:

"The United States never ratified this convention, which, thus, never became 'international law' in any war involving the United States."

[COMMENT: As noted above, this is in reference to the 1899 Hague Convention on the Use of Expanding Bullets. – C.P.]

This is, as anyone who has examined the primary documents knows, a misrepresentation. While the U.S. did not ratify the Convention,

[COMMENT: Which Convention? Mr. Edeiken now hops to Hague IV of 1907, as if they were the same. Is it the contention of Mr. Edeiken that the United States of America never ratified the Fourth Hague Convention on Land Warfare of October 18, 1907, that I make that claim, and that such a claim would be correct? When I read something like this, I begin to wonder whether a writer knows anything. No doubt Mr. Edeiken made this mistake because the electronically scanned versions of the Hague Conventions posted on the Yale University website recommended by Mr. Edeiken delete the signatures, ratifications, adhesions and reservations (4 pages), which are crucial to an understanding of the twentieth century. For example, Serbia was not a signatory to Hague IV. The Germans maintained that Serbian participation in WWI invoked the all-participation clause rendering Hague IV inapplicable, and that German introduction of gas warfare during WWI was therefore legal. The intention was to break the stalemate, capture Paris, and win the war, as in 1870. – C.P.]

it entered a separate convention signed by the president of the U.S. on July 27, 1929.

[SUMMARY SO FAR: Mr. Edeiken takes a comment on the 1899 Convention on the Use of Expanding Bullets as applying to the 1907 Convention on Land Warfare (Hague IV), which it does not, then hops to one of the 1929 Geneva Conventions to get around what he imagines to be the problem of non-ratification by the U.S.. He provides no references to the "convention signed by the president of the U.S. on 27 July 1929", apart from the date. He is referring, somewhat dubiously, to the 1929 Geneva Prisoner of War Convention (not to be confused with the 1929 Geneva Convention on the Amelioration of Sick and Wounded among Armies in the Field). The 1929 Geneva Prisoners of War Convention of War Convention does not contain an all-participation clause, but applies between the signatories only.

ONCE AGAIN: Mr. Edeiken confuses the Hague Convention on the Use of Expanding Bullets of July 29, 1899 – not ratified by the U.S. – with the Fourth Hague Convention on Land Warfare of October 18, 1907 – ratified by the U.S. on November 27, 1909 – then introduces an irrelevant discussion of the 1929 Geneva Prisoner of War Convention to get around what he imagines to be the problem of non-ratification; that is not the problem. The problem with the Fourth Convention is the "all-participation clause" – i.e., that the Convention applies only between signatories to the Convention, and then only when all participants in a conflict are signatories to the Convention – as noted above and below – to which Mr. Edeiken has no answer. If the "all-participation clause" means what it says, then none of the Hague Conventions were in application during either World War, and neither the Germans nor the Allies can be found guilty of violating their provisions. If the "all-participation clause" does NOT mean what it says, then the Allies, on the plain terms of Hague IV, were guilty of more atrocities and "war crimes" than the Germans and Japanese put together, indeed many times over. The question, put crudely, is:

Q: "Hague IV Convention on the wall, who's the worst war criminal of all?"

A: "Thou art, my Queen" – you, the Allies. – C.P.]

[COMMENT OF SECONDARY IMPORTANCE: Note as well that the President of the United States cannot possibly have signed the 1929 Geneva Prisoner of War Convention on July 27, 1929; that is because Mr. Edeiken has gotten the date of signature of the 1929 Geneva Prisoner of War Convention by the national delegations in Geneva – July 27, 1929 – mixed up with the date of ratification by the U.S. Senate; these are two different dates. For example, the Fourth

Hague Convention on Land Warfare of October 18, 1907 – which Mr. Edeiken says was never ratified at all, having confused it with the 1899 Convention on the Use of Expanding Bullets – was ratified by the United States on November 27, 1909, two years later, and the 1929 Geneva Prisoner of War Convention on August 4, 1932. If treaties were referred to by their ratification dates alone, there would be 50 different dates for every treaty. Since Mr. Edeiken never refers to any treaty by its full and correct name, the effect of his writing is confusing to say the least. – C.P.]

Pursuant to this treaty

[COMMENT: Which treaty? Again, he is apparently referring to the 1929 Geneva Prisoner of War Convention, although he does not say so, and appears not to know which is which. Of the 19 different treaties involved at this point, most contain all-participation clauses. The electronically-truncated versions of these treaties posted on the Internet and recommended by Mr. Edeiken delete the signatures, ratifications, adhesions, and reservations, which are essential. The Geneva Conventions did not contain an all-participation clause, but applied between the signatories only. – C.P.]

American forces were instructed to abide by all articles of the various Geneva and Hague Conventions.

[COMMENT: If the Americans were instructed to comply with these treaties, then why did they not do so? Were the Germans bound by the Fourth Hague Convention, while the Allies were not? Or does Mr. Edeiken pretend that the deliberate fire-bombing of civilians and undefended cities, the utilization of millions of German prisoners of war for slave labor for years – even decades – after the war, the conditions in "Eisenhower's Death Camps", etc. etc. were LEGAL? – C.P.]

It should be noted that Germany was, as well, a signatory to the 1929 Convention

[COMMENT: Which Convention? ANSWER, my Queen: The 1929 Geneva Prisoner of War Convention. – C.P.]

which did little more than repeat the provisions of the 1907 Annex.

[COMMENT: of the Fourth Hague Convention on Land Warfare. – C.P.].

[COMMENT: Apart from the confusion, this is just not true. Japan ratified the Fourth Hague Convention on Land Warfare, but refused to ratify the 1929 Geneva Prisoner of War Convention because it required a higher standard of living for prisoners of war than could be provided for Japanese soldiers or civilians. The most significant provision of the 1929 Geneva Prisoner of War Convention is article 63 ("Sentence may be pronounced against a prisoner only by the same courts and according to the same procedure as in the case of persons belonging to the armed forces of the detaining power"), which Mr. Edeiken dares not mention, because, interpreted fairly, it would have rendered all post-war "war crimes trials" impossible. Article 64 guarantees the right of appeal; article 66 stipulates that death sentence may not be carried out in less than three months. – C.P.]

* * *

Porter is even less honest when he deals with the specific provisions of the Convention

[COMMENT: We now hop back to the Fourth Hague Convention on Land Warfare, or Hague IV. – C.P.]

One of the most egregious examples is Porter's analysis of Article 6 in which he states: "Article 6 states that belligerants [sic]

[COMMENT: Mea culpa. My misspelling of the word "belligerent" was due to an unconscious association with the French "gérant" – "commercial manager" – in view of the fact that "war is a racket". – C.P.]

may utilize the labor of prisoners of war, officers excepted, for the public service, for private persons or their own account." To which Porter comments: "German and Japanese 'slave policy' was perfectly legal insofar as it applied to members of resistance groups or lower ranking military personnel."

Leaving aside the point that both Germany and Japan required officers to do slave labor [COMMENT: Note the qualifier: "insofar as". – C.P.], an examination of the Article in question shows a far different text than Porter represents. The actual text is:

"Art. 6. The State may utilize the labor of prisoners of war according to their rank and aptitude, officers excepted. The tasks shall not be excessive and shall have no connection with the operations of the war."

Note how Porter deletes material from the original text which modifies it in a significant manner. It is well-known, for example, that Speer – the director of war production – utilized slave labor for war work. It was one of the charges brought against him at Nuremberg. Another indisputable example is the rubber plant at Monowitz (Auschwitz III) which was staffed by slave labor. By deleting the important modifier Porter fraudulently misrepresents what is allowed.

[COMMENT: Note the manner in which one party to Hague IV

of 1907 is to be held to provisions written during the horse-and-buggy era, while the other is free to expand the provisions of that same treaty, unilaterally and arbitrarily, into the atomic age! Note the manner in which the Allies constantly pretend that everything is "war production" when it suits them. The Germans maintained that "war production" meant the production of munitions and explosives; the Allies maintained that it included more or less everything. Farmers ploughing their fields with horses were "legally" machine-gunned on the grounds that "there are no civilians in this war; even the farmers are raising food for the war effort"; at the same time, Allied prisoners of war working in German industry not involving the production of bombs or explosives, etc. – in at least some cases, voluntarily, for pay, minus taxes, plus German social insurance – were said to be involved in "war production", thus constituting a "war crime"; the atomic bombings etc. etc. were, of course, alleged to be LEGAL. Prisoners of war in Germany were free to volunteer to work in industry, under the same conditions as German workers (wages, social security, taxes), in which case they were released from POW camps; they could not be forced to do so. (Nuremberg Trial transcript *IMT* XVIII, 496-98 [XVIII, 542-44 in the German language volumes].) – C.P.]

This pattern of deception also includes the elision of the clauses that follow the initial statement and which explain it. They are:

"Prisoners may be authorized to work for the public service, for private persons, or on their own account.

"Work done for the State is paid for at the rates in force for work of a similar kind done by soldiers of the national army, or, if there are none in force, at a rate according to the work executed.

"When the work is for other branches of the public service or for private persons the conditions are settled in agreement with the military authorities.

"The wages of the prisoners shall go towards improving their position, and the balance shall be paid them on their release, after deducting the cost of their maintenance."

Thus it can be seen that Porter has deliberately mischaracterized the meaning of the provision. It is not a provision which allows slave labor as he asserts. It is, rather, a provision that allows POWs to enter a labor market unrelated to war production [COMMENT: Definition, please! – C.P.], and receive wages for their work. Needless to say, the Nazis failed to abide by the provisions of Article 6 in their use of slave labor.

[COMMENT: Did the Allies pay their "slave laborers" after the war? – C.P.]

This pattern is repeated in Porter's analysis of Articles 1 and 2 which deal with partisan warfare. This example is quite important for it is the basis for the claims of the deniers that partisan warfare is, per se, unlawful. The meaning of the two articles was crucial to the purpose of the Convention [Hague IV. – C.P.]. This was recognized by the drafters and signatories who, as part of the preamble to the Regulations of the Convention, wrote:

It should be noted that [COMMENT: The quotation begins here. – C.P.] "Until a more complete code of the laws of war has been issued, the High Contracting Parties deem it expedient to declare that, in cases not included in the Regulations adopted by them, the inhabitants and the belligerents remain under the protection and the rule of the principles of the law of nations, as they result from the usages established among civilized peoples, from the laws of humanity, and the dictates of the public conscience.

"They declare that it is in this sense especially that Articles 1 and 2 of the Regulations adopted must be understood."

[COMMENT: Mr. Edeiken is now hopping back and forth between the body of the Fourth Hague Convention, which he refers to as the "Preamble", and the Annex to the same; they are not identical. The quotation above is from the BODY of the Fourth Hague Convention, followed by Articles 1 and 2 of the same, which do not refer to partisan warfare. Article 1 of the body states: "The contracting Powers shall issue instructions to their armed land forces which shall be in conformity with the Regulations respecting the laws and customs of war on land, annexed to the present Convention." Article 2 of the body is the all-participation clause: "The provisions contained in the Regulations referred to in Article 1, as well as in the present Convention, do not apply except between Contracting powers, and then only if all the belligerents are parties to the Convention." Hague IV was specifically repudiated by Soviet Russia, and never ratified by Bulgaria, Greece, Italy, or the national states of Yugoslavia, and therefore never applied during either World War.

What is surprising is that the Fourth Hague Convention has not been entirely forgotten, like all the other Hague Conventions. Nobody accuses the Germans of violating the following (for example):

– Hague Convention of July 29, 1899 (III) For the Adaptation to Maritime Warfare of the Principles of the Geneva Convention (all-participation clause article 11);

– Hague Declaration of July 29, 1899 (IV, I) Prohibiting the Discharge of Projectiles and Explosives from Balloons (all-participation clause page 2, paragraph 1);

– Hague Declaration (IV, 2) of July 29, 1899 Concerning Asphyxiating Gases (all-participation clauses paragraphs 4 and 5);

– Hague Convention (V) of October 18, 1907 Respecting the Rights and Duties of Neutral Powers and Persons in Case of War on Land (all-participation clause article 20);

– Hague Convention (VI) of October 18, 1907 Relating to the Status of Enemy Merchant Ships at the Outbreak of Hostilities (all-participation clause article 6);

– Hague Convention (VII) of October 18, 1907 Relating to the Conversion of Merchant Ships into War-ships (all-participation clause article 7);

– Hague Convention (VIII) of October 18, 1907 Relative to the Laying of Automatic Submarine Contact Mines (all-participation clause article 7);

– Hague Convention (IX) of October 18, 1907 Concerning Bombardment by Naval Forces in Time of War (all-participation clause article 8);

– Hague Convention October 18, 1907 (X) For the Adaptation to Maritime Warfare of the Principles of the Geneva Convention (all-participation clause article 18);

– Hague Convention (XI) of October 18, 1907 Relative to Certain Restrictions with Regard to the Exercise of the Right of Capture in Naval War (all-participation clause article 9);

– Hague Convention (XIII) of October 18, 1907 Concerning the Rights and Duties of Neutral Powers in Naval War (all-participation clause article 28);

– Hague Declaration of October 18, 1907 (XIV) Prohibiting the Discharge of Projectiles and Explosives from Balloons (all-participation clause page 2, paragraph 1), etc. etc..

Since the Allies never complied with the Fourth Hague Convention during the war – or the 1929 Geneva Prisoner of War Convention after the war – the question now arises: why was the Fourth Hague Convention not simply forgotten, like all the others? Answer: Because even a Soviet-style "show trial" like Nuremberg requires some sort of basic legal text. In the Soviet Union, the basic text would be the Soviet Constitution, which guarantees freedom of speech, press, and religion, but which twists them into meaning their exact opposite. Ironically, the 1899 and 1907 Hague conferences which gave rise to these conventions were convened and sponsored by "His Majesty, the German Emperor, King of Prussia". So much for these magnificent accomplishments of the civilized mind. – C.P.]

This important statement of principle enunciated by the

signatory powers about the interpretation of these sections is entirely ignored by Porter.

[COMMENT: Note the manner in which Mr. Edeiken implies that sentences occurring on pp. 2-3 of the photocopy, in the body, are immediately followed by sentences occurring on pp. 8-9 of the photocopy, in the Annex, in an attempt to convince us that one of the principal purposes of the Fourth Hague Convention was expressly to permit partisan warfare. This is done so smoothly that I did not even notice it at first; yet the same person complains of my "elisions" and "mendacity"! Having forgotten to quote articles 1 and 2 of the body, he now hops over to articles 1 and 2 of the Annex. – C.P.]

Pay close attention to what Porter writes and compare it to the actual text of these Regulations. "War Crimes Trials" states:

THE ANNEX TO THE 4th HAGUE CONVENTION

Articles 1 and 2 prohibit guerrilla warfare, stating that belligerants [sic] must be "commanded by a person responsible for his subordinates... have a fixed distinctive emblem recognizable at a distance... carry arms openly... and conduct their operations in accordance with the laws and customs of war."

Porter not only fails to understand these articles, he reports them inaccurately and in a distorted fashion. When the actual language of these two articles is examined it is clear that they have exactly the opposite meaning from that given by Porter. The actual text is:

"Article 1. The laws, rights, and duties of war apply not only to armies, but also to militia and volunteer corps fulfilling the following conditions:

"To be commanded by a person responsible for his subordinates;

"To have a fixed distinctive emblem recognizable at a distance;

"To carry arms openly; and

"To conduct their operations in accordance with the laws and customs of war.

"In countries where militia or volunteer corps constitute the army, or form part of it, they are included under the denomination 'army.' "

"Art. 2. The inhabitants of a territory which has not been occupied, who, on the approach of the enemy, spontaneously take up arms to resist the invading troops without having had time to organize themselves in accordance with Article 1, shall be regarded as belligerents if they carry arms openly and if they respect the laws and customs of war."

Note that contrary to Porter's modified version, the articles do not prohibit guerilla [sic] movements but specifically allow them if certain conditions are met. Because of his creative editing it is made to appear as though Article 1 prohibits partisan warfare and gives as a reason that real "belligerants" have certain attributes which, presumably, partisan groups do not possess. As can be seen from the language which Porter deletes, the actual meaning of the provision is that guerillas [sic] are legitimate as long as they meet certain requirements.

[COMMENT: The point being precisely that these requirements were NOT met, the only exception being in some cases towards the end of the war in France. In the Soviet Union, partisans were treated as prisoners of war if captured in the company of uniformed combatants. International law discriminates against smaller, weaker, and poorer countries which cannot maintain large standing armies and modern armaments. The intention is to prevent situations in which "terror can open the lips that terror has sealed". Americans should know as well as anyone that if uniformed soldiers are ambushed by guerrillas near a village, the village will be burnt down to force the villagers to report future ambushes beforehand. To take another example: the IRA has never had more than an estimated 400 active members at any one time, yet it kept 15-25,000 British soldiers tied down in the Six Counties for almost 30 years. Could it have done so if its members had "carried arms openly" and worn a "fixed distinctive emblem recognizable at a distance"? Actually, the IRA do very well in this situation, because they must be treated as "criminals" in a situation which is not a "war"; if it were a "war", the British would fire-bomb every city in Ireland, burning hundreds of thousands of civilians to death ("women and children first", in the manner of savage tribes). Of course, only the Irish are "terrorists". – C.P.]

Porter's distorted description of Article 2 is even more misleading. Without quoting a single word from the article, Porter declares that it prohibits guerilla [sic] warfare. The article actually expands the definition of legitimate belligerents where military control has not been established. In that case, which would have applied to much of the Ukraine for example, two of the requirements for a guerilla [sic] group to be classified as legitimate belligerents are eliminated.

[COMMENT: When and where in the Ukraine, or anywhere else in the Soviet Union or South East Asia, did the partisans wear a "fixed distinctive emblem recognizable at a distance, carry arms openly, and conduct their operations in accordance with the laws and customs of war"? – C.P.]

Porter uses a similar, but slightly different technique, in his analysis of Article 32. "War Crimes Trials" states in its entirety:

"Art. 32: A person is regarded as a parlementaire who has been authorized by one of the belligerants [sic] to enter into communications with the other... he has a right to inviolability."

Based upon this incomplete rendition of Article 32 and the complete deletion of article 33, Porter asserts: "The detention of Rudolph Hess was illegal."

The text of the Convention is, however, significantly different from the Porter version. The complete text of the Convention provisions concerning parlementaires states:

"Flags of Truce

"Art. 32. A person is regarded as a parlementaire who has been authorized by one [COMMENT: ONE. – C.P.] of the belligerents to enter into communication with the other, and who advances bearing a white flag. He has a right to inviolability, as well as the trumpeter, bugler or drummer, the flag-bearer and interpreter who may accompany him.

"Art. 33. The commander to whom a parlementaire is sent is not in all cases obliged to receive him."

[COMMENT: In which case, he should presumably be returned to his own lines without hindrance. – C.P.]

"He may take all the necessary steps to prevent the parlementaire taking advantage of his mission to obtain information.

"In case of abuse, he has the right to detain the parlementaire temporarily."

[COMMENT: For FOUR YEARS??? – C.P.]

"Art. 34. The parlementaire loses his rights of inviolability if it is proved in a clear and incontestable manner that he has taken advantage of his privileged position to provoke or commit an act of treason."

It can be seen from the actual text that there are two requirements for a person to be qualified as a "parlementaire." The first of these (reported by Porter) is that a parlementaire must be authorized to conduct his negotiations.

This Regulation cannot be applied to Hess. He was clearly not authorized to enter communications with Great Britain. William Shirer writes in *The Rise and Fall of the Third Reich* [! – C.P.] that Hitler was "mystified" at Hess's actions (page 835) and the official communiqué on this incident announced "It seemed that Party Comrade Hess lived in a state of hallucination, as a result of which he felt he could bring about an understanding between England and Germany." (quoted by Shirer, page 838) There is no indication that Hess was authorized to deal on behalf of the Third Reich. In fact, Hess did not claim such a status, relying instead on his position as a cabinet minister (Shirer, page 835).

[COMMENT: Did the British government, in 1940, really know what William L. Shirer was going to write about Rudolf Hess in 1960? How reliable is William L. Shirer, on this subject or any other? Who is William L. Shirer to know what was in Hitler's mind in 1940? Does this sort of technicality really justify Hess's treatment for 46 years, or even 4 years? What makes Shirer an authority on international law? Since Mr. Edeiken claims to possess a law degree, couldn't he at least quote a law book? See also "Sauckel's Exploitation Speech" (pp. 207-222 of this book). – C.P.]

Nor did Hess have the purpose of negotiating with his opponent as is the basic function of a parlementaire. He wanted to negotiate with the Duke of Hamilton – a comparatively low-ranking officer in the RAF – rather than the government and his intent was to provoke an insurrection against the authorities with which a parlementaire is to communicate. As Ivonne Kirkland (former First Secretary of the British Embassy in Berlin) reports:

[COMMENT: As usual, Eideken is making a mistake here, the correct name is Ivonne Kirk*patrick*. – C.P.]

"Finally, as we were leaving the room, Hess delivered a parting shot. He had forgotten, he declared, to emphasize that the proposal could only be considered on the understanding that it was negotiated by Germany with an English government other than the present one. Mr. Churchill, who had planned the war since 1936, and his colleagues who had lent themselves to his war policy, were not persons with whom the Fuehrer could negotiate." (quoted by Shirer, page 836)

[COMMENT: See above. – C.P.]

Not only did Hess not meet the basic requirements for parlementaire status in that he was not authorized to make the trip

[COMMENT: If the British acted correctly, why did they seal the records for seventy-five years? It is entirely possible that, in view of the failure of Hess's mission, Hitler merely pretended that Hess was insane; a similar tale is told about Mussolini's rescue from Gran Sasso. Otto Skorzeny was reportedly told that the Third Reich could not fail; if he failed, it would be alleged that he was insane, and that the rescue attempt had been undertaken without authorization. – C.P.]

and he specifically denied that he was attempting to negotiate with his opponent

[COMMENT: Hague IV simply states "with the other". I repeat: If the British acted correctly, why did they seal the records for 75 years? Were 50 million people killed for reasons known only to the British, and which they refuse to reveal to the world? – C.P.]

but he failed to meet another requirement as well.

[COMMENT: I knew it; the white flag. – C.P.]

Porter deletes the clause of the Convention which requires of a parlementaire that he "advances bearing a white flag." This, again, is a significant omission. It is obvious that a legalistic interpretation of this provision would be unfair. It is silly to expect an airplane to be displaying a flag and it can be argued that, even had Hess provided himself with one, his plane crashed in flames. But there was nothing to prevent Hess from complying with the spirit of this clause. That is, notify his opponent in advance and ask for a parlay

He did not make such a notification which could have been done by radio from his airplane. Further he abuses the concept of a parlementaire in that he gave a false name ("Alfred Horn") (Shirer, page 835). [COMMENT: Shirer again! – C.P.] This vitiated any claim to be a legitimate parlementaire.

The provisions concerning parlementaires are a continuation of the medieval laws regarding the status of the herald and the white flag is not just a technical requirement. It constitutes the manner in which a legitimate parlementaire announces himself. It is the duty of the parlementaire to announce his status before he approaches the opponent so that the opponent has, as stated in Article 33 (which Porter omits) the option of refusing to receive the parlementaire.

It is at this point that Article 33 (also deleted by Porter) becomes crucial. That Article provides that the opponent has the right to refuse the approach of the parlementaire. Hess did not allow the British to exercise this right. Instead, unannounced, Hess popped up in Scotland requesting to meet with a military officer of no great rank (the Duke of Hamilton was not a general officer, he was "a wing commander in the RAF" (Shirer, page 835) [! – C.P.] and demanding that the British government (to which the negotiations of a legitimate parlementaire must be addressed) be dissolved.

Since Hess met none of the conditions of a legitimate parlementaire, the provision of Article 32 concerning his "inviolability" cannot be applied and the treatment of Hess as a prisoner of war was justified. If, as some deniers assert, the Porter version of the Convention should be accepted as authoritative the reader has no opportunity to make a complete analysis of the claim. The simple reason that a reader was not provided with this opportunity is that

Porter decided to present an abridged and modified version of the Convention which distorted its meaning.

* * *

Another example of this patent dishonesty can be found in Porter's analysis of Article 3. Porter represents the text of Article 3 of the regulations as being:

"Art. 3: Belligerants [sic] violating the Convention may be made to pay compensation."

[COMMENT: Mea culpa. The quotation has been corrected. The meaning remains unchanged. – C.P.]

Please note that this is represented as the complete text of Article 3. This is NOT the actual text of the Convention. It is:

"Art. 3. A belligerent party which violates the provisions of the said Regulations shall, if the case demands, be liable to pay compensation. It shall be responsible for all acts committed by persons forming part of its armed forces."

Not only is the text far different from Porter's representation but there is a crucial difference in meaning which Porter creates. The text clearly refers to "a belligerent party" as, from the context of the second sentence (deleted by Porter), means the nation conducting the war. In Porter's version this becomes "belligerants" [sic] which refers not only to the parties but could be interpreted to apply to individuals as well. The drafters of the Convention used the word "belligerents" to mean individuals in Article 2 of the Regulations. It is clear that the meaning forced upon this article by Porter's editorial change was specifically rejected by the drafters who specified that this Regulation applied to "a belligerent party."

Relying on this mendacious rendering of the text, Porter announces: "This is self-explanatory. No trials were contemplated."

This is, at best, a rather audacious assertion.

[COMMENT: It is also one of commonest arguments made by the defence in any "war crimes trial". A cursory examination of pre-WWII standard texts on international law, for example:

– *Wheaton's International Law*, with notes by Richard Henry Dana, 1866 edition, centennial edition reprinted in 1936;

– *International Law*, by Berthold Singer, 1918;

– *Handbook of International Law*, by George Grafton Wilson, 3rd Edition, 1939;

– *The Sources of International Law*, by George A. Finch, published by the Carnegie Endowment for International Peace, 1937;

– *Cases on International Law*, by Charles G. Fenwick, Callaghan and Co., 1935;

– *International Law, A Treatise*, vol. 2, Disputes, War and Neutrality, by L. Oppenheim, published by Longmans, Green and Co., 1935;

– *A Handbook of Public International Law*, by T.J. Lawrence, 11th Edition by Percy H. Winfield (Lawrence died in 1925), published by MacMillan and Co., Ltd, 1938;

reveals that the word "Trial" rarely, if ever, even appears in the index! It does not appear in the index to any of the books listed above, which were selected entirely at random. There are, it is true, many trials mentioned in the texts, but on totally unrelated matters, for example, international prize courts, the seizure and condemnation of contraband, etc. (i.e., blockade running). The word "Trial" began to appear in texts on international law only in about 1943 or 1944, at Soviet insistence (see *Wheaton's International Law*, 7th English edition, vol. 2, War, published by Stevens and Sons Ltd, London, 1944, "Trials of War Offenders", p. 242). Doubts as to the competence of the Soviets – and even the Americans – to try the National Socialists began to appear in texts on international law as early as 1948 (see *International Law*, by Charles G. Fenwick, 3rd edition, published by Appleton-Century-Crofts, Inc., New York, 1948, "Nuremberg trials", p. 673). It is therefore quite correct to state that prior to WWII, "no trials were contemplated".

As for partisan or guerrilla warfare, *A Handbook of Public International Law* by T.J. Lawrence, 11th edition by Percy H. Winfield, 1938, states flatly, on p. 111,

"Non-combatants are exempt from personal injury knowingly and wantonly inflicted, and from pillage, provided that they submit to the lawful demands of the enemy and observe the regulations laid down by him. But when individuals act at one time as harmless civilians and at another as fighting men, interchanging the parts as occasion requires, they may be put to death, if caught.

"The peaceful inhabitants of territory under the enemy's occupation (see Pt. III, Ch. IV), are liable to be called upon to perform any service that is not distinctly military in its character; but they may not be compelled to take part in operations of war directed against their own country. Contributions and requisitions may be levied on them in certain circumstances; and they must not, under pain of death, give assistance or information to their own side."

Similar statements may be found in most – if not all – of the other texts mentioned. – C.P.]

The first and most obvious reason is that – except in Porter's fraudulent version – no reference is made to individuals.

[COMMENT: If there is no reference to individuals, how can there be any trials of individuals? – C.P.]

The text refers only to the liabilities of the state. And, certainly, it contemplates some sort of trial to determine liability. In fact, that was exactly what was done after World War I.

[COMMENT: What exactly are we talking about? Compensation? "War guilt"? "War crimes" in the sense of "atrocities"? "War crimes" in the sense of the "planning, preparation, and waging of war in violation of international treaties and assurances", etc.? The trials held in Leipzig etc. were for standard atrocities. – C.P.]

A fine account of the action against Germany by the United States for sabotage conducted in this country prior to its entry into World War I can be found in "Sabotage at Black Tom" by Jules Witcover (Chapel Hill, 1989).

[COMMENT: Surely we are not to be treated to the "Zimmerman telegram" all over again, are we? – C.P.]

If Porter's point – as the theme of "War Crimes Trials" and Porter's terse comment would indicate – is that Article 3 did not contemplate trials of individual war criminals, he is likewise in error.

[COMMENT: How can this be so if there is no reference to individuals? In any case, a "war crime", traditionally, was an atrocity committed in the field or against prisoners. It did not mean "willing membership in a Conspiracy or Common Plan to Wage Aggressive War", etc. etc. – C.P.]

The crucial question is what Article 3 was meant to do. Porter can only be correct if Article 3 was drafted to provide an exclusive remedy for war crimes [COMMENT: Definition, please! – C.P.]. If, on the other hand, it was drafted to either create a cause of action or to codify an existing right, Porter's statement cannot stand.

Consider an analogy. There is no right under Anglo-American common law to sue for the death of an individual.

[COMMENT: The insurance companies, banks, and industrial concerns being sued by rapacious "Hoaxoco$t survivors" will be very glad to hear of that, not to mention the tobacco companies and gun manufacturers, etc. etc. being sued by champertous Jewish "contingency lawyers". – C.P.]

All such lawsuits are brought under specific statutory enactments known as "wrongful death and survival" statutes.

[COMMENT: Proof that Mr. Edeiken has a law degree: an irrelevant display of irrelevant learning for obfuscation purposes. –

C.P.]

None of these statutes mention criminal law. If Article 3 only creates or codifies a cause of action, as Porter claims, his argument would be similar to a drunken driver who killed somebody asking to have the criminal case against him dismissed on the grounds that the wrongful death and survival statutes make no mention of criminal penalties.

[COMMENT: Does this kind of pettifogging really answer the questions at issue? – C.P.]

A major impediment to the claim that Article 3 creates an exclusive remedy is, simply, that the Convention makes no such statement. The standards of statutory interpretation prohibit the inference of such restrictions. Had the drafters wished to restrict the remedies of an aggrieved party, they would have said so.

[COMMENT: The exact opposite is the truth. Otherwise, either signatory to a treaty could unilaterally increase the obligations of the other party to one's own benefit. – C.P.]

In fact, the drafters went out of their way to indicate that the text of the Convention was neither complete or restrictive in nature:

[COMMENT: Presumably to be supplemented by future treaties; see above. – C.P.]

"According to the views of the High Contracting Parties, these provisions, the wording of which has been inspired by the desire to diminish the evils of war,

[COMMENT: If that is the intent, then why did the Allies commit the most atrocities? – C.P.]

"as far as military requirements permit, are intended to serve as a general rule of conduct for the belligerents in their mutual relations and in their relations with the inhabitants.

"It has not, however, been found possible at present to concert regulations covering all the circumstances which arise in practice;

"On the other hand, the High Contracting Parties clearly do not intend that unforeseen cases should, in the absence of a written undertaking, be left to the arbitrary judgment of military commanders.

"Until a more complete code of the laws of war has been issued, the High Contracting Parties deem it expedient to declare that, in cases not included in the Regulations adopted by them, the inhabitants and the belligerents remain under the protection and the rule of the principles of the law of nations, as they result from the usages established among civilized peoples, from the laws of humanity, and the dictates of the public conscience."

Further it cannot be argued that the trial of war criminals

[COMMENT: Definition, please! – C.P.] was a concept unique to the trial of the Nazis after World War II or unknown to international law. Articles 227 through 230 of the Treaty of Versailles called for such trials of war criminals. As Telford Taylor wrote in *The Anatomy of the Nuremberg Trials* (1992):

[COMMENT: The Treaty of Versailles was never ratified by the United States. As for Taylor, see "Anatomy of a Nuremberg Liar" (pp. 5-26 of this book). – C.P.]

"Under Article 227 the Kaiser was to be tried before a 'special tribunal' of five judges, one each from the United States, Great Britain, France, Italy, and Japan. He was not to be charged with responsibility for war crimes but with 'a supreme offence against international morality and the sanctity of treaties.'

[COMMENT: A crime unknown to international law then as now. The First World War was caused by German fulfilment of international treaty obligations and assurances to Austria, resulting in declarations of war by Russia and France. The Kaiser was not an absolute monarch. What is "international morality"? "State A may consider X a murderer, while State B may consider it murder to execute X"! Source: Dr. Takayanagi, Tokyo Trial transcript, p. 42,251. – C.P.]

The three ensuing articles called for trials of 'persons accused of having committed acts in violation of the laws and customs of war' before 'military tribunals' of the aggrieved nations, and required the German government to "hand over" the individuals so accused to any of the 'Allied and Associated Powers' so requesting. Provisions comparable to Articles 228-230 were included in later peace treaties with Austria, Hungary, and Bulgaria." (paperback edition, page 16)

[COMMENT: Were these provisions a correct interpretation of the Fourth Hague Convention? If so, why did the Dutch refuse to surrender the Kaiser for Trial? – C.P.]

There are, therefore, several reasons to conclude that Porter's conclusion about Article 3 [COMMENT: Of the body of Hague IV, not the Annex. – C.P.] is in error but, more important is his dishonest behavior in re-writing Article 3 and presenting it as the actual text of the Convention. His failure to accurately present Article 3 should call into question the credibility of his work.

[COMMENT: Mea culpa. Same error as above. The quotation has been corrected. The meaning remains unchanged. – C.P.]

This is, by no means, an exhaustive analysis of the defects in the arguments that Porter presents. There are similar defects in his analysis of Regulations 25, 27, and 56 and Regulation 43 [COMMENT: Of the Annex to Hague IV. – C.P.]. In the former case, based upon his paraphrased version, Porter asserts that the bombing of Dresden was improper.

[COMMENT: Does this person maintain the contrary? – C.P.]

He failed to report or comment on the provision of this Regulation which places an absolute duty to indicate or mark such possible targets.

[COMMENT: How do we do that? Paint it red, like Clint Eastwood in *High Plains Drifter*? Draw a circle around it on a map and mail a copy to 10 Downing Street by registered mail with return receipt? Install gigantic electrical displays visible from altitudes of 30,000 feet stating "This Way to Undefended City" (with arrow?). – C.P.]

In the case of a city, that requires the declaration of a city as an "open city." [COMMENT: Who says? – C.P.]

This was not done in any of the cases cited by Porter.

[COMMENT: Do these hair-splitting distinctions really give the Allies the right to burn hundreds of thousands of women and children to death in the deliberate "carpet bombings" of civilian districts with phosphorous and jellied gasoline after dropping heavy explosives to destroy the fire mains? Is this the intention of the Fourth Hague Convention? If the indiscriminate mass bombing of civilians is LEGAL, as clearly alleged here, then why was it declared a "war crime" when allegedly practised by the Germans and Japanese? – C.P.]

Porter's analysis of Regulation 43 – which, he states, mandates cooperation with occupying powers – is based on his assumption that the Hague Convention is the exclusive law covering what was done by the Nazis during their occupation. Whatever the provisions of the Hague Convention the valid laws of a sovereign entity can take a rather jaundiced view of citizens who attach themselves to an invader and engage – as was the case with the Nazi occupation – [in] murder, plunder, and treason. In fact, the prosecutions of collaborators were not based on the Hague Convention but on national criminal law.

[COMMENT: Much of it ex-post facto and based on no objective law whatsoever; or does this person claim that the post-war "purges" in France, for example, were legal? Or the trial of Pierre Laval, which lasted about 15 minutes? How about the hundreds of

Waffen SS-men sentenced to death in absentia and shot within 24 hours after their return home to Belgium after years of captivity in the Soviet Union? Or the hundreds of "slave laborers" returning by boat to Antwerp after the war who were simply thrown off the docks and drowned? (NOTE: One minute they are "slave laborers", the next minute they are "traitors".) How about the women put in the animal cages at Antwerp Zoo? The thousands of torture-murders in southern France? etc. etc. – C.P.]

Porter also fails to state that such co-operation is dependent on the acts of the occupying power being lawful.

[COMMENT: Note the manner in which this person hops back and forth between a moralistic disregard for legal trivialities and technicalities, and a hair-splitting legalistic disregard for all morals and human suffering, no matter what the degree of cruelty, when it suits him. The Germans shall comply punctiliously, while the Allies shall be free to expand their prerogatives (and atrocities) to infinity. How about the actions of the Allied occupation forces – mass looting, rapes, etc.? – C.P.]

Regulations 48 and 49 – as well as Regulation 43 – are clear that it is the affirmative duty of the occupying power to administer the territory in a legimate [sic] manner.

"Art. 48. If, in the territory occupied, the occupant collects the taxes, dues, and tolls imposed for the benefit of the State, he shall do so, as far as is possible, in accordance with the rules of assessment and incidence in force, and shall in consequence be bound to defray the expenses of the administration of the occupied territory to the same extent as the legitimate Government was so bound.

"Art. 49. If, in addition to the taxes mentioned in the above article, the occupant levies other money contributions in the occupied territory, this shall only be for the needs of the army or of the administration of the territory in question."

It should require no reference to demonstrate that the Nazis did not follow these requirements. They murdered,

[COMMENT: Where? At Oradour-sur-Glane? The Germans are supposed to have burned over 500 people to death in a church, but there were no signs of fire. The villagers were conducting partisan operations from the shelter of the village, and were killed by the explosion of their own illegal arms cache. During a recent visit, a child asked why the confessional did not burn. The answer was "shut up, you little fool". – C.P.]

they plundered, and, in the eastern territories, they attempted to eliminate and displace the native population

[COMMENT: What about the millions of Germans, including families, deported to the interior of the Soviet Union to slave for decades, the thousands of German factories expropriated lock, stock, and barrel, the six thousand German aviation and rocket scientists deported to the Soviet Union after the war, etc. etc.? If these actions are illegal during wartime, what makes them legal after the war, when performed by the British, Americans, or the Soviets? – C.P.]

As such the requirement for co-operation with legitimate efforts to administer an occupied territory [incomplete sentence; sic].

* * *

The final point that must be made is a comparison between Porter's paraphrases and the text of the Hague Convention to demonstrate that these errors were, in fact, a major portion of his essay. Every Article of that Convention mentioned by Porter and Porter's complete description of that Article are printed below so that any reader may compare the two texts to determine whether Porter, as he claims, relates "exactly" what the Convention states, and whether there was a consistent – rather than occasional – misrepresentation of the Hague Convention:

[COMMENT: Mr. Edeiken now indulges himself in the nizkoprophagic confusion technique of quoting the same things you do, even it makes no difference, but making sure their quotes are longer than yours. – C.P.]

PREAMBLE, ARTICLE 3

Porter:
"Art. 3: Belligerants [sic] violating the Convention may be made to pay compensation."
Actual:
"Art. 3. A belligerent party which violates the provisions of the said Regulations shall, if the case demands, be liable to pay compensation. It shall be responsible for all acts committed by persons forming part of its armed forces."

REGULATIONS, ARTICLES 1 and 2

Porter:
"Articles 1 and 2 prohibit guerrilla warfare, stating that belligerants [sic] must be 'commanded by a person responsible for his

subordinates... have a fixed distinctive emblem recognizable at a distance... carry arms openly... and conduct their operations in accordance with the laws and customs of war.' "

Actual:

"Article 1. The laws, rights, and duties of war apply not only to armies, but also to militia and volunteer corps fulfilling the following conditions:

"To be commanded by a person responsible for his subordinates;

"To have a fixed distinctive emblem recognizable at a distance;

[COMMENT: Presumably a "fixed distinctive emblem" means more than a mere armband which can be put on before an attack and thrown away afterwards. When and where did partisans and guerrillas ever comply with this article? – C.P.]

"To carry arms openly; and

[COMMENT: When and where did partisans and guerrillas ever comply with this article? – C.P.]

"To conduct their operations in accordance with the laws and customs of war.

[COMMENT: When and where did partisans and guerrillas ever comply with this article? – C.P.]

"In countries where militia or volunteer corps constitute the army, or form part of it, they are included under the denomination 'army.'

"Art. 2. The inhabitants of a territory which has not been occupied, who, on the approach of the enemy, spontaneously take up arms to resist the invading troops without having had time to organize themselves in accordance with Article 1, shall be regarded as belligerents if they carry arms openly and if they respect the laws and customs of war."

[COMMENT: When and where did partisans and guerrillas ever comply with this article? – C.P.]

REGULATIONS, ARTICLE 5

Porter:

"Art. 5: Prisoners... cannot be confined except as an indispensable measure of safety, and only while the circumstances which necessitate the measure continue to exist."

Actual:

"Art. 5. Prisoners of war may be interned in a town, fortress, camp, or other place, and bound not to go beyond certain fixed limits, but they cannot be confined except as in indispensable measure of safety and only while the circumstances which necessitate the measure continue to exist."

[COMMENT: When and where did the Allies comply with this article? – C.P.]

REGULATIONS, ARTICLE 6

Porter:
"Article 6 states that belligerants [sic] may utilize the labor of prisoners of war, officers excepted, for the public service, for private persons or their own account."

Actual:
"Art. 6. The State may utilize the labor of prisoners of war according to their rank and aptitude, officers excepted. The tasks shall not be excessive and shall have no connection with the operations of the war.

"Prisoners may be authorized to work for the public service, for private persons, or on their own account.

"Work done for the State is paid for at the rates in force for work of a similar kind done by soldiers of the national army, or, if there are none in force, at a rate according to the work executed.

"When the work is for other branches of the public service or for private persons the conditions are settled in agreement with the military authorities.

"The wages of the prisoners shall go towards improving their position, and the balance shall be paid them on their release, after deducting the cost of their maintenance."

[COMMENT: When and where did the Allies comply with this article? – C.P.]

REGULATIONS, ARTICLE 7

Porter:
"Prisoners of war shall be treated as regards board, lodging, and clothing on the same footing as the troops of the Government who captured them."

Actual:
"Art. 7. The Government into whose hands prisoners of war have fallen is charged with their maintenance.

"In the absence of a special agreement between the belligerents, prisoners of war shall be treated as regards board, lodging, and clothing on the same footing as the troops of the Government who captured them."

[COMMENT: When and where did the Allies comply with this article? – C.P.]

REGULATIONS, ARTICLE 8

Porter:
"Article 8: Prisoners of war are subject to the laws, regulations and orders in force of the State in whose power they are. Any act of insubordination justifies the adoption towards them of such measures of severity as may be considered necessary."

Actual:
"Art. 8. Prisoners of war shall be subject to the laws, regulations, and orders in force in the army of the State in whose power they are. Any act of insubordination justifies the adoption towards them of such measures of severity as may be considered necessary.

"Escaped prisoners who are retaken before being able to rejoin their own army or before leaving the territory occupied by the army which captured them are liable to disciplinary punishment.

"Prisoners who, after succeeding in escaping, are again taken prisoners, are not liable to any punishment on account of the previous flight."

REGULATIONS, ARTICLE 20

Porter:
"Art. 20: After the conclusion of peace, the repatriation of prisoners shall be carried out as quickly as possible."

Actual:
"Art. 20. After the conclusion of peace, the repatriation of prisoners of war shall be carried out as quickly as possible."

[COMMENT: When and where did the Allies comply with this article? – C.P.]

REGULATIONS, ARTICLE 23

Porter:
"Finally, article 23 (h) prohibits declaring 'abolished, suspended, or inadmissible in a court of law the rights and actions of the nationals of the hostile party' and Article 23 (3) prohibits weapons calculated to cause unnecessary suffering."

Actual:

"Art. 23. In addition to the prohibitions provided by special Conventions, it is especially forbidden –

"To employ poison or poisoned weapons;

"To kill or wound treacherously individuals belonging to the hostile nation or army;

[COMMENT: When and where did the Allies comply with this article? – C.P.]

"To kill or wound an enemy who, having laid down his arms, or having no longer means of defense, has surrendered at discretion;

[COMMENT: When and where did partisans, guerrillas, Soviets, or even the Americans, British, and French, ensure compliance with this article? – C.P.]

"To declare that no quarter will be given;

[COMMENT: When and where did the partisans and Soviets ensure compliance with this article? See *Stalins Vernichtungskrieg* by Joachim Hoffmann. – C.P.]

"To employ arms, projectiles, or material calculated to cause unnecessary suffering;

[COMMENT: When and where did the Allies comply with this article? – C.P.]

"To make improper use of a flag of truce, of the national flag or of the military insignia and uniform of the enemy, as well as the distinctive badges of the Geneva Convention;

"To destroy or seize the enemy's property, unless such destruction or seizure be imperatively demanded by the necessities of war;

[COMMENT: When and where did the Allies comply with this article? – C.P.]

"To declare abolished, suspended, or inadmissible in a court of law the rights and actions of the nationals of the hostile party.

[COMMENT: When and where did the Allies comply with this article? – C.P.]

"A belligerent is likewise forbidden to compel the nationals of the hostile party to take part in the operations of war directed against their own country, even if they were in the belligerent's service before the commencement of the war."

REGULATIONS, ARTICLES 25, 27, and 56

Porter:

"Articles 25, 27 and 56 prohibit bombardment 'by whatever

means' of undefended cities, cultural monuments, etc."

Actual:

"Art. 25. The attack or bombardment, by whatever means, of towns, villages, dwellings, or buildings which are undefended is prohibited.

[COMMENT: When and where did the Allies comply with this article? – C.P.]

"Art. 27. In sieges and bombardments all necessary steps must be taken to spare, as far as possible, buildings dedicated to religion, art, science, or charitable purposes, historic monuments, hospitals, and places where the sick and wounded are collected, provided they are not being used at the time for military purposes.

[COMMENT: When and where did the Allies comply with this article? – C.P.]

"It is the duty of the besieged to indicate the presence of such buildings or places by distinctive and visible signs, which shall be notified to the enemy beforehand.

[COMMENT: Does this minor technicality really justify the Allied fire bombings of millions of civilians in "fire storms" 40 miles high (Hamburg), "carpet bombings" covering hundreds of square miles (examples too numerous to mention), and so on, in a policy initiated for the sole purpose of bringing America into the war? See also *Bombing Vindicated* by Spaight. – C.P.]

"[Art. 56.] The property of municipalities, that of institutions dedicated to religion, charity and education, the arts and sciences, even when State property, shall be treated as private property."

[COMMENT: When and where did the Allies comply with this article? – C.P.]

REGULATIONS, ARTICLE 32

Porter:

"Art. 32: A person is regarded as a parlementaire who has been authorized by one of the belligerants [sic] to enter into communications with the other... he has a right to inviolability."

Actual:

"Flags of Truce

"Art. 32. A person is regarded as a parlementaire who has been authorized by one of the belligerents to enter into communication with the other, and who advances bearing a white flag. He has a right to inviolability, as well as the trumpeter, bugler or drummer, the flag-bearer and interpreter who may accompany him.

"Art. 33. The commander to whom a parlementaire is sent is not in all cases obliged to receive him.

"He may take all the necessary steps to prevent the parlementaire taking advantage of his mission to obtain information.

"In case of abuse, he has the right to detain the parlementaire temporarily.

[COMMENT: For FOUR YEARS? – C.P.]

"Art. 34. The parlementaire loses his rights of inviolability if it is proved in a clear and incontestable manner that he has taken advantage of his privileged position to provoke or commit an act of treason."

[COMMENT: Treason to whom? Was Rudolf Hess a British subject, or have I missed something? – C.P.]

[Actually, this is a reference to "war treason"; see my article "The Meaning of 'War Crime' and 'War Criminal' in Pre-1945 International Law" (pp. 106-115 of this book). – C.P.]

REGULATIONS, ARTICLE 43

Porter:
"Article 43 requires collaboration with occupation governments. 'The authority of the legitimate power having in fact passed into the hands of the occupant, the latter shall take all the measures in his power to restore, and ensure, as far as possible, public order and safety, while respecting, unless absolutely prevented, the laws in force in the country.' "

Actual:
"Art. 43. The authority of the legitimate power having in fact passed into the hands of the occupant, the latter shall take all the measures in his power to restore, and ensure, as far as possible, public order and safety, while respecting, unless absolutely prevented, the laws in force in the country."

[COMMENT: When and where did the Allies comply with this article? – C.P.]

REGULATIONS, ARTICLE 46

Porter:
"Article 46: 'Private property cannot be confiscated.' "
Actual:
[Art. 46.] "Family honour and rights, the lives of persons, and private property, as well as religious convictions and practice, must be

respected.

[COMMENT: When and where did the Allies comply with this article? – C.P.]

"Private property cannot be confiscated."

[COMMENT: When and where did the Allies comply with this article? – C.P.]

* * *

Although Porter claims that he wishes to present "exactly" what is written in the Convention, he does exactly the opposite. Of the Preamble to the Convention and 14 of the Regulations to which Porter refers, only two (Articles 20 and 43) are accurate representations of the text of the convention. Porter's other citations are replete with substantial modifications and deletions which change the meaning of the article which he presents. In several cases an inaccurate paraphrase is presented as a direct quote. Porter, further, ignores any Article which contradicts his thesis that the Third Reich committed no war crimes. [COMMENT: Definition, please! – C.P.]. For example neither Regulations 18 or 50, both crucial to the trials of war criminals was cited. They state:

"Art. 18. Prisoners of war shall enjoy complete liberty in the exercise of their religion, including attendance at the services of whatever church they may belong to, on the sole condition that they comply with the measures of order and police issued by the military authorities.

[COMMENT: When and where did the Soviets, for example, comply with this article? Does "complete liberty of religion" include the right to starve and freeze in open holes in the ground for months, dying of dysentery, in the complete absence of any shelter or adequate food? See *Other Losses* and *Crimes and Mercies* by James Bacque, or *Gruesome Harvest* by Keeling. Or does this writer contend that what would have been a crime in wartime is no crime at all if committed by the victors after the war? – C.P.]

"Art. 50. No general penalty, pecuniary or otherwise, shall be inflicted upon the population on account of the acts of individuals for which they cannot be regarded as jointly and severally responsible."

[COMMENT: Perhaps this is why the British, French and Americans preferred to shoot hostages: the Germans had nothing left with which to pay any "pecuniary penalty". Perhaps this is why entire factories were dismantled and shipped to the Soviet Union or the United States, complete with documentation in violation of all patents;

perhaps this is why six thousand rocket scientists, and at least five million ordinary Germans, were kidnapped for slave labor for years after the war by the Soviets or French; see *The Last Battle* by David Irving, *Are the Russians Ten Feet Tall?* by Werner Keller, etc. etc. – C.P.]

Porter was correct in one respect: as with any statute or treaty, it is important to determine what the Hague Convention "exactly" states. Unfortunately he does not deliver on his promise. A creditable job of cut-and-paste [COMMENT: It is "cut-and-paste" which sent Mr. Edeiken on his wild-goose chase to Geneva. – C.P.] to present "exactly" what the text states is not a difficult task; Porter didn't do such a job. [COMMENT: I respectfully submit that to do so would substantially strengthen my case. – C.P.] He decided, instead, to edit and paraphrase the provisions of the Hague Convention and ignore any provision which contradicted his agenda. [COMMENT: This person prefers to concentrate on German crimes while ignoring Allied crimes and atrocities; which is worse? – C.P.] Porter's presentation is so inaccurate that, in many cases it is impossible to determine the intended meaning of the Hague Convention and, in many cases promotes a defective interpretation of that treaty. [COMMENT: Does this mean that the Americans complied with the Convention, while the Germans did not? – C.P.]

Just as Porter did a shoddy job of cut-and-paste [COMMENT: I prefer the photocopies from the *Carnegie Endowment for International Peace*, with signatures, ratifications, adhesions, and reservations, published in 1915. – C.P.] it would have been a simple matter to check the accuracy of his work. Even a random check would have revealed that 13 of the 15 substantive "quotations" presented by Porter are in error. Obviously CODOH made no check of the easily available primary sources when they published the article.

This brief analysis demonstrates that "War Crimes Trials" is replete with deliberate distortions, fraudulent representations of the text of the Conventions, and factual errors. Porter's work is not only a failure but a rather dismal one. Porter's technique of misquotation and factual error would not be tolerated in any legitimate academic community or any other setting where factual accuracy is required. It would never survive the process of legitimate peer review. It is only in the shadow world of the lunatic fringe of those who deny the Holocaust where efforts like "War Crimes Trials" find acceptability. And it is only the credulous and those with a specific agenda who can consider "War Crimes Trials" as either convincing or authoritative.

The inescapable conclusion is that the process of writing "War

Crimes Trials" was defective or dishonest and the process of publishing it was defective or dishonest. "War Crimes Trials" is so flawed that it is utterly worthless except as an example of a failed attempt to defend the depredations of the Nazis.

[End of Edeiken's article.]

* * *

If it is not legitimate to defend the "depredations of the Nazis", then why did the Americans bother to hold any trials? The statements I made in this article did not originate with myself, nor did I dream them up myself in a fit of moon-struck lucubration. With the exception of Rudolf Hess, every point I have made was presented countless times by American lawyers assigned to the defense of accused "war criminals", both German and Japanese; these points are the subject of argument in countless thousands of pages of the Tokyo Trial transcript, the Trial of Martin Gottfried Weiss (where the defense lawyers were all Americans), and, to some lesser extent, the First Nuremberg Trial (in which the defense lawyers were all German), as well as in hundreds or even thousands of other trials. Of these lawyers, who sacrificed themselves doing a thankless job for many, many years, the best, in my opinion, were Major W. Ben Bruce Blakeney and William L. Logan, George F. Blewett, and George A. Furness. There were many, many, other American, German, and Japanese defense lawyers, hundreds upon hundreds, who defended their clients passionately, brilliantly, with endless erudition, sarcasm, and anger. The defense arguments in these trials, often absolutely irrefutable (for example: "Would it not be blind to the realities of the community of nations to think that the business of government, whether political, economic, or military, can possibly be conducted, if an officer of state has to decide for himself in every case as to whether the command of his government is in violation of international law, treaties, agreements, and assurances, lest he should someday be declared a war criminal by an alien judge?" ["Dr. Takayanagi, Tokyo Trial transcript", p. 42,213.]) were simply ignored in the judgements. Their sincerity cannot be doubted. For example, during the trial of Admiral Toyoda (20 volumes, available at the Peace Palace of the Hague) Major W. Ben Bruce Blakeney said of Lt. General Honma (who had already been hanged): "I hold him in affectionate respect and memory". Why would he say such a thing in an unrelated trial if it were not true? William L. Logan compared the tribunal in the trial of Admiral Toyoda to Caligula "posting his decrees on a high pole so that none might know the offences for which they might be sentenced to death".

In the Trial of Martin Gottfried Weiss, one of the defense attorneys, a Southerner, said that if his grandfather were still alive, he would be a "war criminal" too, because "he once guarded some Yankee prisoners to keep them from escaping": *ipso facto* proof of "willing participation or membership in the Conspiracy or Common Plan."

All these trials contain countless hundreds of quotations and references from classical authorities on national and international law. Why doesn't Mr. Edeiken look them up if he is so interested? Did the atomic bombings really constitute an "advance in international law", while the alleged indiscriminate bombings of Chinese cities by the Japanese were a "war crime"? Were the fire bombings of paper cities filled with women and children an act of "heroism", while the beheading of 7 American bomber personnel under Japanese law was a "war crime"?

One can imagine the screams of indignation if the Germans or Japanese had abrogated the Geneva Prisoner of War Convention by simply declaring prisoners of war to be "Disarmed Enemy Personnel" (DEPs) and therefore no longer subject to the protection of the Convention, as was done by General Eisenhower.

In 1861 Abraham Lincoln declared a naval blockade of the Confederate coastline, and simultaneously announced his intention to hang all Confederates as "rebels". He was informed by the British government that if he wished to hang all Confederates as "rebels", he was quite entitled to do so (since "rebellion", "conflict", and "war" were quite distinct things in classical international law), but that blockade was an act of war requiring a declaration of war, and that once a state of war came into being, he was required to treat Confederate prisoners as prisoners of war: "he was not entitled to combine the conditions of peace and war to his own benefit". The plan to hang all Confederate prisoners of war was in fact only abandoned when Jefferson Davis threatened to retaliate on a "man-for-man" basis. [Source: *1911 Encyclopaedia Britannica*, "War" and related articles.]

Retaliation against prisoners of war was prohibited by the 1929 Geneva Prisoner of War Convention for the first time in history, and it is this which is usually considered its most important feature.

It is clear that Mr. Edeiken knows how to sue somebody in an accident case, but he appears to know relatively little about the matter at hand, and nothing whatever of revisionist history. It is not my contention that the Germans and Japanese never violated any provisions of treaties and conventions signed in 1899 and 1907 [!]; nor do I defend everything they ever did.

It is respectfully submitted that a complete reading of the treaties and conventions in question strengthens my case rather than weakening it, the asseverations of my learned colleague to the contrary notwithstanding.

FURTHER READING:

(Some of the following are available in many editions, having been regularly published and updated for up to 150 years. For "war crimes trials" research purposes, the most useful are probably those published between 1900 and 1940 or 1945.)

— Anderson, Chandler P., *American Journal of International Law* (three articles available on the Internet);
— Andso, Niskuke, *Surrender, Occupation, and Private Property in International Law: Evaluation of U.S. Practice in Japan*. Oxford, Clarendon Press, 1991;
— Bassiouni Cherif M. and Ned Vanda, *A Treatise on International Criminal Law*;
— Black, Henry Campbell, *A Dictionary of Law Containing the Terms and Phrases*, 1891;
— Blewett, George F., *Victor's Injustice, American Perspective*, 1950, pp. 282-292;
— Brierley, Burdick W., *The Law of Nations, an Introduction to the International Law of Peace*, 1949;
— Brierley, Burdick W., *The Prospect for International Law*, 1945;
— Brierley, Burdick W., *The Outlook for International Law*, 1945;
— Cobbett, Pitt, *Cases and Opinions in International Law*, 1913;
— Dickinson, Edwin, *Equality of States in International Law*, 1920;
— Edmunds, Sterling, *International Law Applied to the Treaty of Peace*;
— *1911 Encyclopaedia Britannica*, "Blockade", "Contraband", "Guerrilla", "International Law", "Neutrality", "Peace", "Peace Conferences", "Rebellion", "Secession", "War", etc.;
— *1922 Encyclopaedia Britannica*, "Germany", "Peace Conference", "Poison Gas Warfare", "World War"; many miscellaneous articles;
— Evans, Lawrence Boyd, *Leading Cases on International Law*, 1922;
— Feilchenfeld, E. *International Law of Belligerent Occupants*, 1942;
— Fenwick, Charles G., *International Law*, 1948;

— Fenwick, Charles G., *Cases on International Law*, 1935;
— Finch, George A., *The Sources of International Law*, 1937;
— Flory, *Prisoners of War*, 1942;
— Furness, George A., *Notes of Speech by George A. Furness*, Asiatic Society of Japan (Bulletin), VI June 1976;
— Fuehr, Alexander, *The Neutrality of Belgium: A Study of the Belgian Case under its Aspects in Political History and International Law*, 1915;
— Hackworth, Green Haywood, *Digest of International Law*, 1943;
— *General Index to International Law Situations, Topics, and Discussions*, 10 vol., 1901-1910, published in 1912 (Washington);
— Gallaudet, Edward H. *Manual of International Law*, 1901;
— Hall, William Edward, *Treatise on International Law*, 1904;
— Higgins, *A Treatise on International Law*;
— Holls, Frederick W., *The Peace Conference at The Hague and its Bearing on International Law*, 1900;
— Hull, William I., *The Two Hague Conferences and Their Contribution to International Law*, 1908;
— Hudson, Manley O., *Cases and Materials on International Law*, 1936;
— Hyde, Chas C., *International Law*, 1922;
— Lawrence, T.J., *Documents Illustrative of International Law*, 1914;
— Lawrence, T.J., *Principles of the Law*;
— Main, Henry Summer, *International Law: A Series of Lectures etc.*;
— Markun, Leo, *Principles of International Law*;
— Moore, John Bassett, *A Digest of International Law*, 1906;
— Naval War College of the United States, various publications;
— Nippold, Otfried, *Development of International Law After the World War*, 1923;
— Oppenheim & Lauterpacht, *International Law*;
— Oppenheim, Lassa Francis Lawrence, *The Future of International Law*, 1921;
— Phillimore, *Commentaries on the Law*;
— Phillimore, *Commentaries upon International Law*;
— Politis, Nicolas, *New Aspects of International Law*, 1928;
— Roemer, William Francis, *The Ethical Basis of International Law*, 1929;
— Singer, Berthold, *International Law*, 1918;
— Scott, James Brown, *International Classics of International Law*, 1930 (39 vol.);
— Scott, James Brown, *Recommendations on International Law etc.*, 1916;

— Soule, C.C. & McCauley, C., *International Law for Naval Officers*, 1936;
— Stockton, Chas. A, *Outlines of International Law*, 1924;
— Suter, Keith, *International Law of Guerrilla Warfare*, 1984;
— *The Tokyo War Crimes Trial*, Pritchard-Zaide, Garland Publishing, 22 volumes, 1985;
— Twiss, *The Law of Nations*;
— Vollenhofen, C. Van, *Scope and Content of International Law*, Leiden, 1932;
— Walker, T.A., *Science of International Law*;
— Westlake, *International Law*;
— Wheaton, Henry, *International Law*, 1944;
— Woolsey, Theodore Dwight, *Introduction to the Study of International Law*, 1899;
— Wharton, Francis, *Digest of the International Law of the United States*;
— Wright, Quincey, *Research in International Law Since the War*, 1930;
— Wilson, George Grafton, *International Law*, 1922;
— Wilson, George Grafton, *Handbook of International Law*, 1939;
— Winfield, *Principles of the Law*; and
— *Dissentient Judgement of Justice Pal, International Tribunal for the Far East*, Published by Kokusho Kankokai, Inc.

"When time shall have softened passion and prejudice, when Reason shall have stripped the mask from misrepresentation, then Justice, holding evenly her scales, will require much of past censure and praise to change places." (p. 701, Justice R.B. Pal)

* * *

Note: Mr. Edeiken was once arrested and fined for assaulting an officer of the law during a courthouse brawl; perhaps the carelessness and confusion of his legal writings reflect an impulsive state of mind.

THE MEANING OF "WAR CRIME" AND "WAR CRIMINAL" IN PRE-1945 INTERNATIONAL LAW

In my article "War Crimes Trials" (pp. 66-70 of this book), I said that the 10,000 "war crimes trials" held since WWII have had little or no basis in law; that this is clear from the wording of the treaties which are said to have been violated; that the European and Asian resistance movements were illegal; and that the "collaborators" shot, hanged, or imprisoned after WWII were acting in compliance with international law.

The truth of the above is apparent, not only from the provisions of the treaties said to have been violated, but from many, perhaps all, the recognized and prestigious texts on international law published between ratification of the various Hague Conventions and 1945.

The fact of the matter is, that the Allied victors of WWII stood international law on its head in 1945 by charging the defeated powers, not merely for "crimes" which never existed in pre-1945 international law at all – such as "willing membership in a conspiracy or common plan" to commit "crimes against humanity", "crimes against peace", "planning, preparations and waging of aggressive war", etc. etc., but for actions which were PERFECTLY LEGAL UNDER INTERNATIONAL LAW AS IT EXISTED IN 1945.

Generally, the words "war crime" and "war criminal", in traditional pre-1945 international law, referred to the actions of resistance movements and so-called "war treason", i.e., any action taken by a resident or citizen of an occupied country harmful to the interests of the military occupant.

To a lesser extent, "war crimes" also referred to illegal actions performed on the battlefield by combat troops; various lists are given of between 10 and 20 offences, for example, poisoning wells, abuse of a flag of truce, feigning death so as to kill by treachery, etc. etc.

These latter actions have very little relevance by comparison, and some of them even appear to have been an Allied speciality (in particular, employing assassins, bombarding civilians for purposes of terrorizing the population, the destruction of cultural monuments, robbing prisoners of war of their valuables, abrogating the Geneva Convention in Eisenhower's "Death Camps", etc.).

The following are a few quotations on the subject only.

* * *

The index to *War Rights on Land* by J.M. Spaight, Ll.D., Macmillan and Co., Ltd, London, 1911, a classic of international law, contains no mention of the words "Trial", "War crimes" or "War crimes trials". "Punishment of offenders against the laws of war" is discussed on 462. "War treason" is discussed on p. 333-5.

Page 333-5: "If the inhabitants of an occupied territory do not owe allegiance to the occupying belligerent, they do owe him the duty of quiescence and of abstention from every action which might endanger his safety or success. They are subject to his martial law regulations, and they may be judged guilty of 'war treason' under certain circumstances. 'War treason' ('Kriegsverrath') is distinguished from rebellion (which is the actual taking up of arms) and is thus defined in the German Manual:

"The act of damaging or imperilling the enemy's power by deceit, or by the transmission of messages to the national army on the subject of the position, movements, plans, etc., of the occupant, irrespectively of whether the means by which the sender has come into possession of the information be legitimate or illegitimate' (e.g., by espionage). The French jurist, Professor Bonfils, points out that it is quite immaterial what the motives of the war-traitor are – whether patriotic and noble or base and mercenary – and how he has come by the information he conveys; for these things do not affect the danger to the invading army. So far as touches the latter, it is an act of perfidy when a person who has been respected as a non-combatant abuses his position to render secret aid to his national forces.

"[...] In an occupied country a certain law runs, and that law receives its sanction from the occupying belligerent. He may keep the former Government's laws in force, but still they are, during occupation, the laws of the new ruler, who is alone able to enforce them, and who might abrogate them if he chose. [...] Today, treason means a conspiracy against the established authority in a State. Now, the established authority in an occupied territory is the *de facto* ruler, the occupant. If one likes the phrase, he is the 'war ruler', and it is 'war treason' to conspire against the 'war ruler'. No jurist would deny the occupant's right to deal summarily with an individual who, having been treated as a non-combatant, abused his immunity by sniping the enemy's foragers or stragglers; and the damage done by one individual sniper would probably be infinitely less than that done by sending messages to the national army. Either act is clearly one which the occupant must, for his security's sake, punish rigorously; not because either is morally wrong, but because it is dangerous. But any way, if one compares the two acts from the view-point of morality, less moral blame would appear to attach to the man who takes rifle in hand than to him who pretends to accept the occupant's authority while all the time he is sending secret messages to the other commander. Although no mention of war treason is made in the British Official Manual, as it is in the French, German, and American manuals, the offence is referred to in the Circular Memorandum issued by Lord Kitchener on 2nd May 1900, relative to martial law in the Orange Free State. ..."

* * *

International Law, A Treatise by L. Oppenheim, M.A., Ll.D., Vol. II: "Disputes, War and Neutrality", Fifth Edition, Edited by H. Lauterpacht, Ll.D., Dr. Jur., Dr. Sc. Pol, published by Longmans, Green, & Co., London, New York, Toronto, September 1935, discusses "War crimes" on pp. 177, 178, 211, 219, 221, 337, and 460, stating "See also WAR TREASON". The index continues: "Conception of, 452, 456-461, effects of peace on, 481, superior orders, defence of, 196, 454, violation of capitulations and simple surrender, 432, 433. "Punishment" and "trial" do not appear in the index. "War treason" is discussed on pp. 404, 456, and 457. "Distinguished from real treason" appears on p. 339, "list of kinds of" appears on pp. 458 and 459.

Page 177: "Owing to their position, it is inevitable that he [the occupant] should consider and mark as criminals such of them [the civilian population] as commit hostile acts, although they may be inspired by patriotic motives, and may be highly praised for their acts by their compatriots. According to a generally recognised customary rule of International Law, hostile acts on the part of private individuals are not acts of legitimate warfare, and the offenders may be treated and punished as war criminals. Even those writers who object to the term 'criminals' do not deny that such hostile acts by private individuals, in contradistinction to hostile acts by members of the armed forces, may be severely punished. The controversy whether or not such acts may be styled 'crimes' is again only one of terminology; materially, the rule is not at all controverted."

Page 219: "Section 85. In a sense, the crews of merchantmen owned by subjects of a belligerent belong to its armed forces. For these vessels are liable to be seized by enemy men-of-war, and, if attacked for that purpose, they may defend themselves, may return the attack, and eventually seize the attacking men-of-war. The crews of merchantmen become in such cases combatants, and enjoy all the privileges of the members of armed forces. But unless attacked, they must not commit hostilities, and if they do so, they are liable to be treated as criminals, just as private individuals who commit hostilities in land warfare."

Page 404: "Section 210. Espionage and war treason do not play so large a part in sea warfare as in land warfare, but they may be employed. Since the Hague Regulations deal only with land warfare, there is no legal necessity for trying a spy in sea warfare by court martial according to Article 30, although this is advisable."

Page 452:

"CHAPTER IV. PUNISHMENT OF WAR CRIMES. ...

"Section 251. In contradistinction to hostile acts of soldiers by which the latter do not lose their privilege of being treated as lawful members of armed forces, war crimes are such hostile acts or other acts of soldiers or other individuals as may be punished by the enemy on capture of the offenders. It must, however, be emphasised that the term 'war crime' is used, not in the moral sense of the term 'crime', but only in a technical legal sense, on account of the fact that perpetrators of these acts may be punished by the enemy. For, although among the acts called war crimes are many which are crimes in the moral sense of the word (such, for instance, as the abuse of the flag of truce or assassination of enemy soldiers), there are others which may be highly praiseworthy and patriotic (such as taking part in a levy en mass on territory occupied by the enemy). But because every belligerent may, and actually must, in the interest of his own safety, punish these acts, they are termed war crimes, whatever may be the motive, the purpose, and the moral character of the act.

"Section 253: Violations of rules regarding rules of warfare are war crimes only when committed without an order of the belligerent Government concerned. If members of the armed forces commit violations by order of their Government, they are not war criminals, and may not be punished by the enemy;

[Excerpt from footnote:

"... The contrary is sometimes asserted [extensive references omitted] But [extensive list of authorities omitted] agree with the view expressed in the text. The law cannot require an individual to be punished for an act which he was compelled by law to commit. ..."

Continuation of the text:]

"the latter may, however, resort to reprisals. In case members of forces commit violations ordered by their commanders, the members may not be punished, for the commanders are alone responsible, and the latter may, therefore, be punished as war criminals on their capture by the enemy.

"The following are the more important violations that may occur:

"(1) Making use of poisoned, or otherwise forbidden, arms and ammunition, including asphyxiating, poisonous, and similar gases.

"(2) Killing and wounding soldiers disabled by sickness or wounds, or who have laid down arms and surrendered.

"(3) Assassination, and hiring of assassins.

"(4) Treacherous request for quarter, or treacherous feigning of sickness and wounds.

"(5) Ill-treatment of prisoners of war, or of the wounded and sick. Appropriation of such of their money and valuables as are not public property.

"(6) Killing or attacking harmless private enemy individuals. Unjustified appropriation and destruction of their private property, appropriation and destruction of their private property, and especially pillaging. Compelling the population of occupied territory to furnish information about the army of the other belligerent, or about his means of defence.

"(7) Disgraceful treatment of dead bodies on battlefields. Appropriation of such money and other valuables found upon dead bodies as are not public property or arms, ammunition, and the like.

"(8) Appropriation and destruction of property belonging to museums, hospitals, churches, schools, and the like.

"(9) Assault, siege, and bombardment of undefended open towns and other habitations. Unjustified bombardment of undefended places by naval forces. Aerial bombardment for the sake of terrorising or attacking the civilian population.

"(10) Unnecessary bombardment of historical monuments, and of such hospitals and buildings devoted to religion, art, science, and charity as are indicated by particular signs notified to the besiegers bombarding a defended town.

"(11) Violations of the Geneva Conventions.

"(12) Attack on, or sinking of, enemy vessels which have hauled down their flags as a sign of surrender. Attack on enemy merchantmen without previous request to submit to visit.

"(13) Attack or seizure of hospital ships, and all other violations of the Hague Convention for the Adaptation to Maritime Warfare of the Principles of the Geneva Convention.

"(14) Unjustified destruction of enemy prizes.

"(15) Use of enemy uniforms and the like during battle; use of the enemy flag during attack by a belligerent vessel.

"(16) Attack on enemy individuals furnished with passports or safe-conducts; violation of safeguards.

"(17) Attack on bearers of flags of truce.

"(18) Abuse of the protection granted to flags of truce.

"(19) Violation of cartels, capitulations and armistices.

"(20) Breach of parole.

"Hostilities in Arms by private individuals.

"Section 254. Since International Law is a law between States only and exclusively, no rules of International Law can exist to prohibit private individuals from taking up arms, and committing hostilities against the enemy. But private individuals committing such acts do not enjoy the privileges of members of armed forces, and the enemy has, according to a customary rule of International Law, the right to consider, and punish, such individuals as war criminals. Hostilities in arms committed by private individuals are war crimes, not because they are really crimes, but because the enemy has the right to consider and punish them as acts of illegitimate warfare. The conflict between praiseworthy patriotism on the part of such individuals and the safety of the enemy troops does not allow of any solution. It would be unreasonable for International Law to impose upon a belligerent a duty to forbid the taking up of arms by his private subjects, because such action may occasionally be of the greatest value to him, especially for the purpose of freeing a country from the enemy who has militarily occupied it. Nevertheless, the safety of his troops compels the enemy to consider and punish such hostilities as acts of illegitimate warfare, and International Law gives him a right to do so...

"It must be particularly noted that a merchantman of a belligerent, which attacks enemy vessels without previously having been attacked by them, may be considered as a pirate, and that the captain, officers, and members of the crew may, therefore be punished as war criminals to the same extent as private individuals who commit hostilities in land warfare.

"Section 255. Espionage and war treason, as has been explained above, bear a twofold character. International Law gives a right to belligerents to use them."

Page 458:

"On the other hand, it gives a right to belligerents to consider them, when committed by enemy soldiers or enemy private individuals within their lines, as acts of illegitimate warfare, and consequently punishable as war crimes. ...

"War treason consists of all such acts (except hostilities in arms on the part of the civilian population, and espionage) committed within the lines of a belligerent as are harmful to him and are intended to favour the enemy. War treason may be committed, not only in occupied enemy country, or in the zone of military operations, but anywhere within the lines of a belligerent.

"The following are the chief cases of war treason that may occur:

"(1) Information of any kind given to the enemy.

"(2) Voluntary supply of money, provisions, ammunition, horses, clothing, and the like, to the enemy.

"(3) Any voluntary assistance to the military operations of the enemy, be it as serving as guide in the country, by opening the door of a defended habitation, by repairing a destroyed bridge, or otherwise.

"(4) Attempting to induce soldiers to desert, to surrender, to serve as spies, and the like; negotiating desertion, surrender, and espionage offered by soldiers.

"(5) Attempting to bribe soldiers or officials in the interest of the enemy, and negotiating such bribe.

"(6) Liberation of enemy prisoners of war.

"(7) Conspiracy against the armed forces, or against individual officers and members of them.

"(8) Wrecking of military trains, destruction of the lines of communication or of telegraphs or telephones in the interest of the enemy, and destruction of any kind of war material for the same purpose.

"(9) Circulation of enemy proclamations dangerous to the interests of the belligerent concerned.

"(10) Intentional false guidance of troops by a hired guide, or by one who offered his services voluntarily.

"(11) Rendering courier, or similar, services to the enemy.

"Enemy soldiers – in contradistinction to private enemy individuals – may only be punished for war treason when they have committed the act of treason during their stay within a belligerent's lines under disguise. If, for instance, two soldiers in uniform are sent to the rear of the enemy to destroy a bridge, they may not, when caught, be punished for war treason, because their act was one of legitimate warfare. But if they exchange their uniforms for plain clothes, and thereby appear to be members of the peaceful private population, they may be punished for war treason.

"There are many acts of the inhabitants of occupied enemy country which a belligerent may forbid and punish, in the interests of order and safety of his army, although they do not fall within the category of war treason, and are not therefore punishable as war crimes. To this class belong all acts which violate the orders legitimately given by an occupant of enemy territory.

[...]

"Mode of punishment of war crimes

"Section 257. All war crimes may be punished with death, but belligerents may, of course, inflict a more lenient punishment, or commute a sentence of death into a more lenient penalty. If this be done and imprisonment take the place of capital punishment, the question arises whether persons so imprisoned must be released at the end of the war, although their term of imprisonment has not yet expired. Some answer this question in the affirmative, maintaining that it could never be lawful to inflict a penalty extending beyond the duration of the war. But it is believed that the question has to be answered in the negative. If a belligerent has a right to pronounce a sentence of capital punishment, it is obvious that he may select a more lenient penalty and carry it out beyond the duration of the war. It would in no wise be in the interest of humanity to deny this right, for otherwise belligerents would be tempted always to pronounce and carry out a sentence of capital punishment in the interest of self-preservation."

* * *

Wheaton's International Law, Seventh English Edition, by A. Berriedale Keith, Vol. 2, "War", published by Stevens & Sons, Ltd., 1944, discusses "war crimes" and "war treason" on pp. 183, 184, 185, 240-244. There is a discussion of "espionage and war crimes" on pp. 218-220.

"Punishment of war crimes" is discussed on pp. 586-588, stating "See also WAR CRIMES".

Pages 183-5. [Discussion of punishment of prisoners of war for breaches of discipline; contains very little of any interest.]

Pages 240-4:

"Military government is the government imposed by a successful belligerent, either over a foreign province or over a district retaken from insurgents, treated as belligerents. This supersedes, as far as may be deemed expedient, the local law, and continues until the war or rebellion is terminated, and a regular civil authority is instituted.

"Though the martial law of a commander is not really law at all in the ordinary sense of the term, it does not on that account justify military oppression. Its stringency will, of course, depend on the particular circumstances of each case; for example, on the amount of danger to which the military forces under the commander are exposed, and, in occupied territory, on the conduct of the local inhabitants; but in every case it should be administered in accordance with the universally recognized fundamental principles of humanity and honour, fairness and justice.

"War crimes: Infringements of this martial law are regarded as 'war crimes' . As a rule, no penalty should be inflicted on offenders without previous inquiry and condemnation by a court-martial consisting of a number of officers convened for the purpose. [COMMENT: Note that public trial is not a requirement.] German authorities [COMMENT: and British authorities as well; see above.] speak also of a special kind of war crime, which they call 'war treason' ('Kriegsverrath'). The German Manual defines it as the act of injuring or endangering the belligerent's interests by deceit, or by sending messages to the opposing army with regard to the position, movements, plans, etc. of the belligerent, whether in the field or in occupation. The use of the expression 'war treason' as applied to the nationals of the enemy is, in certain respects, unjustifiable; but, whatever terminology be adopted, the consequences of the offence are the same. Thus certain acts committed openly by members of the enemy's armed forces are legitimate, but are regarded as acts of 'war treason' if attempted or done in occupied territory or within the belligerent's lines, either by enemy civilians or by enemy soldiers in disguise. Between these acts, and those which are sometimes styled 'war crimes', there is really no essential basis of distinction, either in logic or in practice, and it would be as well if the simpler term 'war crime' were alone used, instead of an offensive term which implies, from its ordinary use, moral obliquity. Examples of such acts are the destruction of military stores, bridges, lines of communication, telegraphs, or telephones, or electric works; wrecking military trains; cutting off water supply; setting free captured colleagues; supplying information to the enemy; misleading the belligerent's forces when acting as guides; voluntarily aiding the enemy by gifts of money or supplies or information; damage to or alteration of military signposts and notices; fouling sources of water supply; and concealing animals, vehicles, supplies, and fuel in the interest of the enemy; conspiracy against belligerent authority; opposition to requisitions; possessing arms; entering prohibited places; stealing belligerent property; photographing without authority; bribing the belligerent's forces to surrender or desert; circulating proclamations or making promises calculated to imperil or damage the belligerent, etc.

[...] War crimes of all kinds may be punished by death, and there is something to be said for the view that lesser penalties may include imprisonment extending beyond the duration of the war [footnote refers to Oppenheim, chapter II, Section 257]...

"Of 'war crimes' the number is naturally indefinite, depending as they do on the acts from time to time ordered to be done or forbidden to be done in the martial law proclamation of regulations of the invading or occupying commander. Thus, in the Anglo-Boer War, the British military authorities proclaimed the following to be offences against their martial law: being in possession of arms, ammunition, etc.; travelling without a permit; sending prohibited goods; holding meetings other than those allowed; using seditious language; spreading alarmist reports; overcharging for goods; wearing uniforms without due authority; going out-of-doors between certain hours; injuring military animals or stores; being in possession, without a permit, of horses, vehicles, cycles, etc.; hindering those in execution of military orders; trespassing on defence works. Such offences, together with several others, were specified in the Japanese regulations made in the Russo-Japanese war."

* * *

This is quite simply the fact of the situation; the Nuremberg Trials had no basis in law.

MORE ON THE ILLEGALITY OF RESISTANCE MOVEMENTS AND GUERRILLA WARFARE

Source: *War Rights on Land* by J. M. Spaight, MacMillan and Co., St. Martin's Street, London, 1911, pp. 37-9.

"The separation of armies and peaceful inhabitants into two distinct classes is perhaps the greatest triumph of International Law. Its effect in mitigating the evils of war has been incalculable. One must read the history of ancient wars, or savage wars of modern times – such as Chaka's campaigns, by which he made the Zulu name terrible throughout northern Natal – to appreciate the immense gain to the world from the distinction between combatants and non-combatants. But if populations have a war right as against armies, armies have as strict a war right against them. They must not meddle with fighting. The citizen must be a citizen and not a soldier. Wellington told the inhabitants of southern France in 1814 that he would not allow them to play with impunity the part of peaceful citizens and of soldiers, and bade them go join the ranks of the French armies if they wished to fight [footnote omitted]. It may be said broadly that there is no room in modern war for the resistance of unorganised inhabitants. They have had their chance of joining the armed forces of their country, and if they have not done so, then they must loyally play their part as citizens. For a while their duty to their country must remain in abeyance; with the invader comes the reign of war law, and war law has a short shrift for the non-combatant who violates its principles by taking up arms. 'The civilian who kills without being ordered to do so, and thereby wipes out the line of demarcation (between soldier and inhabitant), cannot be disarmed except by death. The condition of prisoner of war does not exist for him: he must be annihilated in the interests of humanity.'

[Footnote: Moritz Busch, op. cit., Vol. II, p. 207. Professor Holland remarks (Studies in International Law, p. 73), that there are two reasons for not allowing the population of an invaded country to take part in the war: (1) guerrilla warfare has an inevitable tendency to develop into cruelty; (2) if a military commander protects the inhabitants he must be assured that they do not cut off his stragglers or fire on his detachments.]

"Though the sparing of a peaceful population is a fairly modern growth in war usage, the refusal of combatant rights to non-military people is almost as old as history: it is mentioned in *De Officiis*.

[Footnote: Boyd's *Wheaton, International Law* (2nd Edition), p. 428).]

"The idea may be traced from the existence of a peculiar warrior caste in ancient times, through feudalism, with its men-at-arms, jealous of encroachment on their specialised pursuit, to the modern principle of the division of labour, developing a kind of trade-unionism in fighting which would exclude all but professional or semi-professional forces from interference in war. 'It is manifest', says Kipling's Umr Singh, Sikh of the Khalsa, trooper of the Gurgaon Rissala, type and spokesman of a breed of fighters, 'that that he who fights should be hung if he fights with a gun in one hand and a purwana [a permit given to non-combatants for their protection] in the other'. There is a whole chapter of war law – its history and its principle – epitomised in his words. Today the refusal of belligerent rights to unorganised populations has a justification which it lacked in ancient times and those who claim for every citizen the right to take arms at his pleasure against an invader, are really striking at the roots of all clean and civilised war.

"The name of the little French town of Bazeilles, south of Sedan on the road to Montmedy, will be associated with the war law regarding resistance by unorganised populations. There has been much discussion and, no doubt, much false witness, as to what happened there on the 1st September 1870. The German Official History of the War states that the inhabitants took an active part in the struggle which raged in and about the village, and that they spared neither the wounded nor the stretcher-bearers, so that 'the Bavarians found themselves eventually compelled to cut down all inhabitants with arms in their hands.'

[Footnote: German official History (English translation, Part I, Vol. II, p. 316).]

"Whether, as the Germans alleged, the inhabitants burnt the helpless Bavarian wounded alive, pouring hot oil over them before carrying them into the blazing houses, which had been lighted by the German shells, or whether the Bavarians bayoneted old men and women in their beds and threw infants into the burning houses;

[Footnote: See Hozier, *Franco-Prussian War*, Vol. I, pp. 429-31; Cassell's *History*, Vol. I, pp. 95-8, 154; Vol. II, pp. 561-2; Busch's *Bismarck*, Vol. I, pp. 168-70).]

there can be no doubt of the accuracy of two statements, namely, that the village folk resisted the Bavarians arms in hand, and that the Bavarians exacted a heavy vengeance in consequence. The town was made fuel of fire – reduced to the condition of Pompeii, says Sir Harry Hozier – and the bodies of the dead were left to burn where they lay. General Phil Sheridan saw the black ruins and smelt the odour of the burning flesh the next day.

[Footnote: Sheridan's *Personal Memoirs*, Vol. II, pp. 411-12. Bismarck spoke to him of 'those burning Frenchmen – ugh!']

"The *Daily News* correspondent relates that he saw 'the charred corpses of the women and tender little ones – a sight I dream of to this day, and wake in a sweat of horror'.

[Footnote: *Daily News War Correspondence*, p. 190.]

"To point the moral and make it clear that the destruction was not merely the unconsidered act of a maddened soldiery, a German Proclamation of the 29th September spoke of 'the sentence executed against the village in virtue of the law of war.'

[Footnote: Cassell's *History*, Vol. I, p. 154.]

"It is not too much to say that the incident sent a thrill of horror through Europe. But extreme as the punishment was, the inhabitants had undoubtedly broken the law of war in joining in the street fight, and the Bavarians had a clear war right to deal summarily with those taken red-handed in action. Ten years before, a well-informed writer in *Blackwood's Magazine*

[Footnote: Vol. 88, p. 612 (1860).]

pointed out that attacks by the inhabitants of an invaded country directed against the hostile troops would recoil with terrible effect upon their own heads. 'Men, women and children sacrificed, the innocent as well as the guilty, houses burned and property plundered and devastated – are all considered legitimate retribution for acts of aggression by an unorganised population.'"

* * *

Note by C.W. Porter: According to modern research, including an official French investigation, no more than 39 residents of Bazeilles were killed during the fighting. All other claims are dismissed as "propaganda". What is certain is that there was very violent fighting, over 6,000 men were killed, a few partisans were captured and shot by the Germans, and a few houses were burnt.

THE INJUSTICE OF THE ADMISSIBILITY
OF HEARSAY IN WAR CRIMES TRIALS

General discussion of the problem of hearsay

A best-selling English writer, Jennifer Worth, recently cited a Jewish psychiatrist, Dr. Elisabeth Kübler Ross, who claimed that her father and brother both "witnessed" German soldiers machine-gunning Jewish refugees attempting to swim across a river into Switzerland. (Exact quote: "Her father and brother later witnessed Nazi machine gunners shooting a human river" [sic – "a human river", no less! – C.P.] "of Jewish refugees as they attempted to cross the Rhine" [one of the largest rivers in Europe, usually hundreds of feet wide. – C.P.] "from Germany to the safety of Switzerland." (quoted by Worth, *In the Midst of Life*, p. 51; Worth makes no mention of any specific place names or dates. I am unable to find any mention of this incident in the works of Kübler Ross.))

This would, of course, have been an international incident involving a neutral country, Switzerland, Germany's "protecting power" under the Geneva Convention – rather an illogical thing to do, one might tend to think. Any such incident would have resulted in an international letter of protest by the Swiss government, followed by an official investigation and, we may sure, immense publicity. Thus, if any such incident ever actually occurred, it would be easy to verify.

Did Worth lie? Of course not. Worth might be gullible, but she believed what she was saying. Did Kübler Ross lie? Not necessarily. Did her father and brother lie? Again, not necessarily. Kübler may have simply misunderstood them to say that they were witnesses, when in fact they had only heard about the incident. It is very easy to get this impression, even when it was never intended by the speaker: it is very difficult, weeks, months or years later, to be perfectly clear in one's mind as to whether or not a person who tells you a shocking tale ever actually claimed to have witnessed it personally. In most cases, if you can track down the person who told the story and ask him whether he actually saw it, the answer will be something like "No, I didn't see it myself, but everybody knew it". The fact that he didn't see it, that perhaps no one else saw it either, and that it is perfectly possible for "everybody to know" things which are not true at all, is considered perfectly irrelevant. That is the nature of hearsay. For this reason, hearsay is ordinarily inadmissible in criminal proceedings, without some particular guarantee of reliability (i.e., the so-called "exceptions to the hearsay rule").

Hearsay in law

In law, hearsay is an out of court statement (whether oral or written), offered to prove "the truth of the matter stated" (sometimes phrased as "the truth of what it asserts"). If it is offered to prove that the statement was made – but not necessarily that it is true – then it is not hearsay.

In war crimes trials – even those held being in The Hague today – this distinction is always forgotten. Hearsay is simply declared to be admissible – subject, of course, to its "probative value" – after which random accusations are declared to constitute the "truth" unless the defense can disprove them, thus inverting the burden of proof. Yet the defense is in no position to obtain further information. You can question the "witnesses" all day long, and all they will ever say is, "I don't know, all I know is what the other person told me".

"War Crimes Reports"

One particularly prevalent feature of all "war crimes trials" is the so-called "War Crimes Report". There are hundreds of these "reports", undoubtedly thousands. Legally, they are all hearsay, but "admissible hearsay", of highly dubious reliability. For example, at Dachau, the "Chavez Report", which was to have "proven" the existence of a "gas chamber" at Dachau, was never introduced into evidence, and the accusation was dropped before trial. Col. Chavez appeared as an expert witness at Dachau on Nov. 15, 1945, but made no mention of a gas chamber. The Chavez Report was then re-written and introduced into evidence at Nuremberg as documents 2430-PS and 159-L, even though it was known to be untrue. Chavez was never cross-examined on his "report", since his "report" did not form part of his direct testimony.

The Cross Examination of Fernand Gabrillagues

The following article, reproduced in full, appeared on the front page of *The Advocate* – described as "North-Western Tasmania's Only Daily Newspaper" – on January 18, 1947:

"SHOT EN MASSE BY JAPANESE

TOKYO. Friday (A.A.P.) – A French war crimes officer, Fernand Gabrillagues, told the tribunal how 65 French prisoners of war singing the "Marseillaise" were shot en masse by Japanese in Indo China. The Japanese then bayoneted the wounded with unbridled savagery.

On another occasion the Japanese butchered 200 French prisoners with axes and bayonets on "soil running with blood." Witness gave other details of obscene savagery and Japanese treatment of women."

This is the sort of thing which often passes for "fact" in the 20th and 21st centuries. Fernand Gabrillagues was the author of a "war crimes report" regarding Japanese atrocities in French Indo-China. The "report" (referred to as a "deposition"), was introduced into evidence at the Tokyo Trial as "proof" of the "matter stated" – signed by the "expert witness", Captain Fernand Gabrillagues, after which Gabrillagues appeared to testify and was cross-examined on his "report".

On direct examination, he gave his date of birth as January 1, 1918, stating that he was a Bachelor of Letters and Master of Laws, outlining his other apparently impressive qualifications as an expert on "war crimes" and Delegate to the French War Crimes Office. His cross examination was less impressive, to say the least.

Summary of admissions and claims made by Gabrillagues under cross-examination

Gabrillagues was 29 years old at the time of his testimony. On cross-examination, he admitted that he was a student drafted out of university and had never before been employed in any legal capacity before becoming a "war crimes officer". He knew – and hoped – that men would be hanged on the basis of his report; it was written so that "war criminals" could be "rounded up". Yet, as he readily admitted, he conducted no investigation; he interviewed no witnesses; he made no attempt to determine whether any of the accusations might be mistaken or untrue. He made no attempt to discover whether there might have been any reason why the Japanese acted as they did. He performed no checks to prevent the wholesale introduction of falsehood, erroneous information, hearsay or lies. It was "not his work" (i.e., not his job).

He was unwilling or unable to say which army he was in, for reasons which will become obvious; he was unwilling or unable to give the name of his commanding officer in French West Africa; he was unwilling or unable to say which French government his commanding general in Indo-China was responsible to; he claimed he didn't know who the "De Gaullists" were; he even claimed that he didn't know the meaning of the words "resistance" or "underground", although he knew the meaning of the words "guerrilla" and "franc-tireur", which are exactly synonymous.

He was unable to state when the Japanese Army entered Northern and Southern Indo-China. Since the Japanese Army entered these territories in two different years, under an agreement with the Vichy government of France, this might have been important information, depending on when and where the atrocities were committed.

He was unwilling or unable to state whether or not "resistance members" wore uniforms. Finally, and most crucially, under pressure, he repeatedly admitted that the victims of these atrocities were indeed members of the "resistance" and that at least "some" of the civilian victims had been assisting the resistance, thus admitting that he knew the meaning of these words.

Four points should be noted here.

a) The President of the Tribunal did not, at least at this point, dispute the defense contention that the Vichy government was the legally recognized government of France; that non-uniformed resistance is illegal, and that guerrillas are not entitled to protection as prisoners of war;

b) That uniformed armies commit "atrocities" in reprisal for non-uniformed acts of resistance, and that many of the victims of these reprisals will inevitably be "innocent civilians", in name or in fact, is a matter of course. That is the nature of guerrilla warfare, a fact deliberately exploited by all resistance groups. The more people killed in "atrocities" by the uniformed occupant, the more people will join the resistance! This is one of the reasons why non-uniformed resistance is considered illegal under international law.

c) It is obvious that Gabrillagues knew this, and that his refusal to say which army he was in, or which government his commanding officer was responsible to, or to admit that he was well aware of the meaning of the words "resistance" and "underground", were a result of this knowledge, and of an awareness that any such admission on his part would tend to exculpate or explain the actions of the Japanese, at least in part.

Gabrillagues appears to have been a rather strange person: whether he was one of the most uncooperative, uncommunicative and evasive expert "witnesses" in legal history – or the most incompetent – or a mixture of both – is hard to tell. According to his family, he committed suicide in France in the early 1980s saying that his life had been a failure.

d) As far as one can determine, Gabrillagues was the only author of any "war crimes report" ever subjected to cross-examination as to his "report", in any trial, anywhere, ever.

The following is that cross-examination.

* * *

(Excerpted from *Tokyo Trial transcript*, pp. 15,444-72)

CROSS-EXAMINATION BY MR. LOGAN

Q: [...] In your work as investigator, *did you interview any witnesses yourself* and take statements from them or did you get all the information contained in your affidavit from other affidavits?

A: I have misunderstood the question...

Q: When you received the documents respecting these incidents *did you go out and take any statements yourselves* from any of the people involved?

A: I read most of the affidavits and the complaints which were registered by witnesses.

Q: Did you ever question a witness yourself in connection with any of these incidents you have related in your statements?

A: I did not myself interrogate witnesses. It wasn't my work.

Q: Is it a fact that these prisoners of war mentioned in your statement were De Gaullists?

A: I do not know.

Q: Didn't you make any investigation to try to find out what army these soldiers belonged to?

A: Which soldiers?

Q: [The] prisoners of war you mention in your affidavit.

A: They belonged to the Indo-Chinese army.

Q: Were any of them De Gaullists?

A: I do not know.

Q: *Were any of them guerrillas?*

A: *Some of them belonged to the underground.*

Q: On what side were these Chinese troops? Were they on De Gaul's side or were they on the side of the recognized French government, the Vichy government?

A: I have not understood the question.

Q: Didn't you say a moment ago that some of these troops – you didn't know whether De Gaullists or on the side of the Vichy Government – they were Chinese troops?

A: I don't believe I have spoken of Chinese troops.

Q: Indo-Chinese troops, what side were they on?

A: The Indo-Chinese troops were part of the French army of Indo-China.

Q: Were they under the command of the Vichy government at that time?

A: They were under the orders of the commanding general, the senior commanding general of the troops in Indo-China.

Q: For what government were they fighting?

A: The troops were fighting for France.

Q: When you say France, do you mean the Vichy Government?

A: France.

Q: You understand, of course, that the Japanese troops went into Indo-China under an agreement with the Vichy Government. Now, in your investigation did you find out that these Indo-Chinese troops were opposed to the Vichy Government?

A: I do not believe I have the information with me to answer this question.

Q: Didn't you think it important in your work as an investigator to find out what army, if any, these people [i.e., the victims of the alleged atrocities. – C.P] were employed by at the time of these alleged atrocities?

A: I concerned myself solely with the identification and the search for war criminals.

Q: How can you determine who was a war criminal unless you know army he is fighting for?

A: Criminals are judged by the crime which they commit.

Q: That isn't an answer to the question I gave you. Will you please answer the question?

A: Would you please repeat the question?

Q: Do I understand you made this investigation and tried to determine whether or not a person was a war criminal without knowing on which side the prisoners of war were?

A: I made researches regarding prisoners of war from the complaints which I received [...]

Q: Do you know who was the leader of the Indo-Chinese army?

A: General Martin.

Q: And was General Martin a representative of the Vichy

Government?

A: I do not know.

Q: You were in charge of this Investigation Bureau, weren't you?

A: Yes.

Q: Well, wasn't it part of your duties to find out if these prisoners of war were guerrillas?

A: I have never considered these prisoners to belong to bands of guerrillas [this in contradiction to the answer given above and below. – C.P.]

Q: Well, what did you consider them to belong to?

A: To the Army.

Q: Whose army?

A: The French Army.

Q: What do you mean by the French Army?

A: I cannot give you a definition. It seems difficult to give you an immediate definition.

Q: Well, can you give us a definition tomorrow?

A: I think it would perhaps be possible.

Q: Can you tell me how many of these prisoners of war set forth in your statement were members of the Indo-Chinese Army?

A: They all belonged to the Army of Indo-China. [...]

MR. LOGAN: In your investigations did you also come across a document which gave the Japanese Army the right to go into Southern Indo-China in July, 1941?

A: I have never seen such a document.

Q: Now, isn't it a fact, Mr. Witness, that you know that the Vichy forces and the De Gaullist forces were fighting in Indo-China?

A: Fighting how? I don't know.

Q: You don't know? Do you know there two factions in Indo-China, the De Gaullist faction and the faction representing the legal Vichy Government? [...]

May I have an answer to the question? [...]

I think there is a question unanswered, Your Honor. Will the court reporter read the question? [...]

THE WITNESS: You are telling me about it.

Q: Well, is that true and do you know it?

A: What?

Q: Do you know it to be a fact that there were two factions in Indo-China, one representing the legal Vichy Government and one representing the De Gaullists? [...]

Q: During the course of your investigation, you, of course,

found that that the Japanese troops entered Northern Indo-China in 1940, isn't that a fact?

A: The Japanese troops entered Northern Indo-China.

Q: And you also found out that they entered Southern Indo-China in 1941, isn't that so?

A: I have not worried about this question.

Q: Irrespective of whether you worried about it, have you found out that to be a fact?

A: The documentation which I have consulted does not allow me to answer that question – to give an answer to that question.

Q: Irrespective of the documents which you have consulted, is it a fact?

A: I say that it is possible but I cannot give any precisions.

Q: Do you mean to tell us that you have made all these investigations and you do not know when the Japanese army entered Indo-China?

A: I know that there were Japanese penetrated into Southern Indo-China but I do not know the exact date of the penetration.

Q: What is your best recollection on it?

THE PRESIDENT: This is utterly trifling [...] You are not testing his credibility effectively this way, Mr. Logan. It is possible that he does not know the exact date; I do not. I would have to refresh his memory from the evidence.

MR. LOGAN: I am not asking these questions, if the court Please, to test this witness' credibility. I am asking it to try to ascertain the facts...

Q: From your investigation what was the earliest year that you found out that the Japanese were in – entered Indo-China.

[Objection] [...]

MR. LOGAN: I prefaced my question by asking him whether or not he obtained this information from his investigation, which brings it squarely within the statement made by this witness on directly testimony. He has made this statement referring to various alleged atrocities. It is important to find out just when the Japanese army entered Indo-China to see if it was actually present at the time of these alleged atrocities and to investigate the further situation of the resistance troops operating in Indo-China.

THE PRESIDENT: The question is allowed. Objection overruled.

A: I cannot give you any precise date. I recollect some complaints which were – which date from 1943, 1942, 1945, 1946, but my recollections are not very, very clear on this point.

Q: Let me ask this, then. Is it a fact that after the Japanese troops entered Indo-China there sprang up a resistance movement?

A: The documents do not allow me to answer in a precise answer to this question.

Q: Well, what would allow you to answer that question?

A: I was at the war crimes office in charge of researches on crimes committed by the Japanese Army. Complaints were received and on the basis of these complaints I began my investigations. My work was a material work of researching what crimes had been committed and where the criminals were, so that they could be rounded up.

Q: Have you finished?

A: Yes.

Q: Yesterday you referred to the underground. Will you tell us what you meant by that?

A: During my researches I have sometimes found the word "resistance", "underground", in the documents which I have seen.

Q: Did you investigate to find out just what this underground or resistance was?

A: No.

Q: Weren't you interested, as the person in charge of the investigating bureau, to find out what this resistance was?

A: I did not take up that matter.

Q: Did you ask anybody else to take it up?

A: Absolutely not.

Q: Do I understand you, Mr. Witness, that you appear in this Tribunal and present affidavits where you mention "resistance group" and "underground", and you mean to tell this Tribunal that you don't know what it means?

A: I do not understand – I do not very well understand the question as it has been translated.

MR. LOGAN: May I have it re-translated?

(Thereupon, the last question was re-translated.)

A: I did not present any affidavits to this Tribunal. I only —I have only told of them what I had done, or the work that I had done, in the war crimes office.

Q: Well, let me ask you this question: Do you, of your own knowledge, know what the resistance group was?

[Objection by the prosecutor] [...]

THE PRESIDENT: [...] I think the question is allowable and should be answered. It is quite a simple question.

A: I believe that I have already answered this question.

Q: Well, answer it again, will you, please?

A: I answered that in the documents that I had I found a few – several times, the word "resistance".

Q: I understand what you said, Mr. Witness, but that isn't the question I put. I am asking you now. Do you know, of your own knowledge, what the resistance movement was?

A: I have no precise knowledge on movements of the underground – movement of the resistance.

Q: Well, what was that movement?

A: What I could tell you could only be a repetition of what was told to me. That is hearsay, and I want to speak before this Tribunal only of things which I know by myself, in my own knowledge.

Q: Well now, Mr. Witness, as a matter of fact, *your entire affidavit submitted by you on direct is all hearsay*, isn't it?

A: I did not say that what – that my deposition was based on affidavits, but on depositions of witnesses of victims of these crimes.

[Objection as to translation]

THE PRESIDENT: [...] After consulting with my colleagues, I think that the following questions are pertinent and I will ask the witness to answer them:

Did the members of the resistance wear uniforms?

THE WITNESS: I have not been able to ascertain it. [...]

[Probably *"Je n'ai pas pu le vérifier"*, a sort of halfway-house between "No" and "I don't know". – C.P]

MR. LOGAN: Well, tell us what you heard this resistance was?

A: I practically have no knowledge of the movement – concerning the resistance movement. I only received complaints from victims of atrocities of the Japanese Army, and I confined my activities to that.

Q: Isn't it a fact that the resistance Movement was started in Indo-China against the Japanese and the Vichy Government in Indo-China?

A: The documentation which I have seen does not allow me to answer your question.

MR. LOGAN: If the Tribunal please, I think I have been patient about this. I think we ought to have a direction and make this witness answer these questions.

THE PRESIDENT: Witness, do you, in fact, know anything more than appears in the documents?

THE WITNESS: All that I have heard beyond that I considered as hearsay, and I cannot give evidence of these before this Tribunal.

THE PRESIDENT: You can. You are mistaken. You must

answer from hearsay, but you can say the sources of your information.

THE WITNESS: I haven't heard any information on this point.

BY MR. LOGAN: (Continued):

Q: When you were in the Colonial Services of the French colonies, were you in the Vichy army or were you in the resistance Movement from that point onward?

A: I was mobilised – I was drafted February 1, 1943 – no: 1944.

Q: Do you understand English?

A: (In English) Very small.

Q: Was that year incorrect that was just given over the translation system?

A: (In English) It seems that the number – (In French) I think that the number given "4", is not exact – is not correct. It is "43".

Q: What time were you a member of the resistance Movement?

A: I was drafted February 1, 1943 in the French Army of Africa.

Q: Was that under the Vichy government or was that in the resistance Army?

A: In the French Army of Africa.

Q: Was that as a member of the resistance Group or a member of the forces of the Vichy government?

A: It was as a French citizen who was still under military obligations.

THE PRESIDENT: It is suggested to me that if you words "Free French" instead of "resistance", you might get more satisfactory answers.

Q: Were you a member of the Free French?

A: Since February 1, 1943 I belonged to the French Army of Africa, the only army which was in Africa.

Q: Were you under General Le Clerc?

A: I did not say that I was in Africa. I was in West of Africa – in French West of Africa.

Q: I didn't ask you that. Were you under General Le Clerc?

A: General Le Clerc was not in the West of Africa.

Q: Were you under him?

A: Absolutely not.

Q: Then you were under some general of the Vichy Government?

A: I do not think so.

Q: *Do you seriously want this Tribunal to understand from your testimony that you were fighting for France but you didn't know which army you were in?*

A: I was only thinking of fighting for France.

Q: And you didn't care which army you were in, is that it? And, furthermore, you don't know which army you were in, is that it?

A: I was in the French Army.

THE PRESIDENT: The French Government employed him on war crimes, apparently, and that is the Free French Government.

Q: From whom did you receive your pay from 1943 on?

A: The Disbursing Officer of my unit.

THE PRESIDENT: Mr. Logan, this is trifling. I say it again to any Member of the Tribunal having a similar view.

MR. LOGAN: It may be trifling, Your Honor, but to me it is more serious than that. A witness comes here and testifies the way he has. I'm trying to find out just what the situation was as he investigated it so that he can give this Tribunal some information on these alleged crimes.

BY MR. LOGAN: Tell me this: *Did you ever check to find out if any of the charges made in these affidavits which are submitted by you are false?*

A: It was not for me to judge whether the witnesses have made false depositions...

Q: And you made no check to find that out, is that it?

A: It was not in my province to judge of the exactitude of the directness of witness – of the depositions made.

Q: Now, is it a fact that these people who claim to have suffered these alleged atrocities were members of the resistance Force?

A: Yes, certainly.

Q: And the civilians also mentioned in these affidavits, were they assisting the resistance Force?

A: Some did and some did not.

Q: And General Martin was the one in charge of the resistance Force in Indo-China?

A: I do not know.

Q: Did you make any investigation to find out?

A: I did not try to find out.

MR. LOGAN: That is all.

CROSS-EXAMINATION BY MR. SHIMANOUCHI

Q: Mr. Witness, what is your age?

A: I was born on January 1, 1918.

Q: You testified, Mr. Witness, that you were a student prior to the war. Then you were drafted in the Army in September, 1942?

A: I stated that it was on February 1, 1943.

Q: Up to that time were you occupied in some profession or vocation?

A: I was a student, and then I went to Africa as a Colonial civil servant.

Q: What duties were you assigned to after you were drafted?

A: I was infantry platoon leader.

Q: Have you, Mr. Witness, before you took up your work with the War Crimes Office in September 1946, engaged in any legal business, either as a prosecutor or a lawyer?

A: Not at all. [...]

CROSS-EXAMINATION BY MR. BROOKS

Q: Mr. Witness, in your investigation, did you investigate to see if any of these alleged acts were taken by way of reprisal?

A: I think that in certain localities the Japanese may have been irritated by the actions – by the attitude of the French population.

Q: Did your investigation show that certain actions complained of were to suppress and deter the activities in resistance of franc-tireurs or others?

A: The massacres at Langson and other places certainly did not aim at suppressing the activities of franc-tireurs.

Q: Did your investigations uncover any actions that would classify the participants as franc-tireurs?

A: In my deposition I have not spoken of relations between the Japanese and those that may be called franc-tireurs.

Q: In other words, *you never made any investigations as to matters that might have been in justification of some of the actions to which you have referred*?

A: (No answer)

MR. BROOKS: I didn't get the answer.

THE PRESIDENT: *Did you try to discover any reason why the Japanese acted as they did*?

THE WITNESS: I did not try to discover any reasons [...]

MR. BROOKS: That is all.

MR. LOGAN: No further cross-examination. If the Tribunal please, at this time I move to strike out and disregard all the evidence presented of alleged atrocities in Indo-China on the ground that the evidence shows that these resistance troops were not lawful troops of

France, they were fighting contrary to the orders of their own legally recognized government, and cannot claim rights are prisoners of war under international law but fall into the classification of guerrillas or franc-tireurs.

THE PRESIDENT: Of course, there is no such evidence as you claim, Mr. Logan. We will, at the proper time, pass judgement on the evidence we've heard [...]

[This despite the witness' clear admission that the victims were, in fact, members of the resistance.

Q: Now, is it a fact that these people who claim to have suffered these alleged atrocities were members of the resistance Force?

A: Yes, certainly.

Q: And the civilians also mentioned in these affidavits, were they assisting the resistance Force?

A: Some did and some did not. – C.P.]

* * *

The real problem is the admissibility of hearsay. As noted in the famous Dissentient Judgement of R.B. Pal of India:

"Exhibit 1574 is a statement taken out of court.... The name of the airman was given by this man as 'Stan Woodbridge of Chingford, Essex, England'. *We do not even know whether there was really any such airman in the R.A.F. and whether he is really dead.*" (p. 1,212 of the section dedicated to the Dissentient Judgement of R. B. Pal of India, volume 21, Tokyo Trial transcript.)

Pal noted that nothing in international law gives the victor in war the power to legislate in international law. If the nations of the world wished to create such authority, they were free to do so, but the proper way to so would be by means of a treaty; but no such treaty exists.

Historically, most European wars were brought to a conclusion based on the terms of negotiated peace treaties containing an amnesty for all acts committed during the war, thus avoiding endless recriminations, renewed injustice, and serial wars related to the same problems. The modern world has largely abandoned this approach.

For further information in a relatively accessible form, search for Pal, Radhabinod. "Judgment".

The Dissentient Judgment of R.B. Pal is available on line in PDF form at http://www.sdh-fact.com/CL02_1/65_S4.pdf. Published in book form in *The Tokyo Judgment: The International Military Tribunal for the Far East (IMTFE)* 29 April 1946 – 12 November 1948. Edited by B. V. A. Röling and C. F. Rüter. Amsterdam: University Press Amsterdam, 1977. Also published separately in Calcutta and Japan. Currently out of print and nearly impossible to find.

All quotations taken from the complete 52,000 page, 21-volume transcript. Currently out of print and almost impossible to find except in a few large law libraries. 30 years ago there were said to be only 4 copies of the original in the whole world.

THE MYTH OF THE ILLEGALITY OF CONCENTRATION CAMPS

To the generations of people having grown up – like hot-house plants – in the suffocating atmosphere of Holocaust propaganda, it may come as a surprise to learn that concentration camps are not illegal.

There is nothing in international law prohibiting concentration camps, even today. (See * Footnote.)

The following are a few quotes on the subject only:

"That, in case of general devastation, the peaceful population may be detained in so-called concentration camps there is no doubt." (*International Law, A Treatise*, L. Oppenheim, Vol. II, Disputes, War and Neutrality, Longmans, Green and Co., London, Fifth Edition, September 1935, footnote 2, p. 289.)

"The practice, resorted to during the South African War, of housing the victims of devastation in concentration camps, must be approved. The purpose of war may even oblige a belligerent to confine a population forcibly in concentration camps." (*Ibid*, p. 332.)

"Concentration camps are practically internment camps for non-combatants... Such an extreme measure is only to be justified by very extreme circumstances; in fact, by such circumstances as make concentration not only imperatively necessary for the success of the belligerent's operations, but also the lesser of two evils for the inhabitants themselves..." (*War Rights on Land*, J.M. Spaight, McMillan and Co., London, 1911, p. 307.)

(It should be noted that *War Rights on Land*, a classic of international law, was written only 4 years after the Second Hague Conference, which – in the form of the Fourth Hague Convention on Land Warfare of October 18, 1907 – formed the basis for nearly all the so-called violations of "international law" invoked to hang the defendants at Nuremberg.).

"If devastation is justified, then some system of concentration is not only justified, but demanded by considerations of humanity." (*Ibid*, p. 310.)

"A similar policy of devastation was carried out by the British in the former Boer Republics. Whole regions were laid waste to prevent their being used as a base by the enemy, the non-combatant families having first been removed from them and sent to concentration camps.

There is no doubt that these camps were essential for the security of those deported to them, both against natives and to secure for them the means of life." (*Wheaton's International Law*, Seventh English Edition, Stevens and Sons, London, 1944, Vol. 2, WAR. Page 214.)

"Devastation on a broad scale was carried out by Spain in Cuba in 1897. The practice of 'concentrating' the civilian population in garrison towns, which accompanied the devastation, led to protests from the United States which ultimately formed part of its grounds for war. In 1901 The British armies in South Africa interned the civilian population in 'concentration camps', with the result of serious loss of life. At the same time the country was laid waste far and wide as a means of cutting off the supplies of the guerrilla forces." (*International Law*, Chas. G. Fenwick, Third Edition, New York, Appleton-Century Crofts, Inc., 1948, p. 567.)

The same work, one of the most objective, points out the difficulties involved for a defeated power:

"How could Germany, blockaded by Great Britain during the four years of the first World War, be expected, even had there been the will to do it, to feed prisoners according to the standard of its own army which had to bear the burden of the war, or even according to the standard of its factory workers whose work was essential to the winning of the war? And if prisoners revolted against the meagre fare to which they were subjected, disciplinary punishment appeared to be justified." (*Ibid*, p. 575.)

The fact is that "concentration camps" were, and are, legal under international law, and have existed in one form or another in practically all countries. One reason why they cannot be abolished is because no objective definition of the term "concentration camp" appears possible. Note that, to J.M. Spaight, a concentration camp is an "internment camp for non-combatants", during wartime only. Whether American Civil War (more correctly: "Secession War") prison camps can be assimilated into the same category as "concentration camps" is entirely a matter of definition.

What has not changed is the spirit of American-British hypocrisy and contempt for human life. For example, had it not been for Northern refusal to exchange prisoners, there wouldn't have been any Northern prisoners in Confederate prison camps, at Andersonville or anywhere else in the South. Despite the fact that the problem was the North's own doing, and that the Southern armies and population were starving as a result of the blockade and Union destruction of Southern crops and infrastructures, Confederate prisoners in Northern prisons were starved deliberately, in retaliation for the alleged "deliberate" starvation of Union prisoners in the South.

The commander of Andersonville prison camp in Georgia, Commander Hartmann Wirz, was a Swiss-German who visited Europe as an official representative of the Confederacy several times during the war, running the blockade. After the war, he was indicted for "conspiring with Jeff Davis and his rebel cabinet" to "render Union prisoners unfit for service through a policy of deliberate mistreatment and starvation", and for killing a Union prisoner with a right-handed blow to the head.

Wirz was subjected to a medical examination during his trial. He was found to be suffering from malnutrition; and atrophy and paralysis of the right arm as the result of unrepaired fractures. Wirz was convicted and hanged with a short drop, taking 14 minutes to die.

Photographs and engravings of Union prisoners from Confederate prison camps suffering from malnutrition, diabetes, gangrene and cancer [!], in addition to all the usual contagious diseases, were then printed by Congress and widely distributed for 30 years after the war to keep the Republican Party in power. This was known as "waving the bloody shirt".

Since one lie requires another, and since Andersonville provides a perfect explanation for what happened at German camps in 1945, the more irresponsible of the Holocaustians have now come full

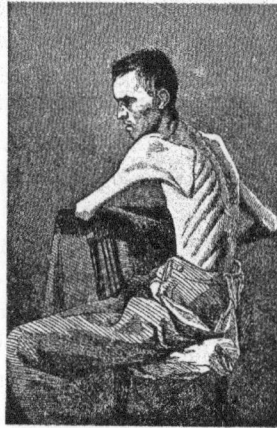

1865-1870

THE MARTYRS OF ANDERSONVILLE

and other Confederate prison pens were widely publicized during the Reconstruction period to justify the Radical policy toward the South. These drawings of living skeletons rescued from the prison at Belle Isle were published in a book by the Radical Congress. Yet General Grant himself had refused to save these men by exchange because—as he said—the South needed its soldiers back to carry on the war, while the North could always get new ones. Almost as many Southerners (25,-976) died in Northern prisons as Northerners in the South (30,218).

circle, and are referring to Andersonville as "America's Auschwitz".

Concentration camps in their modern form are generally thought to have been invented by General Valeriano Weyler y Nicolau, a Spanish General in Cuba, in 1897. Weyler was Spanish, but of Prussian descent, leading to the myth that such camps were a "Prussian invention".

The Cuban War of Independence was fought with enormous destruction of property on both sides. Rebel guerrillas moving along the length of the island burned Spanish sugar plantations and other property in an attempt to render the island valueless to Spain; Weyler moved all "loyal" Cubans into "campos de reconcentramiento", announcing that all civilians outside the camps would be treated as guerrillas and shot on sight. The intention was to cut the island in two and hamper the movements of the guerrillas.

The camps were shut as a result of American protests and Weyler was recalled to Spain, a concession which failed to satisfy American greed for Spanish overseas possessions. Weyler served as Minister of War 3 times and died in 1930; there is a monument to him in Madrid. Modern Cuban sources estimate 25,000 deaths in the camps, down from a propaganda figure of 250,000.

[NOTE: The Spanish point of view is somewhat different. They argue that the strategy of the Cuban rebels, under the leadership of Máximo Gómez, was to drive all civilians unwilling to cooperate with the guerrillas into the towns, which were then to be deprived of food through the destruction of crops. Weyler simply reversed a situation created by the rebels: all civilians unwilling to cooperate with the Spanish were to be driven into the countryside, after which the COUNTRYSIDE was to be deprived of food by the same methods. The rebels could never have defeated the Spanish and never tried; their only hope was to involve the United States.]

Following the Spanish-American War, Cuba was granted its independence, while all other Spanish overseas possessions were retained. Following Filipino defeat in regular warfare intended to free the country from its American "liberators", guerrillas under the leadership of Emilio Aguinaldo continued the war using irregular tactics. At this point, the Americans imitated the tactics of "Butcher" Weyler, building concentration camps on the island of Mindanao, "to protect non-combatant civilians". The number of civilian deaths in these camps is unknown.

If, as is usually estimated, 28,000 Boer women and children died in British concentration camps during the Second Boer War, this amounts to a death rate of 10-20% of the total civilian population in enemy-occupant "death camps". The only historical parallel to concentration camp mortality on this scale must be sought in Stalinist policies in the Baltic States. Special taxes were levied upon "loyal Boers" to enable the British to pay the costs of interning their relatives. The population of the camps amounted to virtually every white woman and child in the Transvaal and Orange Free States; the western Transvaal, in J.M. Spaight's own words, was turned into a "smoking desert" on the grounds of "military necessity".

In 1914, with the invasion of Belgium, Britain became the champion of the "independence and neutrality of small nations", a chief propaganda aim of the First World War.

The 1944 Edition of *Wheaton's International Law* (published in London) alleges that the South African Republics "warred against Great Britain" (p. 99), and that the British went to war to defend the rights of British subjects abroad (a right never conceded to National Socialists where ethnic Germans in Poland were concerned).

At Nuremberg, concentration camps were held to be "criminal" (as long as they were German), while members of resistance groups were held to be patriots and heroes; shooting or imprisoning them ("Night and Fog") was held to be "criminal".

With the advent of alleged Al-Qaeda prisoners at Camp X-Ray at Guantanamo Bay Naval Base in Cuba in 2002, it was once again discovered (by the idealistic Americans) that concentration camps are "legal", and that irregular combatants are "criminals". Where was this knowledge at Nuremberg?

Since Camp X-Ray is "not on American soil", and since the inmates are "not U.S. citizens", they are not protected by U.S. law; but since it is a "domestic matter", they are not protected by "international law" either. How very convenient.

The manner in which international conventions are intentionally drafted in vague language permitting interpretation in any manner one likes, has been brilliantly described by G. Lowe Dickenson in *The International Anarchy 1904-1914*, Century, New York, 1926 (for example, the Hague Conferences were never expected to produce any practical results and were ridiculed privately by all the statesmen involved, pp. 347-358).

That the same is increasingly true of almost all law, is probably obvious to anyone who has ever been involved in legal proceedings.

Thus, like "weapons of mass destruction" (another undefined term), "concentration camps" are illegal, immoral and emaciating only when possessed by our enemies; our own concentration camps are perfectly legal, lawful and laudable.

All nations intern enemy aliens during wartime. The Fifth Hague Convention even requires the internment of belligerent troops on neutral soil. How are they to be interned, if not in "camps"?

That the Jews were "enemy aliens" resident in National Socialist Germany is apparent from their own many "declarations of war" against Germany, beginning on March 24, 1933. Yet only a minority of all Jews were ever interned, even during wartime (the highest percentage occurring in Holland as the result of fears of an Allied invasion) – a degree of moderation never imitated by the United States, Britain, Australia or Soviet Russia.

It appears to me that, far more important than the nomenclature of the penal institution in which one is incarcerated, are the procedures and rules of evidence according to which one is imprisoned, and the conditions of confinement. American prison conditions, despite expensive infrastructures, are among the worst in the world. See *No Escape: Male Rape in U.S. Prisons*, a 378-page report from Human Rights Watch, 350 Fifth Ave., New York, NY, 1018-3299 USA, also available from http://www.hrw.org/reports/2001/prison/report.html. See also *Scottsboro Boy* by Haywood Patterson, Bantam Paperback, 1952, a book which, in many respects – forced sodomy, prison rackets, slave labor for outside private commercial firms – could have been written yesterday, describing almost any prison in America. If anything, the situation is far worse as a result of the inversion of racial roles and the abolition of segregated prisons. When Americans solve their own problems, they will be qualified to preach to the rest of the world.

Why exclusive attention should be focused on Jewish "suffering" in German prison camps 60 years ago, is something only the Jews can explain, particularly in view of the fact that their complaints of hardship are neither unique, nor, in many respects, even true.

* **Footnote:** To verify the truth of this statement, go to
http://iate.europa.eu/iatediff/SearchByQueryLoad.do?method=load
or click "Source Language: English", "Target Language: English", "Hit List Only" or "All Fields" (it makes no difference), and search for "convention concentration camps", "treaty concentration camps", or any combination of these words, for example, "convention concentration", or "treaty camps".

The Eurodicautom is an official dictionary for use by the European Commission, and lists hundreds of treaties and conventions. For example, if you search for "convention concentration", you will find many international conventions relating to concentrations of food additives, etc. But you will find nothing under "internment camps" or "concentration camps", and nothing under "camps". Try the same with "Treaty".

FURTHER READING:

— *Konzentrationslager 1896 bis Heute, Eine Analyse*, [*Concentration Camps 1986 to Today, An Analysis*], Andrjez J. Kaminski, Verlag W. Kohlhammer, 1982 (exceedingly extensive bibliography, somewhat marred by wholesale acceptance of Holocaust propaganda);
— *First Guidebook to the USSR: Prisons and Concentration Camps of the Soviet Union*, Avrahim Shifkin, Stephanus, 1980 (illustrated by 170 maps and drawings; the author is an Israeli whose father was murdered by Stalin);
— *The Brunt of the War, and Where It Fell*, Emily Hobhouse, London, 1902;
— *War without Glamour, or Women's War Experiences Written by Themselves, 1899-1902*, Collected and Translated by Emily Hobhouse, Bloemfontein, no date;
— *The Martial Spirit*, Walter Millis, Literary Guild of America, 1931 (Cuban guerrilla war tactics; "reconcentration centres", "camps" and "garrisoned towns"; anti-Spanish atrocity propaganda);
— *Belgian Neutrality under International Law*, Alexander Fuehr, Funk and Wagnalls, New York, 1915;
— *Jüdische Kriegserklärungen an Deutschland. Wortlaut – Vorgeschichte – Folgen* [*Jewish Declarations of War against Germany. Text – Prior History – Consequences*], Hartmut Stern;
— *The German Presence in Queensland*, Manfred Jürgensen, Alan Corkhill and Raymond Evans, University of Queensland, Brisbane, Australia, 1988 (expropriation and internment, etc. of German nationals during First World War);
— *The American Past*, Roger Butterfield, Simon & Schuster, NY, 1947 (quote on p. 191: "Yet General Grant himself had refused to save these men by exchange because – as he said – the South needed its soldiers back to carry on the war, while the North could always get new ones.");
— *Other Losses*, James Bacques;
— *Crimes and Mercies*, James Bacques.

DISCLAIMER:

I expressly repudiate any and all philosophical or moral conclusions which may appear to arise from the above article. I merely describe the legal situation as it exists.

If British actions during the Boer War – travelling six thousand miles to invade the Boer Republics and steal the gold mines of the Transvaal, murdering 10-20% of the total White population of the country in concentration camps in so doing, etc. etc. – were not, and are not, illegal under international law, then "international law" is a mockery and a cynical farce.

We would be far better off if there were no such thing as "international law", because, in that case, there would be no basis whatsoever upon which to make fraudulent, sanctimonious and hypocritical accusations against the Germans – in 1933-45, or at any other time.

* * *

Eisenhower's "death camps" were *illegal* under international law, for a wide variety of reasons. They were set up *after the war,* in violation of *every single treaty* relating to the treatment of prisoners of war. The link is included only to show that this is the way Americans have *always treated people.*

There appears to be little or nothing on the Internet about General Weyler's concentration camps in Cuba; I have seen photographs of inmates from these camps at photographic exhibitions on the history of Cuba, and they are in no way different from the photographs of sick and dying inmates at Bergen-Belsen or anywhere else. In Spanish, the inmates were referred to as "reconcentrados" and the camps as "campos [or "centros"] de reconcentramiento". Obviously there were no gas chambers in Cuba.

JAZZ IN THE CONCENTRATION CAMPS

Examples of true conditions in the German camps as opposed to American prisons and camps

A review of *Musik am Rande des Lebens* [*Music on the Edge of Life*] by Milan Kuna

(Partial translation from *Deutsche Geschichte*, issue 60, by Carlos W. Porter.)

One of the most astonishing chapters in the history of the concentration camps was jazz [a particularly snide and stupid remark by the author of the book review is omitted here]. "It seems all the more unbelievable that jazz could be played in German concentration camps, as if the SS and camp management were completely unaware of the racist and chauvinistic Nazi cultural policy", Kuna wonders (p. 266). In actual fact, jazz played by inmates was not only tolerated, but even gladly listened to by SS men. The guards ignored the brown boycott, and the inmates were allowed to jazz whatever came out of their saxophones. In Buchenwald, jazz was played by a 14-man combo called "Rhythmus". The French Communist Louis "Marco" Markovitsch set the tone musically, playing tenor saxophone and clarinet, while his countryman Ives Dariet, better known under his professional name as Jean Roland, wrote the arrangements. Finn Jacobsen, from Denmark, and Lena, a Dutchman, played trumpet. The "Rhythm-Boys", with the Russian Nikolaj on guitar, John Verden on drums and Herbert Goldschmied on piano, played hits by Duke Ellington, Cole Porter, Glenn Miller, W.C. Handy and Irving Berlin. This was in addition to hits by jazz geniuses ranging from Louis Armstrong to Artie Shaw and Fats Waller (p. 270 f). In addition to larger-scale entertainment concerts in the camp movie theater, the jazz musicians, working in smaller groups with constantly changing personnel, wandered from barracks to barracks: "On these occasions, for example, they were allowed to play Glenn Miller's 'In The Mood', which could not be heard almost anywhere else in Europe" (p. 272). [?] [sic]

Kuna notes that, to permit the Buchenwald jazz orchestra to continue playing, influential inmates had to create jobs for them which left the musicians with sufficient energy and leisure time to play music. The allocation of "jobs fit for jazz musicians" was taken care of by Professor Herbert Weidlich, an inmate of Buchenwald since 1942, who rendered great services to jazz in [Buchenwald] concentration camp, exploiting his position to protect the musicians.

The jazz-playing inmates in Sachsenhausen included young Czechs interned for participating in prohibited student demonstrations. The so-called "Sing-Sing Boys" sang Jaroslav Jezek hits which were actually forbidden in the Third Reich because of their lyrics (p. 122 ff) [!]. The group broke up once and for all when the "boys" were released and sent home in 1942.

Jazz in Mauthausen, too

Carefully-rehearsed Czech jazz was played in Mauthausen as well: the barracks barber, Dr. Jaroslav Tobiasek, who belonged to the large camp classical orchestra but was also the driving force behind the Mauthausen mini-jazz band, resisted the hostility of the conductor of the Mauthausen classical orchestra, Rumbauer, who considered the combo "competition" and placed a great many obstacles in its way. The band members came from all over Europe; the saxophonist was [the Czech] Rudolf Dudak. Jazz was also played in Bistriz, near Beneschau, a small concentration camp near Prague: the pianists Kopecky, Mancl and Zschok played piano melodies from Gershwin's works "Rhapsody in Blue" and "An American in Paris", while Fischer's dance orchestra played songs by Cole Porter, Duke Ellington, Charlie Chaplin and Irving Berlin. This was in addition to all types of other songs, interpreted by Pospili, Sobesky or the "Camp Caruso", Kabourek (p. 278).

Among Theresienstadt jazz groups, the Weiss Quartet competed against Erich Vogel's Dixieland Orchestra. Bedrich Weiss, known as "Fricek", one of the best known jazz musicians in Prague in the mid-1930s, composed his "Doctor Swing" in the camp. Not only did he look like Benny Goodman – slandered by the National Socialists as the "Swing Jew" – he even played in the same style. Under the leadership of gifted German Jewish pianist Martin Roman, the two bands merged, forming what then became known as the "Ghetto Swingers". Roman, a well-known Goodman fan just like Weiss, had emigrated from Berlin to Amsterdam on racial grounds, accompanying the well-known Americans Louis Armstrong, Coleman Hawkins and Lionel Hampton on pre-1940 tours, and had also toured with "gypsy baron" Django

Reinhardt. Transferred to Theresienstadt from Westerbork concentration camp in Holland, Roman took over the artistic lead and, with Weiss, arranged thirty new compositions. Gershwin's "I Got Rhythm" was used as set-chaser. The vocalists consisted of tenor Freddy Haber and a girl trio in the style of the Andrews Sisters.

The "Ghetto Swingers" at the Marktplatz Café

The "Ghetto Swingers", who played at the Café am Marktplatz [in Theresienstadt], also appeared in the film "The Führer Gives the Jews a City", in which, for propaganda purposes, the Jewish director, Kurt Gerron, depicted the ideal concentration camp on film. The band members – gigging the "Bugle Call Rag" in the film sequence – wore blue blazers with a Star of David. In one of the following scenes in the film, a string orchestra, led by Karel Ancerl, plays selected classics. The Jewish camp self-government in Theresienstadt had a great concern for art and culture. The first opera performed after the opening of the camp was Smetana's "Bartered Bride"; another was "The Kiss" by the same composer. Other operas included Mozart's "The Marriage of Figaro", "Bastien and Bastienne" and the "Magic Flute". There was also a wonderful children's opera, "Brundi Bear", by Hans Kräsa, from Prague. Conductor Rafael Schacter's performance of Verdi's "Requiem" was a subject of religious dispute, and was greatly disliked by Orthodox Jews (p. 196 ff).

The night club pianist Carlo S. Taube worked up his impressions into a symphony climaxing in a distortion of "The Song of the Germans", with horrendous dissonances (p. 215 f).

The Theresienstadt City Orchestra

The City Band of Theresienstadt was led by Peter Deutsch, former conductor of the Royal Danish Orchestra. The repertoire included various Strauss waltzes, a few songs by Kmoch, a potpourri of songs by Karel Vacek and finally the Bohemian folk song, "Schaffers Annerl" [Schaffer's "Little Annie"] [?] (p. 244). "Isn't it all miraculous?" wrote Willi Mahler, a music-lover, describing his impressions of the Great Holiday Concert of 25 June 1944 in his diary. "The German soldier is losing the struggle for his existence in the West, South and in Eastern Europe, and the Jews, sealed off in the [...] atmosphere of Theresienstadt, are allowed to listen to promenade concerts and have their own band, at the order of the German administration of our own settlement" (p. 225). Upon the approach of the Red Army, the lyrics of the Czech musical numbers got even cheekier: "... in the end, we'll all laugh when everybody shits on Germany" (p. 292).

[COMMENT: *Plus ça change, plus la même chose.* – C.P.]

Perhaps with this in mind, the Prague musician Karel Hasler, composer of "Our Czech Song", was cold-bloodedly murdered in Mauthausen by his fellow prisoners (p. 286 f.). Saxophonist Rudolf Dudak's instrument saved his life when an American war-criminal fighter pilot machine-gunned the "victims of fascism" out of a clear blue sky on a clear day: "The attack took place in broad daylight, just while the camp band was playing on the parade ground. The musicians stumbled all over each other, trying to take cover. Rudolf Dudak was lucky enough to be wearing his saxophone on a strap around his neck, so that the instrument protected his abdomen. A bullet grazed the metal, ricocheted off as if it were a steel helmet, and Dudak survived" (p. 357).

Catastrophe on the *Cap Arcona*

Emil Frantisek Burian, a Marxist musician from Prague, was among the inmates evacuated from Neuengamme near Hamburg on the luxury liner *Cap Arcona*, immediately before the end of the war, with the intention of transferring them to the care of the British victors. "Astonishingly, Christmas was celebrated in Neuengamme every year", Kuna summarizes. "On the parade ground stood a great fir tree, decorated with bright light bulbs. What a paradox! The symbol of a peaceful and contemplative Christmas time in the concentration camp! Christmas celebrations were held in the stone barracks opposite the kitchen, in a great hall capable of seating 500 people, with the participation of inmates from every country in Europe. Jaromir Erben sang Dvorak's song "We Are Attracted to What Is Strange" in this hall every year since 1941. For the Christmas celebration, Burian sang the very first performance of a song of his own called... "The Song of the Cold" (p. 308).

On board the *Arcona*, Burian continued composing songs in praise of Marxism-Leninism. Although the war was almost completely over, the *Arcona*, and its sister ships the *Deutschland* and the *Theilbeck* – also filled with refugees – were attacked by British aircraft on the orders of Arthur ["The Butcher"] Harris. "The ships burst into flames and sank within an hour. The passengers jumped into the water while the pilots machine gunned everything that moved. Anybody who wasn't burnt to death or shot was sucked down and drowned by the sinking ships. Of the 7,500 people on board, there were only 500 survivors, who had been lucky enough to keep their bearings in the ice-cold waters..."

Burian's compositions disappeared in the depths, but their composer was one of the few who succeeded in staying afloat, finally landing on the shores of the Baltic, totally exhausted and suffering from exposure, after many long, terrifying hours in the icy water.

(End of translation.)

* * *

The book by Milan Kuna, 400 pages long in fine print, is chiefly concerned with classical music, and contains many reproductions of piano sonatas, orchestral scores, etc. etc. composed by Bohemian or Czech inmates in all German concentration camps, including Auschwitz, and pen-and-ink sketches of the musicians. At the same time, the ridiculous pretense is maintained of German barbarism and cruelty and the existence of an "extermination program". I wonder how much classical music is composed in American prisons?

THE INJUSTICE OF CONSPIRACY ACCUSATIONS IN WAR CRIMES TRIALS

In war crimes trials, "conspiracy", "design", and "plan", are used sometimes synonymously, and sometimes not. The doctrine of conspiracy was borrowed from American state and lower Federal Court decisions, particularly Marino v. US, 91 Fed. 2d. 691, Circuit Court of Appeals. The rest of the world, of course, was not placed on notice to obey these decisions. In 1945, conspiracy was a concept unknown to international law. An example of the unfairness of this doctrine in practice is provided by the case of Schoepp and Gretsch, in the Trial of Martin Gottfried Weiss, Dachau, Nov. 15 – Dec. 13, 1945, M1175 National Archives, beginning on microfilm page 000691.

* * *

DEFENSE: I would like to make a statement to the court relative to the defendants Schoepp and Gretsch. There has been no evidence against either of these men, either by the prosecution or by any witness for the defense. Therefore, they have nothing that they have to defend. But they ask me to say to the court that they throw themselves on the court, if there are any questions that any member of the court would like to ask them. They have nothing to hide, and it would be up to the court to ask them any questions they might have.

PROSECUTION: May it please the court... whether or not there is any evidence before the court as to the criminality and culpability with respect to Schoepp and Gretsch, is a matter which this court has already decided, in their rulings on the motion for a directed verdict of not guilty. It may be the position of the defense counsel that there is no evidence, but I think it is grossly improper to put the court into the position of asking the accused to be put on the stand. I think it is highly improper for the defense counsel to ask the court to reveal their attitude by putting them in the position of asking the accused Schoepp and Gretsch to take the stand. I think that that is an election which should be made by the accused themselves, after they have conferred with counsel, and it is certainly improper to ask this court whether or not they have any questions that they want to ask the accused at this time.

DEFENSE: May it please the court, that isn't the point at all.

These men have nothing to say on the stand, but they don't want the court to get the impression that they are refusing to take the stand, or refusing to answer any questions. They are merely throwing themselves on the court, with these words: "I have nothing to hide". There is no point in their taking the stand. I wouldn't know what to ask them. The prosecution has not brought one thing out against them. There is nothing for them to defend. But they don't want the court to get the idea they are hiding anything, and for that reason they open themselves to the request of the court. There is nothing improper about that. The burden of proof is on the prosecution to prove that these men are guilty of what they are charged with. There has been no evidence brought out against them. The prosecution takes the position that the burden is on them to prove that they are innocent.

PROSECUTION: The answer to that is that these men are charged with acting in pursuance of a common design to subject these prisoners to killings, beatings, tortures, starvation, abuses, and indignities. We have shown by our case that these men were guards, and as such they acted in pursuance of a common design to subject these people to the beatings, killings, starvation, and so forth, as charged in the particulars. I again say that it is entirely up to the accused, with the advice of their counsel, to either take the stand or remain silent, as they see fit, but to try to put this court into the position of making an election, or even attempting to disclose their opinion as to their guilt or innocence at this time, is grossly improper.

PRESIDENT: The defense will proceed with their case.

DEFENSE: Do I understand, Sir, that the court desires them to take the stand?

PRESIDENT: The court is not going to express itself one way or the other. We have already passed on your motion for a directed verdict of not guilty, at the conclusion of the prosecution's case. You can proceed with your case in any way you think best.

ALBIN GRETSCH, one of the accused, was then called to the stand by the defense as a witness in his own behalf, and testified through the interpreter as follows:

DIRECT EXAMINATION:
Questions by the defense:

Q: What is your name?
A. Albin Gretsch.

Q: How old are you?
A: Forty-six years.

Q: Where were you born?
A: Augsburg.

Q: Did you ever participate in a common design to murder or to mistreat any prisoners, or any persons?
A: No.

DEFENSE: No further questions. (!)

On cross examination, the prosecution showed that he was a guard, that he had a gun, and that there were bullets in that gun.

On redirect, the defense showed that he never fired a shot.

Gretsch was convicted of *"aiding and abetting in a common design"*.

JOHANN SCHOEPP, one of the accused, was called to the stand by the defense as a witness in his own behalf, and testified through the interpreter as follows:

DIRECT EXAMINATION:
Questions by the defense:

Q: What is your name?
A: Johann Schoepp.

Q: How old are you?
A. Thirty-four and half years.

Q: Where were you born?
A: In Alcen, Rumania.

Q: Are you a Rumanian citizen?
A: Yes.

DEFENSE: No further questions. (!)

On cross examination, the prosecution showed that he was a

reserve guard on a transport.

On redirect, the defense showed he had no gun, no orders, nothing to do, and was a conscript assigned to the German Army from the Rumanian Army.

He was convicted of *"aiding and abetting in a common design"*.

EXCERPTS FROM PROSECUTION SUMMATION
(beginning on microfilm page 000857)

PROSECUTION (Lt. Col. Denson)
... The case has been long. This court has heard the oral testimony of over 170 witnesses...I would like to call the court's attention and wish to emphasize the fact that the offense with which these 40 men stand charged is not killing, beating, and torturing these prisoners but the offense is aiding, abetting, encouraging and participating in a common design to kill, to beat, to torture, and to subject these persons to starvation.

[Note that there is no mention of a gas chamber. That accusation was dropped before trial, but reintroduced into evidence at Nuremberg, even though it was known to be false. – C.P.]

It may be, because of the testimony submitted here, that this court may be inclined to determine the guilt or innocence of these forty men by the number of men they killed, or by the number of men they beat, or the number they tortured. That is not the test that is to be applied in this case... We are not trying these men for specific acts of misconduct. We are trying these men for participation in this common design... as a matter of fact, this case could have been established without showing that a single man over in that dock at any time killed a man. It would be sufficient, may it please the court, to show that there was in fact a common design, and that these individuals participated in it, and that the purpose of this common design was the killings, the beatings, and the tortures and the subjection to starvation... The evidence before this court demonstrates beyond all peradventure of a doubt the existence of this common design. It is not contended, nor is it necessary to sustain, the charges that this common design had its origin in Dachau, nor was it first conceived in January 1942. ...

[Note that the word "conspiracy" is avoided at all times, apparently to give the prosecution more leeway than allowed in conspiracy cases. It was never revealed where the "design" originated, who made it, when and where, whether it was in writing or oral, or who was present. – C.P.]

EXCERPTS FROM JUDGMENT: 13 December 1945

PRESIDENT: The evidence presented to this court convinced it beyond any doubt that the Dachau Concentration Camp subjected its inmates to killings, beatings, tortures, indignities, and starvation to an extent and to a degree that necessitates the indictment of everyone, high and low, who had anything to do with the conduct and the operation of the camp. This court reiterates that, although appointed by a conquering nation as a military government court in a conquered land, it sits in judgment under international law and under such laws of humanity and customs of human behavior that is recognized by civilized people. Many of the acts committed at Camp Dachau had clearly the sanction of the high officials of the then customs of the German government itself. It is the view of this court that when a sovereign state sets itself up above reasonably recognized and constituted law or is willing to transcend readily recognizable constituted customs of human and decent treatment of persons, the individuals effecting such policies of their state must be held responsible for their part in the violation of international law and the customs and laws of humanity.

[Note that no references are given to any provisions of any laws constituting the legality of the court, the trial, or the crimes of the defendants. – C.P.]

The accused and counsel will stand. The accused will present themselves individually in the order in which they are numbered before the bench.

Thirty-six of the forty defendants were sentenced to be hanged, two to life imprisonment, and Schoepp and Gretsch to ten years. Appeal was permitted as to sentence, but not as to the merits of the case. Twenty-eight of the defendants were actually hanged. Most of the rest were released in the 1950s.

THE INJUSTICE OF AFFIDAVITS IN FOREIGN LANGUAGES

The production of "diaries" was a growth industry in the post-war years.

In one of these efforts, the top floor of a house disappears behind a book case; the house is sold to an architect who does not realize that the top floor is missing; with many other magical events.

In war crimes trials, "diaries" are produced by something resembling magic; the conjuror takes a mimeograph, utters an incantation and – presto! – reams of secondary evidence appear where none existed, usually in the form of "copies" or "translations".

In the Tokyo Trial, the incantation goes something like this:

* * *

We offer in evidence IPS document no. 2707-K, which is the English translation of extracts from a diary...

"We are ordered to kill all the males we find... our aim is to kill or wound all the men..."

* * *

We offer in evidence IPS document no. 415, which is the English translation of extracts from a captured diary...

"27 Mar. 45 (correct Japanese year: 20th year of Showa)... we went out to kill the natives. It was hard for me to kill them because they seemed like good people. Frightful cries of the women and children..."

* * *

We offer in evidence IPS document no. 426, which is the English translation of an extract from a captured diary...

"My turn was the second one... I bayonetted him... after bayonetting them we covered them with soil".

* * *

We offer in evidence IPS document no. 2776, which is the English translation of extracts of a captured notebook diary...

"7 Feb 45 – 150 guerillas were disposed of tonight..."

* * *

We offer in evidence IPS document no. 428, which is an English translation of an excerpt taken from a loose, handwritten sheet containing a battle report...

"All were either stabbed or shot to death..."

* * *

We submit in evidence IPS document no. 2749, which is an English translation of an extract from a bound, printed and mimeographed file containing censored papers...

"It was pitiful, so I couldn't watch. They also shot them and speared them to death with bamboo lances. Indeed the Japanese army does extreme things..."

* * *

We offer in evidence IPS document no. 2777, which is the English translation of an excerpt from the bound handwritten notebook diary dated 14 November 1943 to 17 April 1945...

"All inhabitants of the town were killed..."

* * *

We offer in evidence IPS document no. 425, which is the English translation of extract from a captured bound diary-notebook dated July 1944...

"Every day is spent hunting guerillas and natives. I have already killed over 100. The naiveté I possessed at the time of leaving the homeland has long since disappeared. Now I am a hardened killer and my sword is always stained with blood. Although it is for my country's sake, it is sheer brutality. May God forgive me! May my mother forgive me!"

* * *

We offer in evidence IPS document no. 2707-H, which is the English translation of a captured Japanese "Memorandum"... which mentions and makes admission and confirmation of the practice of cannibalism...

"... those who eat human flesh (except that of the enemy) knowing it to be so, shall be sentenced to death as the worst kind of enemy against mankind..."

* * *

We tender in evidence IPS document no. 2850, which is an extract from statements made by prisoner of war YANAGAZIWA, Eiji...

"Cannibalism..." (pp. 12,565-77).

* * *

Extract from diary, apparently belonging to an officer, unit unknown.

Vivisection took place...

"... to prevent their escaping a second time, pistols were fired at their feet, but it was difficult to hit them. The two prisoners were dissected while still alive by Medical Officer YAMAJI and their livers taken out, and for the first time I saw the internal organs of a human being. It was very instructive..." ... (p. 14,140) (SPAC "translation").

* * *

(The following is the document of which Justice Pal said, "We were not given the captured diary... I hope it was written in Japanese":)

"The head, detached from the trunk, rolls in front of it... a superior seaman of the medical unit takes the Chief Medical Officer's sword and... turns the headless body over on its back, and cuts the abdomen open with one clear stroke... not a drop of blood comes out of the body. (Maybe he was anaemic. – Ed.) If ever I get back alive it will make a good story to tell, so I have written it down." (pp. 14,075-80)

* * *

(Speaking of "confessions" in foreign languages...):

"They made much reduced official reports in the Japanese language and characters which we could not read but were nevertheless compelled to sign, without being told the contents. Afterwards, these reports turned out to be our "confessions", in which we were charged with the queerest facts..." (p. 13,680-1)

* * *

(In the following case the "witness" read about his "testimony" in the newspaper and showed up to repudiate his affidavit entirely and testify for the defense).

"I was summoned to the U.S. Military Government in Saipan and examined by a young American Lieutenant... He knew Japanese and interrogated me in that language. His Japanese was not fluent, but good enough to make himself understood. He wrote down my statement in English and had me sign it but he did not translate it and read it to me... I do not understand spoken English. I can only understand written English if I have an English-Japanese dictionary before me and considerable time to ponder over the written material. On the original document is a statement by Ensign Charles D. Shelton which reads as follows:

"I swear that I am familiar with the English language and the Japanese language and that before the above statement was signed I read same in the Japanese language to the person who signed same".

"This statement is in error. A translation of the English document was not given to me either orally or in written form. The manner in which I was questioned is as follows: the American lieutenant asked me questions in Japanese to which I responded. Then, writing with a fountain pen on a piece of paper, he appeared to be making a statement. The interview lasted about 20 minutes, at the end of which time the Lieutenant gave the handwritten piece of paper to a Navy enlisted man who typed out the piece of paper which I ultimately signed..."

* * *

Cross examination by the prosecution:
Q: "How did things proceed; what happened?"
A: "In accordance with some notations made on a memo paper he asked questions... he apparently had some kind of list of questions..."
Q: "Did you ask what it was you were being asked to sign?"
A: "I asked no questions... I learned about it for the first time when it appeared in the newspapers in October last year". (Testimony of Wakamatsu Makoto, 22 August 1947, pp. 26,532-42).

THE MYTH OF
"VOLUNTARY CONFESSIONS"

In "war crimes trials", confessions are usually typewritten by the interrogator, often entirely in English. Paragraphs in the prisoner's handwriting have usually been dictated by the interrogator. The First Dachau Trial (Trial of Martin Gottfried Weiss and Thirty-Nine Others), offers an insight into the manner in which these confessions were obtained.

* * *

(TESTIMONY OF KICK, microfilm pages 000145-9).

Q: Are either of these two statements 96 or 97 in your handwriting?
A: The post-script on page 4 of 96 is in my handwriting.

Q: The rest of it is written in what manner?
A: The other part of it is typed.

Q: Did you dictate the typing?
A: No.

Q: Who did?
A: The interrogating officer.

Q: Who was the interrogating officer?
A: Lt. Guth.

Q: Is the language contained in either of those statements your language or the language of Lt. Guth?
A: Those are the expressions of Lt. Guth.

Q: And at the end of your statements you signed them, and swore to them as being the truth, did you not?
A: Yes.

Q: ... will you describe to the court the treatment that you received prior to your first interrogation anyplace?

(Prosecution objection as to whether beating received on the 6th of May could be relevant to confession signed on the 5th of November).

Q: ... Kick, did the treatment you received immediately following your arrest have any influence whatever on the statements that you made on the 5th of November?

A: ... The treatment at that time influenced this testimony to that extent, that I did not dare to refuse to sign, in spite of the fact that it did not contain the testimony which I gave.

Q: Now, Kick, for the court, will you describe the treatment which you received immediately following your arrest?

A: I ask to refuse to answer this question here in public.

President: The court desires to have the defendant answer the question.

A: I was here in Dachau from the 6th to the 15th of May, under arrest; during this time I was beaten all during the day and night... kicked... I had to stand to attention for hours; I had to kneel down on sharp objects or square objects; I had to stand under the lamp for hours and look into the light, at which time I was also beaten and kicked; as a result of this treatment my arm was paralysed for about 8 to 10 weeks; only beginning with my transfer to Augsberg, this treatment stopped.

Q: What were you beaten with?
A: With all kinds of objects.

Q: Describe them, please.
A: With whips, with lashing whips, with rifle butts, pistol butts, and pistol barrels, and with hands and fists.

Q: And that continued daily over a period of what time?
A: From the morning of the 7th of May until the morning of the 15th of May.

Q: Kick, why did you hesitate to give that testimony?
A: If the court hadn't decided I should talk about it, I wouldn't have said anything about it today.

Q: Would you describe the people who administered these beatings to you?

A: I can only say that they were persons who were wearing the United States uniform and I can't describe them any better.

Q: And as a result of those beatings when Lt. Guth called you in, what was your frame of mind?

A: I had to presume that if I were to refuse to sign I would be subjected to a similar treatment.

* * *

(TESTIMONY OF KRAMER, microfilm pages 000298-9).

Q: Kramer, were you interrogated after your arrest anywhere except Dachau?

A: Yes, in Fuerstenfeldbruck.

Q: Did that interrogation have any effect on the statement that you made here?

Prosecution: I object to that question as being immaterial and irrelevant.

President: Explain exactly what happened.

Q: Will you explain exactly what happened at that interrogation?

A: I do not want to talk about it.

Q: The court desires you to explain what happened.

A: I was beaten by an interrogation officer. Several prisoners were also present. I was supposed to tell how many people I shot or hanged. I can say with a conscience that I never killed a person. Thereupon, I was beaten over the head with sticks and rubber hoses until I broke down.

Q: Anything else to say about that?

A: No ...

* * *

(TESTIMONY OF DR. WITTELER, microfilm pages 000327-331).

A: During my interrogation I had to sit in front of the desk of Lt. Guth. A spotlight was turned on me which stood on the desk. Lt. Guth stood behind the spotlight and the interrogation started. "We know you, we have the necessary records about you..." I started to make an explanation. I was immediately stopped. I was yelled at. He called me a swine, criminal, liar, murderer, and that is the way the interrogation continued. I couldn't give any explanations. I was only told to answer "yes" or "no"... I was interrupted immediately and told that all I had to do was answer "yes" and "no". I couldn't even explain it. I was told to shut up and to answer "yes" or "no"... since it was not like he thought it was, I had to get up and stand. So I stood up until 1:30 in the morning – seven hours.

Q: ... at the conclusion of the drafting of this statement you signed it?

A: No, I answered that it is not correct... this statement was not written in my presence. It was written in another room. The reporter was with me in the room all the time, but the statement was written in another room. After I couldn't stand up any more this statement was put in front of me at 1:30. And then when I said that this testimony... is not by me, that is the testimony of Dr. Blaha – who was present for several hours that night... so that I didn't want to sign it. Lt. Guth said he would interrogate me until tomorrow morning, that he had other methods...

[Dr. Blaha was a Czech Communist who claimed the Germans forced him to skin people and make slippers, saddles, purses, handbags, gloves, and trousers out of human skin. He also was the only witness at the Dachau Trial who claimed there was a gas chamber at Dachau. His testimony was introduced into evidence at Nuremberg as "proven fact" – C.P.]

Q: How many people were present at the time you were interrogated?

A: Altogether, three: Lt. Guth, Dr. Leiss, and I, and, for a short time, Dr. Blaha.

Q: This writing in your own handwriting. Was that dictated or did you make it up?

A: When I found that the interrogation would end that way, I wrote down this last part and signed my name to it.

Q: Was it your own words or was it dictated to you?
A: Lt. Guth dictated those words...

Q: Prior to the time that you signed that statement, have you been served with any papers in this particular case?
A: No, I didn't know why I was in Dachau. I had no idea I was one of the accused. After the interrogation at 1:30 I was sent to the colonel and the colonel then read the charge to me. The first time I heard I was supposed to be a murderer, was then.

Q: You mean Col. Denson read the charges to you?
A: Yes.

[Col. Denson acted as prosecutor in this trial and delivered the prosecution summation. Lt. Guth appeared as a witness and denied all accusations of improper conduct. Guth was a Viennese who came to the United States in 1941. – C.P.]

* * *

(TESTIMONY OF GRETSCH, microfilm pages 000701-3).

Q: Gretsch, is this statement in your handwriting?
A: No, that isn't my handwriting.

Q: What part of this paper is in your handwriting?
A: This is my handwriting here.

Q: And what is this? What part of the paper is this?
A: That is, "I have made the above statements without compulsion, and I have read and corrected it and understand it fully. I swear before God that it is the pure truth".

Q: That is the oath, is it not?
A: Yes, that is the oath.

Q: And is the oath the only part of this statement that is in your handwriting?

A: Yes...

Q: ... Gretsch, you signed each page... did you not?

A: Yes, I signed it on the bottom, but I didn't read it. It was in a hurry...

Q: ...Were you told to sign your name to each sheet of paper?

A: Yes...

* * *

(PROSECUTION REBUTTAL – TESTIMONY OF COL. CHAVEZ, microfilm pages 000712-4).

Q: Kick testified that he was beaten daily from the 7th of May until the 15th of May... did you have occasion to examine Kick?

A: Yes.

Q: ... did you have occasion to observe his physical condition?

A: I did.

Q: Did he have any black eyes?

A: He did not.

Q: Did he show any evidence of violence having been used upon him?

A: He did not.

Q: Was any one or both of his arms paralysed?

A: Not that I observed. He was just as natural as he is now. In fact, he looked better at that time than he does now. I observed nothing. He was very co-operative, and the record will so indicate. He was sworn and he gave his testimony in a very gentle manner.

Q: Did he at any time state to you, Colonel, that he had been beaten or in any manner mistreated?

A: He did not.

Q: ... how often did you see him?

A: Just during the time that he was interrogated.

Q: ... of course he was fully clothed?

A: Yes.

Q: But there is no question about it – at the time you talked with him he was quite cooperative?
A: He was...

[Col. Chavez was the author of the "Chavez Report", which was to have "proven" that a gas chamber existed at Dachau. The report was never introduced into evidence, and this accusation was dropped before trial. Col. Chavez appeared as an expert witness at Dachau on Nov. 15, 1945, but made no mention of a gas chamber. The Chavez Report was then re-written and introduced into evidence at Nuremberg as documents 2430-PS and 159-L, even though it was known to be untrue. – C.P.]

* * *

(TESTIMONY OF LT. LAURENCE, microfilm pages 000714-5).

Q: Did you have occasion to examine Albin Gretsch?
A: Yes, Sir.

Q: ... and did he complain of any mis-statements?...
A: Not at all, sir... they are mostly his own words, sir. And I may add, sir, that I wasn't in a hurry at all. He took many hours and as he was rather slow in answering, I gave him all the time he wanted...

Q: The statement, with the exception of the oath, is in your handwriting, is it not, Lt. Laurence?
A: Yes.

* * *

[Of course, while German allegations of mistreatment are always dismissed as baseless, similar accusations from prosecution witnesses are accepted as "proven facts". Among the offenses for which Kick was hanged was knocking 15 teeth out of the lower jaw of Llewellyn Edwards of 12 Nora St., Cardiff, Wales, who claimed to have lost 15 upper teeth at some other time [!]. See below. – C.P.]

Q: At the time you went in Kick's office, how many teeth did you have in your head?

A: Fifteen, sir. On the bottom, sir. Fifteen of my own, sir. On the top I had artificial teeth. (microfilm page 000722)

THE RIDDLE OF ATROCITY ALLEGATIONS INVOLVING PRISONERS

In the Far Eastern war crimes trials, Japanese defendants were commonly convicted of killing POW's by fiendish torture (possibly for tenderizing purposes), after which the victims were eaten. Today, of course, it is recognized that the Japanese are a nation of fastidious eaters who consume little meat; nor do they devour dogs, cats, rats, and bird's nests like the Chinese.

In the German war crimes trials, the evidence concerning fiendish torture is much the same, except that we are spared this final culinary insult (or perhaps the food was less appetizing).

Certainly no one familiar with the average year's "Holocaust survivor" crop could get his taste buds in a twist for such cuisine-on-the-hoof. In addition to its often unsavoury appearance, there is the danger that such fare, like polluted shellfish, might prove toxic to the eater.

With "eating" eliminated, there remains "beating". A survivor, like an egg, spends a great deal of time being beaten (when he is not being steamed, fried, or poached); this may explain the scrambled nature of his testimony.

The evidence in prison camp trials (both Japanese and German) is very repetitive. Dozens of witnesses appear and describe horrific tortures in which inmates are beaten to a pulp with hands, fists, boots, and a variety of objects.

The defendant then appears and testifies, in effect: "I slapped them; sometimes I hit them with my fist; once in a while I kicked them. But I never hit them with an object, or beat them so badly as to cause serious injury. If I am serving food and they are all trying to steal it, what am I supposed to do? Write out a written report, in which case they will all be punished more severely later, or just hit them and make them stop?"

This, of course, is taken as a "confession". "Hit" is translated as "beat", giving the impression of repeated blows and serious injury. Since thousands of inmates died of disease (this is always admitted by the prosecution somewhere or other), many of these he "hit" have died; therefore, he has "beaten thousands of people to death". He is then hanged on the basis of his "confession", corroborated by "eyewitness evidence".

The following testimonies, from the Trial of Martin Gottfried Weiss, are probably typical of thousands of cases.

* * *

(The testimony of Tempel, microfilm pages 000445-50. Tempel was a member of the SS. The SS overseers claimed that the prisoners beat each other, since most of them were criminals and there were not enough guards. Tempel was hanged.)

A: I used the whip once that I can remember... seven bottles of wine were stolen... each block elder received three over his buttocks. There was no report handed in... I always hit them with the hand. I was strict but just. It was entirely necessary, because... these blocks elders and the capos took their own rations from their own people. Butter and other things were stolen from the kitchen or taken outside and sold, and in some instances cases of eggs were missing...

Q: ... you slapped prisoners every time you came into contact with them, did you not?
A: No, prisoners weren't beaten without a reason.

Q: ... you always had a reason for beating them, didn't you?... you beat prisoners, slapped them in the face and hit them in the head? Is it not true that you broke bones and hit them in other places besides their buttocks?
A: No, it never happened that I hit a prisoner in the face or broke bones or drew blood.

* * *

(The testimony of Becher, microfilm pages 000608-9, 000615-6. Becher was a Communist who claimed that the SS had beaten people, but denied beating people himself.)

Q: Did you ever beat, or beat to death, prisoners?
A: I never beat anyone to death, or else I would be in jail today. Now and again I administered a slap in the face as a reprimand, but that was necessary to avoid punishment reports to the SS...

Q: Did you ever kick with your feet?

A: I never kicked with my feet, but I told people while marching "get up, see that you get up".

Q: The witness Siebold said that you beat Russians to such an extent that their noses bled as a result. Is that correct?
A: It is possible that a slight bleeding of the nose occurred on a person whom I slapped on the face. I cannot remember any such case...

Q: ... Becher, there was a witness who testified that you beat another prisoner, Kowalski, to such an extent that he had to be sent to the hospital, and died.
A: I can remember the case of Kowalski exactly... I gave him two slaps in the face, and he had to go to the plantation for easy work. When he came back he had dysentery. He remained in the block for three days, made the beds filthy, and then I took him over to the hospital. After five or six days, the report came in that he had died of dysentery... it sometimes happened that certain prisoners attempted to make homosexual advances on other prisoners, and naturally, these people had to be corrected. It happened that people stole. For example, the smoking tobacco of a man was stolen. Thereupon I asked him whether that was true. He said, "No, it was not true, I could swear to it". Then the other prisoner told me to search him, he had the tobacco in his pocket. And that was actually true. I found the tobacco belonging to the other man in his pocket.

Q: ... and you beat Kowalski in the face, did you not?
A: With the flat of the hand.

Q: And you beat Kowalski in the body, did you not?
A: No, only in the face...

Q: ... now Becher, how many of these men did you beat while you were block eldest?
A: Me, beat people? I didn't beat people. I only corrected them. If somebody stole from his companions, or if he was a homosexual. What else could I do?

Q: It is a fact, isn't it, that you corrected them by beating them?
A: Yes. with the hand. I beat them with the hand, and never with an object, and never so that they would be injured or go to the hospital...

* * *

(The testimony of Kick, microfilm pages 000619-20. Kick was another Communist. Kick was hanged for making mole-skin coats out of Jewish inmates.)

Q: Do you admit to having beaten people?

A: No. But I did give out slaps in the face, where, according to my feeling, I had a right to do so. Or else, if I didn't, I would have to make a report to the SS. Or in order to save the prisoner from getting the twenty-five and the usual things that accompanied it, because I myself experienced the twenty-five and the other things.

Q: You said before that you did that in order to correct them. What made you correct them?

A: In order to tell that to the court I would have to talk until tomorrow, in order to explain all those things that could happen in a block with one thousand people. I would like to tell you only one case. One evening, while passing by a block, I see somebody there using a newspaper instead of the toilet. I wanted to look in to see what he is doing, but I didn't look in for long, because the whole mess flew in my face... or else if the room eldest gave jam and bread to somebody else for distribution, at noon when they fall in again, ten or twelve complain that they didn't have any marmalade... or else when you were trying to select fifty or sixty people for work, you picked out ten because they were the strong ones. By the time you picked out ten more, the first ten would have disappeared. And these various cases, I could continue to tell about them into tomorrow morning...

THE TOKYO WAR CRIMES TRIAL

On October 30, 1938, an actor named Orson Welles pretended to be a sole surviving radio announcer broadcasting from the ruins of a city destroyed by Martian invaders. Thousands of people abandoned their homes and fled in terror to escape octopus-like monsters ravaging the countryside in flying saucers equipped with death-rays; yet, a simple flick of the radio dial would have revealed that other stations were broadcasting normally.

Three years later, America faced another, even graver threat – a second invasion of flying-frying people-eating monsters and non-octopoidal humanoids: not this time from outer space, nor even yet from the Black Lagoon; but from a small island in the Pacific called Japan.

Known to naturalists for its omnivorous feeding habits – in contrast to the European variety – and for its aggressive nature – *Fascisticus japanicus* subsists on a diet of Japanese, Chinese, Filipinos, Americans and raw fish (Americans in particular are hard to clean, rendering this diet expensive).

That the Japanese are a nation of habitual cannibals has been repeatedly "proven" in "War Crimes Trials" (a sort of zoo).

The most famous of these "War Crimes Trials" was the International Military Tribunal for the Far East, or Tokyo Trial. The transcript is available in book form from Garland Publishing, 1000A Sherman Ave., Hamden CT 06514, or 136 Madison Ave, New York 10016-6753, under the title *The Tokyo War Crimes Trial*, edited by R. John Pritchard and Sonia Magbanua Zaide, ISBN 0-82404755-9.

The following "eyewitness testimony" is taken from these volumes.

* * *

"Two men fled and hid nearby as the Japanese approached, but the Japanese bayoneted to death all five occupants of the house, one of whom was a three-year girl. The six Japanese ate the flesh from some of the bodies of their victims... the flesh of the little-girl was cut into small pieces, put on the ends of sticks and roasted over an open fire... the flesh of another victim was roasted or boiled with native vegetables. The flesh of three of the victims was consumed in this manner... After the Japanese left, two observers went into the house and saw a piece of human flesh inside of a bag left by one of the Japanese and also inside one of the kettles..." (JAG Report 137, pp. 12,468-9 of mimeographed transcript; these reports "quote" "testimony" of unknown persons, often illiterates identified by first name only who are allowed to repeat hearsay and who could not be cross-examined.)

* * *

"I saw this from behind a tree and noticed Japanese cut his flesh from arms, legs, chest and hips... I was shocked at the scene and followed the Japanese just to find out what they do to the flesh. They cut the flesh to small pieces and fried it. About 1800 hours a Japanese high official (Major General) addressed about 150 Japanese. At the conclusion of the speech a piece of the fried flesh was given to all present, who ate it on the spot." (Affidavit of Havildar Changiram, p. 14,130; Changiram was a totally unknown person who never appeared in court.)

* * *

"Towards the end of the Pacific War the Japanese Army and Navy descended to cannibalism, eating parts of the bodies of Allied prisoners whom they had unlawfully killed... At times this consumption of the flesh of their enemies was made into something of a festive occasion at officer quarters. Even officers of the rank of General and Rear-Admiral took part. Flesh of murdered prisoners or soup made from such flesh was served at meals..." (Judgment, *IMTFE*, pp. 45,674-5; hearsay repeated in interrogation written in English is taken as fact and upheld in the judgment.)

* * *

"Sake was served... it was said we should come to a party... Colonel KATO did not have enough drinks and things to go with the drinks... the question came up of where to get something in the line of meat and more sake. The general asked me about the execution and about getting some meat. Therefore, I telephoned personally to my headquarters that meat and ten sho of sugar cane rum be delivered to the 307th Battalion Headquarters. I do not recall now if the sugar cane rum was delivered or not, I know that the meat was... After the party at the 307th Battalion Headquarters where human flesh was served and eaten, on my way back I talked to Admiral MORI, and told Admiral MORI of the party. It was then that he told me to bring down a little human liver from the body of the next flyer to be executed... I also heard that flesh from this flyer was served in soup... human liver was eaten in the officer's mess... MIYAZAKI returned to the naval headquarters with a portion of the liver... I then ordered Doctor TERAKI to go and cut out the liver... I ordered the removal of the liver previous to the execution... I had it cut and dried... It wasn't exactly a party, but they ate the liver at the 308th Battalion Headquarters that night. It was Hall's liver... yes, definitely they ate it... During the Chinese-Japanese war human flesh and liver was eaten as a medicine... they were all saying that liver was good medicine for the stomach... these are the three times that I ate human flesh... I ate a small pill made from human liver in Singapore... ORDER REGARDING EATING OF FLESH OF AMERICAN FLYERS... The battalion wants to eat the flesh of the American aviator... attend the execution and have the liver and gall bladder removed..." (pp. 15,033-42; note use of gall bladder as culinary delicacy; above passages are from an interrogation written in English.)

* * *

Here they are forbidden to eat each other:
"Those who eat human flesh (except that of the enemy) knowing it to be so, shall be sentenced to death..." (p. 12,576; the document is an "English translation" of an original document which was not brought to court.)

* * *

Here they are executed for eating each other:
"Troops must fight the Allies even to the extent of eating them... troops were permitted to eat the flesh of Allied dead but must not eat their own dead... four men were executed... for disobeying this order." (p. 12,577; the document is an "English translation" of an original document no one has ever seen.)

* * *

Here they hate the taste of human flesh:
"Of course, nobody relished the taste." (p. 15,034)

Here they love the taste of human flesh:
"The evidence indicated that this cannibalism occurred when there was other food available... this horrible practice was indulged in from choice and not of necessity." (Judgment, *IMTFE*, p. 45,675.)

* * *

Here they only eat people when they are hungry:
"The flesh of the enemy should be eaten... all prisoners of war would be executed... the flesh would be eaten... we should fight and live on the flesh of our comrades and that of the enemy" (pp. 15,134-5; hearsay quoted in an interrogation written in English.)

* * *

The existence of gas chambers on remote islands is proven on page 40,535:
"Journal of Taiwan POW Camp Headquarters date 1 Aug 44.
(Note: Japanese did not use Western system of dating)
"... sets out plan for the final disposition of POWS... they may be disposed of in any way such as poisoning, bombing, gassing, drowning, decapitation..." (The document is an "English translation" of an original which was not produced.)

* * *

There were no acquittals. One of the Tokyo defendants, Umezu, petitioned for clemency on the grounds that he was 70 years old and was dying of rectal cancer. The Americans hanged him anyway. That takes gall.

"JAPS ATE MY GALL BLADDER"

OR
THE INDESTRUCTIBLE WITNESS

In his famous dissentient judgment at the Tokyo Trial Justice R.B. Pal of India used the term "vile competition" in reference to propaganda and atrocity charges. One gets the impression that "witnesses", "affiants" and "deponents" are striving to outdo each other in improvements upon the same tale, each claiming to have personally suffered the most.

What follows are some of the entries from that "competition".

* * *

I WAS BAYONETED FIVE TIMES

"I fell down with five bayonet wounds, three in the neck and chest and did not move again..." (p. 15,415)

I WAS BAYONETED FIVE TIMES TOO

"I got five bayonet wounds – one on the upper part of my right arm, another on the upper right of my chest passing through my breast, another on my waist again passing through my right side, and another on my right shoulder. Because of the force of the bayonets that passed through my body..." (pp. 12,442-3)

I WAS BAYONETED SEVEN TIMES AND BURNED

"All were bayoneted and stabbed, thrown into a pile, saturated with gasoline, and then set on fire. The only survivor of this group described how she was bayoneted four times in the back and three times in the front..." (p. 12,444)

I WAS BAYONETED FIVE TIMES, NO, ELEVEN TIMES

"I received five stabs. I pretended death and held my breath... when I breathed, he heard it and stabbed me another six times. The last thrust went through my ear, face, and into my mouth, severing an artery... I lay there for approximately one hour... I managed to get my leg between my two hands and I chewed at the knob until it became undone." (pp. 14,107-8)

I WAS BAYONETED THIRTY-EIGHT TIMES

"Q: Now, you say that you have sustained 38 bayonet wounds. On what part of your body were you wounded?

"A: In different parts of my body." (Answer continues for two pages; pp. 12,430-2.)

I WAS BEHEADED

"There was a Japanese sword sticking into the earth close to the grave... My head was bent forward, and after a few seconds I felt a dull blow sensation on the back of my neck... I had a large wound on the back of my neck..." (pp. 12,885-6)

I WAS BEHEADED TOO

"Four natives were put to death by beheading, without trial. One of them, Mairuhu, however, was not killed and has reported this crime in his statement, prosecution document 5530, with a photograph showing the scar in his neck." (p. 13,927)

SO WAS I

"The officer took out his sword, and I saw him hand it to one of the soldiers and point to me. Japanese soldiers approached me from behind and suddenly I felt a sharp pain in my neck, also I felt the blood running over my face... The following sunrise I came to my senses and found that I was soaked in blood. I looked around and found that my five comrades were all dead with their heads partly severed from their bodies." (pp. 12,984-5)

ME TOO BUT I FELL OFF A CLIFF

"Two Japanese attempted to behead them, one of the soldiers striking the victims across the neck with a sabre while the other pushed the decapitated bodies over the cliff. Apparently all of this group were killed except two. The bodies of four were later identified. One man survived the attempted beheading..." (pp. 12,457-8)

I WAS BEHEADED BUT CARRIED SOMEONE ON MY BACK

"They made us stand at the edge of a trench and began to massacre us by sword strokes on the back of the neck. When this was finished they went away. I understood later that they had gone to fetch gasoline. I fled with the two sharp-shooters – one of whom had untied my hands and then run off – and I carried one of them on my back." (p. 15,417)

I SURVIVED SHOOTING, BAYONET WOUNDS AND A 750-FOOT FALL

"At the moment when the Japanese took aim at us the condemned struck up the 'Marseillaise'... many of us were wounded... during the two hours which followed, scenes of unparalleled savagery took place, beginning with the Japanese throwing themselves upon us, yelling and using our bodies as fencing targets for the bayonet. Then they amused themselves by firing rifle or revolver shots in the ear of those who did not appear quite dead. The least tremble called forth roars of laughter and loud shouts of joy and marked a new victim whom they immediately set upon with the bayonet. I myself was wounded four times, in the arm, in the chest, and in the right buttock.

"When the Japanese considered that not a single one more remained alive they had us removed by Anmanites (our irregulars) and thrown into a ravine. The bodies thus thrown rolled for 200 to 250 meters. I came to myself, lying head downwards..." (pp. 15,420-1)

I WAS SHOT, BAYONETED, AND NEARLY BURNED ALIVE

"Finally, they were all herded into a group and shot with rifles and machine guns. The Japanese removed the bodies, but not the witness, who feigned death... The Japanese brought tins of petrol and poured it over the prostrate prisoners, other than the witness... they then set fire to the petrol amidst the screams and yells of pain and the prisoners were burnt to death. The witness could smell the burning flesh. He lay still until the Japanese departed. Many Japanese passed him and kicked him and some pricked him with their bayonets. One actually drove a bayonet into his side..." (pp. 12,951-2)

I SURVIVED BEATING AND DROWNING WITH MY HANDS TIED

"The submarine made its appearance in the near vicinity... orders were given to come aboard the submarine... after all the survivors had gained the deck of the submarine, the Japanese proceeded to fire upon the life boat...

"I learned then that the Japanese crew were employing a tactic somewhat similar to the old Indian practice of running the gauntlet wherein they forced survivors to pass between two lines of men armed with clubs, bars and other blunt objects and, when reaching the end, being either shoved or knocked into the sea to drown... I was struck a terrific blow at the base of my head... I was shoved down through the two lines of Japanese who rained blows upon my body and head with various objects which I was too stunned and dazed to identify, although I was later advised by my doctor that I had been cut with a bayonet or sword in the process.

"When I reached the end of the gauntlet, I fell into what appeared to me to be a white foamy sea".

(Note: this is from an "affidavit" which is being "quoted" by the prosecutor.)

"THE PRESIDENT: Lord Patrick has pointed out to me you have not read that part where this witness or this deponent explains how he kept afloat although his hands were tied... You stopped at the words 'foamy sea'... it is desirable that you should read on and explain how this man, according to his testimony, kept afloat although his hands were tied... You need not worry. He says that he kept afloat by treading the water." (pp. 15,144-5)

ME TOO BUT I WAS SHOT

"The sub came closer and closer... they told the Europeans to board the sub... two Japs were making us stand by in front of us, one with a revolver and one with a coil of rope... one was preparing himself to tie us up... when I arrived at the very end of the deck, above the propellers I heard a bang and felt a terrific shock on my head and I toppled over into the water. The Japs tried to make a good job of it indeed, as they did it above the propellers. How I missed them I do not know. I must have been unconscious for a little while. When I came to I was in the water, with plenty of blood around me... I spotted the sub now about a mile distant... I inspected my head with my hand and found no hole in the bone..." (pp. 15,170-4)

I WAS TORTURED ON A SUBMARINE DECK FOR FOUR HOURS

"The Japanese officer then came out on deck. He had a sword... they marched them down the port side of the sub... another one ran him through once or twice with a bayonet. Then they pushed him over the side.

"Q: How long were you a prisoner on board the submarine?
"A: Approximately four hours." (pp. 15,116-9)

(Note: For a submarine to sink a merchant vessel and then surface is extremely dangerous. A surfaced submarine is defenseless against aircraft called on ship's radio, to say nothing of radar and sonar. Procedure after sinking is to submerge and leave the area immediately. If it does not do so, it must be prepared to submerge in less than one minute, meaning that the crew cannot be on deck. For these reasons, the above atrocities can only be perjured: referred to are the sinkings of the *Jean Nicolet*, S.S. *Ascot*, and other ships. The Japanese government, in response to wartime protests, conducted an investigation and concluded "there are no facts that correspond to such attacks".)

I ESCAPED LIVE CREMATION BY CRAWLING THROUGH A DOUBLE BARBED-WIRE FENCE WITH A BULLET IN MY LEG, AFTER WHICH I JUMPED OFF A 50-FOOT CLIFF, KILLED THREE JAPS IN HAND-TO-HAND UNDERWATER COMBAT, SWAM A BAY, WANDERED IN THE JUNGLE FOR FIVE DAYS WITHOUT FOOD OR WATER, THEN JOINED UP WITH GUERRILLA FORCES

"Q: On this document what does the 'X' line stand for?

"A: It represents a double barbed wire fence which encircled the complete compound, which is approximately seven feet high, and the two fences were about two feet apart.

"Q: On the left, or southeasterly side of the fence, what is indicated?

"A: A sharp cliff, with some underbrush, bordering Puerto Princesa Bay. This cliff is approximately fifty to sixty feet high... these buckets of gasoline, they were thrown into the entrance of A Company shelter, then a lighted torch was thrown in to ignite the gasoline; and as the men were forced to come out on fire, they were bayoneted or shot or clubbed or stabbed. I saw several of these men tumbling about, still on fire, and falling from being shot... I quickly emerged from the entrance of my shelter and somehow scrambled through the double barbed wire fence... in the few seconds that I was exposed I was hit by a bullet in the right leg... I then let go of the bluff and scrambled down the cliff... after proceeding fifty to a hundred feet, the rocks ended and I stumbled upon three Japanese sailors... attempting to set up a Lewis gun... I had no alternative but to jump these three Japanese sailors in an attempt to get this machine gun away from them.

"We finally fought out into the water, where, due to their weight, I fell under the water and remained under the water, holding them under with me, forcing them finally to release their hold on the gun and me, and they attempted to return to the beach.

"Coming out of the water, I pulled the actuator on the Lewis gun and managed to kill these three Japanese sailors. But seeing another machine gun being set up a little further down the beach, I was forced to return the way I had come, in an effort to find a hiding place among the rocks. In order to get in a small crevice that I found, I was forced to throw the machine gun in the water... Patrols continued to patrol the rocks and beaches for the rest of the day... that night, myself, along with four others, swam the bay and managed, after a few days in the jungle, to join up with the Filipino guerillas." (pp. 15,229-240, testimony of Douglas William Bogue.)

"For five days and nights, without food or water except rain, Bogue tramped through the jungle..." (Statement of Philippine prosecutor, p. 12,671.)

(Note: This incident was also the subject of a wartime protest made for propaganda purposes.)

I SURVIVED A THROUGH-AND-THROUGH MACHINE GUN WOUND RECEIVED IN THE OCEAN, AFTER WHICH I LOST CONSCIOUSNESS FOR TWO DAYS, ENGAGED IN HEAVY PHYSICAL EXERTION, AFTER WHICH MY WOUND HEALED WITHOUT A TRACE IN THE ABSENCE OF ANY MEDICAL TREATMENT

"The bullet that hit me struck me in the back about waist level and passed straight through. It knocked me over, and the waves brought me in to the edge of the water. I continued to lie there for ten or fifteen minutes, and then I sat up and looked around, and the Japanese party had disappeared. I then took myself up into the jungle and lost consciousness...

"Q: You had been unconscious, then from Monday to Wednesday?

"A: Yes... I managed to get him up into the jungle, then I went into the village...

"Q: How many trips to the village did you make for food...?

"A: On two or three occasions I went into the village.

"Q: And how long was it after the shooting on the Monday that you and Kingsley decided to give yourselves up again?

"A: About twelve days.

(Note: They gave themselves up to the Japanese twice even though the Japanese were killing all prisoners.)

"THE PRESIDENT: What attention did your wound get after you had given yourself up?

"A: I did not get any.

"THE PRESIDENT: Did the Japanese know about it?

"A: No, I did not tell them about it." (pp. 13,457-76, testimony of Sister Vivien Bullwinkel)

I MARCHED SEVENTY-FIVE MILES IN NINE DAYS WITH A 105.6 FEVER AND NO FOOD OR WATER CARRYING A WOUNDED COMRADE ON MY BACK, AFTER WHICH MY FEVER DISAPPEARED WITHOUT TREATMENT

"I did have bronchial pneumonia and malaria. My temperature was 105.6...

"Q: Despite the fact that you were sick you were forced to join the Death March?

"A: Yes.

"Q: How long did it take you to make it?

"A: 9 days.

"Q: During the march did you have food and water provided for you by the Japanese?

"A: For the first five days not a drop of food or water or rest was given by any of the Japanese?

"Q: Where did you get your water?

"A: Well, there were many that didn't get any, many that died that tried to get water. All that was available was from an occasional artesian well along the side of the road or possibly a caribou well. That water in the ponds was so polluted that it was highly dangerous to drink and that which came from the artesian wells was of such small amount that when the great numbers of men tried to get it, well, the troops would simply raise their weapons and fire into the group...

"Q: During the first five days how were you able to manage to get some food, if at all?

"A: The Filipino civilians tried on many occasions to give food to the men that were marching. However, they done so at the risk of their lives and a lot of the civilians did lose their lives trying. Other than that, only an occasional sugar cane patch offered food... even the lack of food could have been stood and I suppose that going without water could have been taken, but a person must have rest. But the continued marching and sitting for hours in the hot sun...

"Q: After the Chaplain was wounded did you aid him, Mr. Ingles?

"A: I was one of several that helped to aid him. I personally helped to carry him until the next rest period and throughout the following days we took turns...

"Q: I understand that when you were taken prisoner your temperature was 105.6... how many days did you help him?

"A: That happened on the third or fourth day. We assisted him from then on until the ninth day which was the termination of our hike.

"Q: Did your sickness become worse during this march?

"A: I seemed to have sweated out a portion of the malaria and temporarily I felt somewhat better." (pp. 12,611-31, testimony of Donald F. Ingle)

(Note: according to the prosecution, 53,000 captives at Bataan were forced to walk 75 miles in 9 days without food, water or medical supplies. Everyone who attempted to obtain water or food was shot or bayoneted; persons attempting to give them water or food were shot or bayoneted.

Obviously, if this were literally true, none of the men would have reached their destination: yet most of them got there. The death rate was about 10%, mostly from disease.

According to the defense, the march was dictated by absolute military necessity: the surrender was due to disease and lack of food; the Japanese had insufficient supplies; ammunition was plentiful. The surrender site was under artillery fire from Corregidor and Fort Drum; transport was needed for military purposes.

The Fourth Hague Convention places no restrictions on the distances which POWs may be made to march while in captivity. Under the terms of the 1929 Geneva Prisoner of War Convention, prisoners may be made to walk 20 kilometers per day, or more in case of necessity. Nothing requires transport by vehicle, although some were so transported.

Under the Fourth Hague Convention, prisoners are subject to the same discipline as the troops capturing them; beating, slapping and kicking are methods of discipline in the Japanese army; thus, anything short of arbitrary execution or extreme torture was legal. Japan did not ratify the Geneva Prisoner of War Convention because it required a higher standard of living for prisoners than could be provided for Japanese soldiers and civilians; but it permitted less discipline. Hearsay about crimes committed by soldiers could be collected by anyone, even in post-war Japan; conspiracy was not proven; the defendants could not be linked with these events; the only function of this evidence was to prejudice the court.

The prosecution claimed that transport was available for all prisoners, but could not say how much there was. The quantity of vehicles and fuel was not known because the trucks and fuel were with the units; many had been destroyed. The officer who claimed that the transport was "enough" (Maj. King) did not appear in court; he "testified" by "affidavit". (See pp. 12,592-5; see also testimony of Sgt. Moody, pp. 12,578-90; testimony of Col. Stubbs, pp. 12,736-75.)

It was admitted by Col. Stubbs that the transport was "enough" only if each vehicle shuttled back and forth (pp. 12,762-3; such as one Jeep making 27,000 round trips.)

The defense summation on prisoners of war by Mr. Freeman (pp. 42,618-91) is quite impressive, but some of the evidence on which it is based seems rather poor (pp. 27,117-963). The National Archives do not reply to letters requesting photocopies of cannibalism confessions or Red Cross reports describing excellent conditions in Japanese prison camps.)

I HUNG 24 HOURS BY MY WRISTS WITHOUT FOOD OR WATER

"This usually pulled both arms out of socket. While at this camp, I personally hung as long as twenty-four hours in that position. No food or water was given me..." (pp. 12,607-8)

I STOOD FOUR DAYS IN THE SUN WITHOUT WATER OR MAYBE IT WAS ONLY TWO DAYS

"On another occasion an Australian officer was ordered to stand for four days outside the guardhouse without food or water. He collapsed after two days and was released." (p. 13,040)

I HUNG BY MY WRISTS FOR TWO DAYS AFTER ELEVEN DAYS OF OTHER TORTURE, THEN LOST CONSCIOUSNESS

"For the next ten days I was beaten with a big stick... on the eleventh day water was forced into my stomach, and when my stomach was full, the Japs jumped on it and I became unconscious. I was brought around by two Jap soldiers who threw cold water over me. For the next two days I was suspended from a beam by the wrists, with my toes barely touching the ground. There was a wire tied to my wrists and a clamp fastened to my waist. Electricity was passed through these wires and my arms and body were burned. The pain made me cry out continually, and there seemed to be hooks plucking at my whole body. After two days of almost continual current being passed through me, during which time I was only given small quantities of water to drink, I became unconscious...

"Before this, the Japs accused me of being a British spy... as I cannot even write my name, I tried to point out that this charge was ridiculous." (pp. 13,109-10)

(Note: this passage is taken from an "affidavit". Evidence is presented in the form of written statements in foreign languages signed by illiterates.)

MORE "EVIDENCE"

"After an orgy of drinking, the Japs caught a pig and permitted it to lick the blood off the floor." (p. 12,409)

(Evidence is from "summary" of "war crimes report".)

"When they saw the body of fourteen-year old Fortunata SALONGA lying in an exposed position, attempted to have intercourse with her although she had been dead from eight to ten hours and rigor mortis had set in." (p. 12,413)

("Summary" of "report" quoting Communist propaganda, hearsay, lies and other entries in the Tokyo "Suffering Contest".)

* * *

Was the Holocaust in Europe "proven" in a similar manner?

THE MYTH OF JAPANESE ATROCITIES AT NANKING

Another illustration of the "methods of proof" used in War Crimes "Trials"

The tropical landscape of the Tokyo Trial transcript is rich in strange fauna and flora. A variety prevalent on the lowlands of Central China is known for the hypertrophic development of its organs of locomotion and perception (particularly hearing). He is called the Universal Witness.

Despite its name, ("Ah See" in Chinese), the vision of this specimen is quite poor.

Like the Indestructible Witness, the Universal Witness is immune to shooting, bayoneting, and other forms of capital punishment; however, the Universal Witness is everywhere and sees everything; he sees though doors, walls, and obstacles.

I SAW JAP ATROCITIES IN 12 CITIES AND WAS BAYONETED TEN TIMES BUT ONLY HAVE ONE SCAR

"I was the eye-witness... in such places as (list of 12 Chinese place names)... many others were killed in various other places... ten Japanese stabbed the left side of my abdomen with bayonets... The scar on the left side of my abdomen is an evidence." (pp. 4,650)

(Note: Affidavit was written in English in 1946 describing events in China in 1937, "translated orally" into Chinese prior to signature.)

THE JAPS TOOK ME ALONG AS A WITNESS, THAT'S WHY I SAW SO MANY ATROCITIES

"I and another were put to one side, and the Japanese used light machine guns to kill the rest... I helped throw the bodies in a pond by order of the Japanese... the same day in the afternoon I saw three Japanese rape a dumb girl... I was taken by Japanese soldiers again...

they killed with the bayonet... on the same day in the afternoon I was taken to... and saw three Japanese soldiers set a fire... I saw another raping case..." (p. 2,609)

(Note: This affidavit was written in English in 1946 describing events in China in 1937, complete with names of the Japanese responsible, with the names of their units, and was "translated orally" from English to Chinese prior to signature).

I SAW JAPS HANG AROUND AFTER RAPING

"I see with my very eyes the Japanese soldier raping a woman in a bath room, and his clothes outside, and then afterwards we discovered the bathroom door and found a woman naked and also weeping and downcast...

"Now we went to the camp to try to get... to catch two Japanese who were reported to be living there... we saw one Japanese still sitting there, with a woman on the corner and weeping... and that man was sitting there with his head low there... once we caught a Japanese raping, and he was naked. He was sleeping... I know another case where because of the boatman... he told me this: where he saw that too on his boat, it happened on his boat... after raping, the Japanese asked the old man in that family, isn't that good?... I forgot to say that when the Japanese asked the older man whether it is good or not, he wanted the old man to rape that young girl so all the girls – now I saw this – they all jumped into the river. So the whole family jumped into the river and all drowned. This is not second-hand story. This is real, real and genuine, and we have, we know that, the boatman has been with us for a long time." (pp. 2,569-2,573)

(Note: The witness claimed to have a Ph. D. from the University of Illinois at the age of 13.)

I TREATED A BEHEADING VICTIM AND HEARD ABOUT MASS RAPES AT NANKING

"I can say the few instances of patients that I treated during the time immediately following the fall of Nanking, but I will not be able to give their names, except in the case of two... one case... is that of a young woman of forty, who was brought to the hospital with the back of her neck having a laceration severing all the muscles of her neck, and leaving the head very precariously balanced... there was no doubt in our minds that the work was that of a Japanese soldier...

"Q: You say that the woman of about 40 had a wound in her neck and the muscles were cut and were hanging loose. But what was this caused by?

"A: A Japanese sword..." (pp. 2,534, 2,552-3, Testimony of Dr. Robert O. Wilson)

THEY CUT MY HEAD OFF BUT I CRAWLED TO THE HOSPITAL

"They attempted to cut off her head. The muscles of the neck had been cut but they failed to sever the spinal cord. She feigned death but dragged herself to the hospital... Dr. Wilson is trying to patch her up and thinks she may have a chance to live..." (p. 4,476)

(Note: This is the same woman. First quotes are from Dr. Wilson. Wilson's hospital at Nanking had 180 beds. Wilson claimed that 500,000 people were in Nanking at this time; many patients were turned away, but he could not say how many. If the Japanese injured 200 people, Wilson's testimony is "true".

Second quote is from mimeographed "diary" of James H. McCallum; McCallum was an unknown person who did not appear to testify; one of the American defense attorneys had defended a James H. McCallum on a charge of mail fraud in Ohio; the defendant jumped bail and was never caught. It was never learned whether this was the same James H. McCallum.)

HOW THE JAPS KILLED 200,000 OR MAYBE 260,000 OR MAYBE 278,586 OR MAYBE 300,000 OR MAYBE 500,000 AFTER MASS RAPES AT NANKING

"... approximately 260,000 dead... over 300,000 victims were reported... it is believed that over 200,000 more are yet to be confirmed... more than 200,000 were murdered... more than 300,000 people killed... the total number of victims killed totalled – I wish to say there is a typographical error there – the number should read 278,586... the total number of bodies buried... totalled more than 155,300...

"OBJECTION: Mr. Brooks calls my attention to the fact that in another portion of the affidavit is contained the statement that 300,000 were killed in Nanking, and as I understand it the total population of

Nanking is only 200,000...

"THE PRESIDENT: ... the judges will be just as vigilant as the defense to see that evidence which is indefinite or vague, or sweeping assertions which are not supported by evidence, are rejected" (pp. 4,537-51).

(Note: The quotes are from two "war crimes reports" prepared by the Nanking Procurator General's office in 1946 relating to events of 1937. Material on which conclusions are based are not attached to the reports. Also included are several "reports" of "burial societies". The "reports" are quite short.

According to the defense, 20 cases of rape by young recruits were reported to headquarters in Tokyo, 3 trials were held; 1 officer was executed and 2 soldiers imprisoned. Elsewhere it is stated that up to 100 trials of Japanese soldiers were held; elsewhere, that 180 cases per week were being reported from possibly hostile sources. One defense witness admitted that atrocities in Nanking were "very severe"; what this means in terms of numbers is hard to guess.

Mass rape was a crime allegedly committed by Japanese in all theatres of war as part of a "Common Plan". It seems obvious that such a "plan" would be incompatible with discipline and that any army following such a "plan" would be immediately defeated.)

At the time of these events, the Chinese Nationalists were co-operating with the Communists under the terms of the Shan Agreement to expel the Japanese from China, and the Japanese were the victims of considerable Communist propaganda, not only in China, but elsewhere.

It appears that Japanese atrocities at Nanking (to the extent to which they have any reality at all) were a reprisal for Chinese atrocities against Japanese residents in China at Tung Chow on July 29, 1937, atrocities which included rape. It was pointed out by the prosecution that murder could be justified on the grounds of reprisal, but that rape could not be.

See also:

— *What Really Happened at Nanking: The Refutation of a Common Myth* by Tanaka Masaaki;
— *The Alleged Nanking Massacre: Japan's Refutation to China's Forged Claims* by Tadao Takamoto, Yasuo;
— *Nanking: Anatomy of an Atrocity* by Masihiro Yamamoto.

THE MYTH OF JAPANESE ATROCITIES AGAINST POWS AT MUKDEN

OR
HOW I SURVIVED MIRACULOUSLY
WHILE ALMOST NOBODY DIED

In the post-war Japanese film *Rashomon*, a single event takes on radically different shapes when seen through the eyes of different people, including the ghost of a dead woman.

In the Tokyo Trial transcript, a similar phenomenon may be observed.

PROSECUTION VERSION OF MUKDEN PRISONER OF WAR CAMP

(Prosecutor, International Military Tribunal for the Far East, 3 January 1947.)

"These two affidavits describe the conditions under which prisoners lived at Hoten Camp near Mukden. Over two hundred inmates died of malnutrition, lack of medical care, and lack of fuel. The buildings were inadequately heated although plenty of coal was available for issue. During the first month and a half the prisoners received maize and Chinese cabbage soup and two sour buns a day. The food was frequently so contaminated that the prisoners could not eat it. All requests for additional food, fuel and medical supplies were refused..." (pp. 14,188)

"Deponent states that during the first few months he was at Mukden Camp about 250 American prisoners died either from starvation or dysentery. No medical care supplies were available. The food consisted of maize and soy beans.

"The prisoners worked in nearby factories making steel helmets for the Japanese army, airplane parts and gears for large calibre guns. Deponent worked in a steel mill sixteen hours a day. During his stay in Mukden Camp as a result of the hard work and poor food, he lost over sixty pounds in weight." (pp. 14,194-5)

"Deponent was confined at Camp Hoten, Mukden. The camp was about six hundred yards from a large Japanese ammunition factory. There was no designation on the prisoner of war camp. During a B29 air raid nineteen prisoners were killed and about thirty were injured." (pp. 14,193-4)

RED CROSS VERSION OF MUKDEN PRISON CAMP

(Excerpts from two Reports published by the International Red Cross in Geneva: (i) From the Report of January 1944; an Extract from the Report filed by Max Pestalozzi, a Representative of the ICRC, following his inspection of the Mukden Prisoner of War Camp at Mukden, Manchuria (Manchukuo), on November 13, 1943; (ii) From the Report of March 1945; an Extract from the Report filed by Mr. Angst, a Representative of the ICRC, following his Inspection of the same Camp on 6 December 1944.)

(i) "Delegation to Japan – on November 13, Mr. Max Pestalozzi has visited the camp of prisoners of war at Mukden, Manchukuo, which confined Britishers, Australians, Americans, in total, more than a thousand prisoners of war.

"The dwellings are satisfactory; they are brick buildings, well-constructed and well-equipped. The prisoners there are provided with straw mattress and complete bedding. As for clothing, the prisoners possess two suits of clothing; one for summer and one for winter. The prisoners of war are satisfied with the nourishment, however they find it a little monotonous in the long run.

"The sanitary arrangements are sufficient. The camp has an infirmary attached to it, fully-equipped, which, considered as military hospital, is given all necessary things. The dental cares are also much appreciative. All the prisoners have been inoculated against typhoid, paratyphoid, and dysentery and vaccinated.

"A large sport ground and many indoor games are available to prisoners, but prisoners who desire are given books, as much instructive as recreative.

"In regard to correspondence, the prisoners can send a plenty of messages.

"The discipline is somewhat relaxed, because the prisoners came from several units of army and navy.

"The delegate of the International Red Cross Committee express much satisfaction of his visit and the kindness of the Red Cross of Manchukuo, and signalize at the same time, that the officers attached to the camp are making the utmost effort in order to ameliorate the treatment of the prisoners of war."

(ii) "On Dec. 6 again, Mr. Angst has made the second call at the camp of prisoners of war at Mukden, which assembled more than a thousand Americans, approximately a hundred Britishers, several Australians, and a French.

"The measures to protect against aerial attacks have been taken; the hygienic institutions are satisfactory, and this camp is disinfected whenever it seems to be necessary.

"The rations correspond in quantity to those which are distributed to the camp guards, but the quality of them looked better; the energy values attained about 3500 calories.

"The supplemental foods are prepared for the prisoners who do heavy labours, and for the patients, as well as in the special occasions as, for example certain fete days.

"The hospital of the camp is a brick building, which can receive one hundred fifty patients. It is composed of a separate ward, a tuberculosis patients rooms, a room of test, operations, X-rays, pharmacy and a recreation room. The medical and surgical equipment is complete, and only the patients who suffer from special diseases are transferred to the Mukden Military Hospital, which gives equally dental care.

"The medical inspections take place three times a week and the patients receive doctor's visits every day. All the prisoners have been vaccinated for small pox, and inoculated against typhoid, paratyphoid, dysentery and cholera.

"The money which they use is given them out of their savings.

"It is above all expended in the canteen, where they are informed that these pocket money serve to buy musical instruments, sporting goods, food, seeds and toilets articles. The prisoners also can send the funds to their families if they wish.

"Most of the people are able to work. The duty hours are eight hours a day, with recesses of morning, noon, and afternoon. Sunday is a holiday. Some men work in factory, and the rest are occupied in conversations in the camp.

"There is no Chaplain in the camp; the religious services are celebrated in English by a Japanese clergyman.

"The prisoners can play sport, music and cards; visitors from outside are not admitted, no more than the visits to outside are non authorized; but they can go out of the camp to visit the graves.

"The camp commander has reported to the delegate that their morale and spirits have been, on the whole, ameliorated, and that the relations between the camp authorities and the prisoners have been satisfactory, and with the camp guards they have talked in a like manner; the state of health has been equally ameliorated, and they have seemed also to be satisfied with the fact that they can have these special considerations given them at that time." (Defense document 3136, introduced into evidence on 8 September 1947, pp. 27,918-21.)

THE MYTH OF THE GAS CHAMBER
AT DACHAU

Shower bath, Dachau

We are all familiar with an instrument called the kaleidoscope, in which loose bits of glass are reflected by planar mirrors showing each bit of glass in 6 places at once, creating the illusion of a symmetrical design.

A similar phenomenon occurs in "War Crimes Trials," in which gas chambers are shown in 3 different places at once, and anywhere from 1 to 6 in number, creating the illusion of a Common Design (sometimes referred to as a Common Plan) for the extermination of human beings.

An example of this illusion is the Gas Chamber at Dachau, which appeared in April of 1945, disappeared from Dachau by November of that year, only to reappear at Nuremberg in December, after which it disappeared from Nuremberg and only entered the scene again as "proven fact" in the trial of Oswald Pohl in 1947 (along with the steam chambers of Treblinka).

The following is, I believe, a complete list of pretrial exhibits mentioning this "gas chamber", which was to be "proven" in the First Dachau Trial (trial of Martin Gottfried Weiss). The gas chamber accusation was dropped before trial. It is apparent that the U.S. Army Corps of Engineers knew before November 15, 1945, that no gas chamber could function in the manner described, and that other stories of gas chambers functioning in a similar manner were not true. Yet a decision was made to continue this accusation in other trials for political reasons.

Microfilm page 00005052: "Report of the Atrocities Committed at Dachau Concentration Camp. Vol. 1. War Crimes Investigation Team No. 6823. Signed by David Chavez Jr. Colonel, JAGD, 7 May 1945."

Microfilm page 0000713:
"Exhibit F photograph of gas panel.
"S3 photograph of gas chamber
"V2 plan of water and gas installations
"V10 shower nozzle removed from gas chamber.
"V11 label removed from cans (Zyklon) found in or near gas chamber."

Page 25 of "Chavez Report", microfilm page 00089:
"The new building had a gas chamber for executions... the gas chamber was labelled 'shower room' over the entrance and was a large room with airtight doors and double glassed lights, sealed and gas proof. The ceiling was studded with dummy shower heads. A small observation peephole, double glassed and hermetically sealed, was used to observe the conditions of the victims. There were grates in the floor. Hydrogen cyanide was mixed in the room below, and rose into the gas chamber and out the top vents. (Exhibit 34)
"Dr. Blaha witnessed the first test of the gas chamber in the new crematorium in early 1944, and examined the 7 victims used. Two were killed in the first test, an experiment to determine the amount of gas needed to kill a person. (Exhibit 5)
"Weight of general testimony shows that the gas chamber was

developed successfully to get the desired results. Witness after witness mentions seeing living persons herded into the crematorium and never being seen again. When the chamber was not used it was because of the shortage of the materials to make the gas, the same reason for not using the crematorium continually, and certainly no change of heart on the part of the SS in charge. No witness can testify as an eye witness to an execution by gas except Dr. Blaha, because the crematorium and gas chamber was made up of condemned prisoners who lived in the crematorium yard and once in there, never left the area alive. Men picked for such duty knew that they were to be killed as persons too dangerous to the SS as possible future witnesses."

Col. Chavez testified at trial on November 15, 1945, and made no mention of any gas chamber. There is no mention of any gas chamber in the testimony of Col. Lawrence Ball, another government expert witness. There is no mention of any gas chamber in the prosecution opening statement, summation, or judgement. No mention in the defence summations. No mention in the testimony, except for a few sentences in the testimony of Dr. Blaha. Not one of the forty defendants was asked a single question concerning any gas chamber. Dr. Blaha testified twice. In his second appearance as witness during prosecution "rebuttal", he also makes no mention of any gas chamber. The Chavez report was rewritten and introduced into evidence at Nuremberg as "proven fact", even though it was known to be untrue (Documents 159-L, 2430-PS).

The existence of a gas chamber at Dachau was not upheld in the judgement at Nuremberg.

Page 56 of this same report, the "Chavez Report" (microfilm page 000120, reel 1, M1174, Trial of Martin Gottfried Weiss et al., National Archives): "This new building also contained a gas chamber for execution... the gas chamber was labelled 'shower room'. The first test of a gas chamber was in 1944, when prisoners were used to determine the amount of gas required to kill a person."

000132: "(Diagrams) drawing of piping section above chamber, ventilator, galvanized piping, open into gas chamber. Insulated piping. Gas chamber... gas chamber. Dachau prison camp."

000133: "Grill covered inlets. Hinged door. Water [?] drains. Gas chamber. Dachau prison camp."

000134: "Vents. Ceiling. Gas Chamber. Dachau prison camp. Shower heads flush with ceiling."

000135: (Diagram) Gas Chamber. Gas tight doors. Wooden

shed believed to contain pump or compressor [?]. Piping system above chamber ceiling, dimensions of chamber 24' × 18' × 6'. Chamber constructed of smooth, pale-yellow brick like refractory brick, with small cement joints. Elevation. Gas chamber. Dachau prison camp."

Pre-Trial Witness Interrogations and Other Exhibits:

000199: "In February 1945, 65 Jewish children... arrived in the camp..; the children started crying and said: Please don't put us into the gas chamber. When we replied there was no such thing as a gas chamber, they said: oh yes, our parents told us that we were going into another camp and that we would be put into a gas chamber. We repeated there was no such thing, but they answered: oh yes, oh yes, our father or mother, or uncle or cousin, ... were put into the gas chamber because they were Jews. The children were kept in the camp for 2 or 3 weeks and were sent to the extermination camp in Auschwitz. Even old and hardened prisoners who had witnessed great inhuman treatment were deeply moved by the sight of the children."

000204: "There was no gas chamber in the camp in working order [!]. A gas chamber was being built in the crematorium and in January 1945, work was going on at a high speed. The chamber was soon completed except for the gas boiler [?]. A railway worker who had to go in and out of the camp told me that a boiler had arrived at the Ostbahnhof, Munich, from Auschwitz. But this boiler, together with many gas cylinders had been destroyed in an air raid."

000212: "The years 1940/43 seem to have been the worst period in Dachau and other similar camps. I was told by eyewitnesses of the mass extermination of Jews who were sent in a gas chamber 500 at a time..." (Report on Prison Camp conditions dictated by Captain P.M. Martinot, 23 May, 1945)

000248: "Another specific provision was for a crematorium of four ovens and *one* gas chamber (called 'desinfection chamber') [!]. I do not know whether this camp was ever built."

000250: "The most important building projects which were planned and executed during my presence were as follows:... one crematorium called 'Barracke X' in the concentration camp at Dachau, containing *six* individual gas chambers [!] and 2 combustion ovens."

000277: "The Polish priests were compelled to build the well-known crematory and gas chambers (plural)... they were dragged by their legs to the chambers of death..."

000379: "Source said he visited a building that was designated as a shower room, but which in reality was a gas chamber."

000417: "The following Signal Corps photos are contained in 1222614 and have been retained in the War Crimes Office in Washington D.C. Gas Chambers [plural]."

000420: Photo of soldier in front of door reading 'Gaszeit: (illegible) Vorsicht! Gas! Lebensgefahr! Nicht Öffnen!'... Dachau Atrocity Camp: Gas Chambers [plural], conveniently located to the crematory, are examined by a 7th Army soldier. These are part of the horror chambers used by the Nazis before the 7th Army liberated the camp."

000445: "The following Signal Corps photos are contained in 12226 and have been retained in the War Crimes Office in Washington D.C.... (Gas Chamber) [singular]."

000455: "Photo... Yank examines fake showerhead in the gas chamber [singular] at the Dachau Concentration Camp. Located in the crematory, unknowing prisoners were brought into the shower room marked 'showers'. Here they were stripped and after the door was closed, they were gassed."

000485: "Here also, there were gas chambers [plural] camouflaged as 'showers' into which prisoners were herded under the pretext of bathing and the huge crematory ovens."

000486: "Inside as well as outside [?] were gas chambers [plural] with adjacent crematory ovens... almost 100 naked bodies were stacked neatly in the barren room with cement floors. They had come from a room on the left marked 'Brausebad' for 'shower bath'. It really was a gas chamber [singular] a low ceilinged room about 30 feet square. After 15 or 20 were inside, the doors were firmly sealed and the faucets turned on and poison gas issued [!]. Then the bodies were hauled into a room separating the gas chamber from the crematorium. There were four huge ovens with a huge flue leading to a smoke-blackened stack."

000489: "The troops also discovered gas chambers, torture chambers and ovens."

000496: "We saw the original gas chambers, four huge cells [!] into which victims apparently were crowded and put to death. Later on this method was improved by construction of a large chamber with a jet in the ceiling, similar to shower bath sprinklers. The prisoners undressed in a room, where a man sat, with flowers on his desk, who gave them soap and a towel. Herded into the shower room, the gas was turned on while the operator watched its effect through a telescopic peephole."

000497: "Gas chamber executions."

000506: "Here one can see for oneself the lethal chamber where the people the Nazis doomed were gassed. It has imitation shower baths, installations with dummy sprinklers set in a pipeless ceiling [!], and gratings looking like water drains in the floor through which gas was sent." (So did it come through the floor or through the ceiling?)

000508: "Shower rooms [plural again] where gas was poured [!] into chambers [plural]."

000509: "Jarolin [deputy camp commander at Dachau, defendant in Trial of Martin Gottfried Weiss]... said he thought they had gone to the gas chamber [singular]."

000513: "Gas chamber deaths at Belsen."

It was admitted by the prosecution that many inmates were mentally ill, had lost their minds, or were wandering around in a mental daze, yet their statements were accepted as "fact", no matter how contradictory. It was also admitted that Dachau had 6 hospitals and that 15,000 people died of disease in the last few months, and that emaciation is a symptom of dysentery. Defendants were convicted of "aiding and abetting in a common design", even if no accusations were made against them by inmates (case of Gretsch and Schoepp).

GASKAMMER
getarnt als „Brausebad"
– war nicht in Betrieb

GAS CHAMBER
disguised as a „shower room
– never used as a gas chamber

CHAMBRE A GAZ
„chambre de douche" camouflée
– ne fut jamais utilisée

CAMERA A GAS
camuffata da „bagno a doccia"
– non fu messa in funzione

Камера для газа
маскированная как „душ"
– не был в действии

"Gas chamber" at Dachau – "never finished", "never used", etc. etc. In reality, simply another shower bath, remodelled after the war, with lowered ceiling (originally 10 feet high).

THE MYTH OF SHRUNKEN HEADS AND OBJECTS OF HUMAN SKIN

Objects of human skin feature prominently in war crimes trials. As a rule, no such objects were found; no forensic tests were performed. Prosecution testimony as to the existence of such objects is taken as "proven fact", while defence testimony is ignored.

At Dachau, the prosecution claimed that Jews were skinned; that the skins were hung in the sun to dry; then tanned and used to make slippers, saddles, purses, gloves, and trousers (!).

The following is defence testimony from the First Dachau Trial (Trial of Martin Gottfried Weiss and Thirty-Nine Others, Nov. 15 – Dec. 13, 1945, microfilm M1175, National Archives, Washington D.C.).

* * *

"Q: Isn't it a fact that here in Dachau you had a room where you had a collection of human skin of all persons who had committed suicide?

"A: No, I had no room where I had skin or healthy organs. Naturally, I had a room where I had pathological organs which you have in each hospital. They are taken out and set up in that room for that purpose. In order to teach medical knowledge to students.

"Q: And in that room you also had human skin, did you not?

A: No, I don't know anything about human skin and I don't keep human skin unless I was concerned with cancerous human skin.

"Q: Now, doctor, isn't it a fact that during your time here the skin was taken off the prisoners and tanned and used as hand bags?

"A: No.

[Note: No human skin hand bags were ever introduced into evidence and apparently none were ever found.]

"Q: Isn't it also a fact that during that time you had on your desk the skull of a prisoner?

"A: Yes, I had a skull on my desk. And I had this skull brought from the pathological station and it had already been prepared. I had that brought to my office so that each doctor had the opportunity to look at it.

"Q: It was a shrunken head, was it not?

"A: It was a skull, a bone can't be shrunken." (Testimony of Dr. Wittler, microfilm pages 000341-2. Wittler was sentenced to death, with sentence commuted to life imprisonment. No shrunken head was introduced into evidence.)

"A: ...I came to a construction hut, and saw that there was some skins there. I asked what the skins were doing there. The prisoner told me that the kapo, Knoll, had given him an order to catch the moles, to take their skins off, and to save the skins. Then I went to kapo Knoll, together with the prisoner, and I asked him who had given the order. He told me that Hauptsturmbahnfuehrer Zill gave the order, in order to make a fur jacket." (Testimony of Hirner, microfilm page 000635)

"A: ...he caught mice and moles and I don't know what all he caught.

"Q: Did you know that he had caught some moles, and that he later on sold the skins of the moles?

"A: I know that he had some skins during my time and that he got cigarettes for them, but I don't know just how far this reached.

"A: But you know that it is a fact that he did catch moles?

"Q: If that was his business or not, I don't know." (Testimony of Keller, microfilm pages 000637-8)

"Q: The witness Kaltenbacher [Kaltenbacher was a Communist] said that at Christmas you bragged that you had killed ninety-seven Jews, and you needed only three more, I forget the number it was, to get extra food from the commandant?...

"A: ... I was kapo, head kapo... there were many moles in that plantation. The detail at the time was very great – 14, 15 or 18 hundred prisoners. They caught those, skinned them, and baked them. The Hauptsturmbahnfuehrer saw that and asked where the furs are. He gave me the orders to collect them and he would have a fur jacket made for his wife out of them. He needed at least 100-150. I had them stored at the construction site, and the gypsy brought dyes and things and had the hides prepared. I could not deliver the required number, because in the year 1939 the entire camp was evacuated. Besides, I myself did not catch any moles... now and again I received some mole skins and delivered the same to Zill...he said, 'Knoll, how is it going?' I told them I still had to kill thirteen until I had the first hundred. I said that aloud and as clear as I am saying it in court today. The listeners didn't know what it was about. After that they talked about what I could kill. Naturally the question came: only Jews!

"In the same moment the word was born that I was a killer of Jews. There was no talk of a Jew... I would have had to kill more than one Jew every day and I still would have not reached the named number of 87..." (Testimony of Knoll [a prisoner] microfilm pages 000623-4)

* * *

No human skin was introduced into evidence. All 40 defendants were found guilty on all counts with 36 death sentences.

Note the sloppiness implied in assuming that a skull and a shrunken head are one and the same thing, as if the difference really did not matter – all based on hearsay, in the absence of any forensic tests or physical evidence whatsoever. In war crimes trials, as in the witchcraft trials of the Middle Ages, truly anything will do, no matter how irrational, self-contradictory, or insane.

* * *

In the 1980s, on one of several occasions, I visited the Peace Palace of the Hague, in the Netherlands, where the "original documents" from the Nuremberg Trials are alleged to be kept, except that they are not there. As a rule, they have only copies.

One of the officials immediately said, "Oh, you want to see the human soap, of course? Everybody wants to see the human soap. It smells." His face wrinkled up in a sneer of disgust.

"Has it been forensically tested?" I inquired, innocently.

"Oh yes," he replied casually, with a breezy smile.

"Do you have a copy of the report?" I said.

The smile instantly disappeared. "No", he replied, in a much lower voice. He had never thought of that.

"If it hasn't been forensically tested, I don't want to see it", I said.

"Well, how about the human skin?" he replied. "With the human soap, I know there is nothing, but there might be a report with the human skin." (The "human soap" is Exhibit USSR-393, the "human skin" is Exhibit USSR 394. They are kept together.)

He then pulled out a huge object wrapped in crude brown paper and tied up with crude twine, undid all the knots, and pulled out a huge piece of "human skin" (which looked like cow hide to me). There was nothing else in the package whatsoever: no report, no legal documents, nothing. I left him looking at it with a look of intense bewilderment. He couldn't figure out how it could be "known" that these exhibits are authentic, and yet not be accompanied by any forensic report.

Some time later, I wrote to the Peace Palace of the Hague asking what procedures would be required to subject the "human soap" to forensic testing by an independent laboratory. I never received an answer. The problem, of course, assuming that these exhibits are authentic, would lie in proving that the Germans made them, and not the Soviets. Perhaps those who believe in the authenticity of these objects will do us the favour of testing them and proving their origins.

JAPAN WAS PROVOKED INTO A WAR OF SELF-DEFENSE

SYNOPSIS OF ARGUMENTS BY LAWYERS FOR THE DEFENSE. INTERNATIONAL MILITARY TRIBUNAL FOR THE FAR EAST

Illustrations of the real situation in international law as opposed to American fantasies

On December 7, 1928, a group of distinguished Senators gathered in the Capital Building at Washington D.C. to discuss ratification of the Briand-Kellogg Peace Pact, an instrument whose purpose was to "abolish aggressive war".

Among those present was the author of the Pact, Secretary of State Frank B. Kellogg.

During the course of the recorded discussions, the following exchange took place:

"Q: Suppose a country is not attacked – suppose there is an economic blockade...?

"A: There is no such thing as a blockade [unless] you are in war.

"Q: It is an act of war?

"A: An act of war absolutely... as I have stated before, nobody on earth, probably, could write an article defining 'self defense' or 'aggressor' that some country could not get around; and I made up my mind that the only safe thing for any country to do was to judge for itself within its sovereign rights whether it was unjustly attacked and had a right to defend itself and it must answer to the opinion of the world."

The above was quoted during the Tokyo Trial by American defense counsel to show that Japan's War of the Pacific, according to the very terms of the Brian-Kellogg Pact itself, did not and could not constitute "aggression".

Japan's War of the Pacific was a war of self-defense for the following reasons:

– blockade is an act of war (p. 43,051);

– every nation is the judge of what constitutes self-defense (*Ibid*);

– no submission to any tribunal is required by the Pact (pp. 42,162; 42,240);

– self-defense is not limited to defense of the national territory (p. 42,239);

– the Pact does not contain any sanctions, express or implied (pp. 42,163);

– breach of treaties does not constitute aggression (p. 42,191);

– American aid to the Chinese made America a belligerent in that war (see Note, below);

– declarations of war are not required in self-defense (pp. 42,431-5);

– no treaty requires any warning prior to attack (pp. 42,447-8);

– declaration of war prior to attack was intended, but was delayed due to clerical errors on the part of Embassy staff in Washington (pp. 43,704-18; see also p. 42,448-51).

It was argued further that:

– the attack on Pearl Harbor was not illegal under international law (pp. 42,403-513; 43,493-738);

– Japan was provoked into a war of self-defense (pp. 43,050-175);

– Japan was not prepared militarily for war (pp. 43,177-222);

– Japanese military preparedness was not aggressive (pp. 43,224-263).

Japan is an island nation devoid of natural resources, overpopulated, dependant on imports of nearly all commodities for manufacture. Most of Japan is mountainous or infertile; most cities are on the coast.

Japan must be a naval nation; every major city in Japan can be destroyed by coastal shelling from battleships, to say nothing of airplanes.

Japan was not prepared for war in the Pacific.

Japan never prepared for combat in tropical regions; military supplies and equipment were designed for combat in cold climates (pp. 26,949; 43,244).

Most Japanese ships were small, for the coastal trade; many were built of wood (pp. 24,915; 43,076; see also p. 24,929).

2 destroyers were added to the Japanese fleet in 10 years, 1931-1941, reaching a total of 112 in 1941 (*Ibid*).

Japan had no long-range aircraft carriers. Japanese carriers could not refuel at sea (pp. 26,719-20; 43,221).

Japanese ships were built for patrolling shallow Japanese coastal waters (pp. 11,272; 43,202).

Japan did not stockpile any commodity except oil for any purpose in 1941.

Japan planned to store 36,000 kiloliters of oil by 1943 (pp. 24,855; 43,241).

Japan did not store ammunition or oil in Formosa or southern parts of Japanese territory overseas (pp. 26,951; 43,246).

Japan did not develop a merchant marine (pp. 24,965; 43,076).

Japan had few civilian aircraft or ships capable of conversion (pp. 26,671; 43,201).

Japan suffered from an acute food shortage in 1939-40 (pp. 25,050-2; 43,101).

The American embargo applied to foodstuffs, including rice, tea, soy beans, wheat flour, fertilizer, fodder, edible fats and seeds (pp. 36,966-8; 43,131; 25,255-9; 43,162-175).

Synthetic oil could not be produced due to a lack of high pressure steel pipes, coal and cobalt (pp. 24,870; 43,134).

Japan possessed 11,654 military aircraft (pp. 8,030-1; 43,070) and 65 submarines in 1941 (pp. 11,261; 43,194).

Japan built 1,380 army planes in 1941 (pp. 18,293; 43,240).

Japan's initial conquests after Pearl Harbor were achieved using 1,175 land planes; 475 carrier planes; 13 divisions of army; and a "handful" of marines (pp. 39,391; 43,262).

Japan negotiated for 9 months prior to the attack. In the course of these negotiations, the Americans demanded a guarantee of freedom from attack by Japan regardless of any action taken against Germany (pp. 43,517-21).

Japan agreed, repudiating the Tri-Partite Pact (pp. 43,522-39).

Japan gave the Americans permission to publish the text of the repudiation (p. 43,642).

Japan offered to withdraw all troops from China (pp. 25,856; 43,588) or at least 90% (p. 43,604).

Japan received no response to either concession (43,602).

Japanese cables (decoded by the Americans in violation of international law) were so badly mistranslated by American Nisei that they probably helped cause the war (pp. 43,607-21).

(As far as one can tell, no Nisei translators of Japanese were used in war crimes trials of Japanese military personnel. Affidavits in English were supposed to have been translated orally and accurately on sight to Japanese affiants prior to signature by translators who were British or American, frequently with Jewish names.)

The Americans froze Japanese assets (in violation of a treaty) and began to embargo oil. It was demanded, as a condition to restoring normal relations, that Japan sign an agreement with various other nations who had never before been party to the negotiations, including Thailand and Soviet Russia (pp. 43,678-98).

To obtain agreement with the other nations in accordance with this demand could have taken months or years; and might never have been possible. Japan had enough oil for a few months only. A conference was held at which it was decided that if there was to be war, it must come now; by spring Japan would be too weak to fight. In any case, the attack on Pearl Harbor was an act of utter desperation. The oil embargo meant the destruction of Japan's independence and perhaps survival as a nation.

Japan faced immediate military defeat in China; total industrial collapse at home; and destruction through coastal shelling of all the major cities by any one of five traditional enemies (America, Britain, China, the Netherlands, and particularly the Soviets).

Oil had been supplied to Japan for two years in the teeth of hostile public opinion. It was believed essential to keep war out of the Far East; Roosevelt wished to import rubber, tin, etc from the South Pacific, supplying the British in the Near East with meat, wheat, corn, troops, and military supplies (pp. 25,316-7; 43,121).

When this did not work, Japan was forced into war, crushed with atomic bombs, and her leaders hanged for "aggression".

War with Japan had been avoided – as long as it was believed that Germany could be provoked into a declaration of war through bombing and ramming attacks on German and Italian ships and submarines, and many other violations of international law (pp. 42,436; 43,639).

Japan attempted to negotiate a surrender for 11 months prior to the atomic bombings (pp. 23,582-610).

That America, Britain and Holland conspired "aggressive war" against Japan is proven by the report of the conversations at the Most Secret American-Dutch-British Conversations held in Singapore in April 1941:

"It was important to organize air operations against Japanese occupied territory and against Japan itself. It is probable that her collapse will occur as a result of economic blockade, naval pressure, and air bombardment".

Space does not permit further discussion of the crimes of this nation of monsters (we are not referring to the Japanese).

Note: Almost no use was made of the argument that America was a belligerent in the China Incident. The Incident was a "conflict" rather than a "war" in the sense that belligerent and neutral rights were not invoked: diplomatic relations were undisturbed; enemy aliens in Japan were not interned, etc. Rather, it was maintained that if it was a war, then American aid to China made America a belligerent subject to attack without formality. The Americans claimed it was a war in which they could participate without becoming a belligerent.

ERNST SAUCKEL'S
"EXPLOITATION" SPEECH

Translated by Carlos W. Porter

Most Nuremberg Trial documents have never been translated into English in their entirety. Typically, a single paragraph or even sentence is taken out of context, often mistranslated, to offer "proof" of German crimes. The rest of the document is ignored; the correctness of the translation is never questioned.

For example, the following quotations appear in a footnote on p. 948 of William L. Shirer's *Rise and Fall of the Third Reich* (page 1128 of the 1960 Pan paperback edition):

"One of his [Sauckel's] first directives laid it down that the foreign workers were 'to be treated in such a way as to exploit them to the highest possible extent at the lowest conceivable degree of expenditure.' He admitted at Nuremberg that of all the millions of foreign workers 'not even 200,000 came voluntarily.' "

Sauckel was, of course, hanged at Nuremberg for his "slave labour policies".

The second quotation comes from an unsigned document (124-R) stating that factory foremen were sent to concentration camps for giving their "slave workers" so much as a box on the ear; the first is a falsified translation of a single sentence, taken out of context, from a speech (016-PS) in which Sauckel is explaining the necessity for labour service by both Germans and foreigners, and is demanding the best possible treatment for his workers, both German and foreign! The verb "exploit" does not even appear in the sentence! The verb is to "bring forth".

The original German reads: "Alle diese Menschen müßen so ernährt, untergebracht und behandelt werden, daß sie bei denkbar sparsamsten Einsatz die größtmöglichste Leistung hervorbringen."

A better translation would be: "All these people must be fed, housed, and treated so as to produce the greatest possible output with the greatest possible economy of industrial effort".

The meaning is to achieve the highest possible production per man with the lowest possible number of workers, a perfectly ordinary sort of concept in any undertaking (for example, the basic principle of judo is said to be: "maximum efficiency, minimum effort").

The full text of the document is as follows:

* * *

Translation of Document 016-PS, Nuremberg Trial Draft directive by Ernst Sauckel

[cover letter to Alfred Rosenberg omitted]

The Commissioner for the Four Year Plan
The General Plenipotentiary for the Labour Service

20.4.42

The Labour Service Programme

On Remembrance Day 1942, the Führer announced to the German people the most gigantic and most difficult German military achievements in history. In addition to the heroic and victorious struggle against an enemy unprecedentedly superior in numbers and materiel, an enemy fighting with the courage of the most extreme desperation and the most bestial cruelty, there has been the endurance of a hard winter, without parallel in the history of the past 140 years, in terms of cold, ice, snows, and storms. Overcoming the unprecedented hardships caused by such a climate, and by such extraordinarily bad weather conditions, has turned our soldiers on the Eastern front, measured against all previous human and military achievements, of all time – we may say without exaggeration – into Supermen.

These soldiers are now entitled to expect the homeland itself to bring forth a comparably powerful concentration of the forces of the nation in order to ensure final, complete, and the earliest possible victory.

All related burdens and other necessary restrictions, even in nourishment, must be borne with proud determination, precisely in view of the example set by our soldiers.

Our Greater German Army has shown an excess of heroism, endurance, and overcoming, on the Eastern front, in Africa, in the air, and on the sea. To ensure their victory under all circumstances, we must now ensure that they are supplied with increasingly better and more numerous weapons, material, and munitions, as the result of an increasingly greater production effort on the part of the entire German people, that is, of all creative workers, both intellect and manual, both men and women, and of all German youth.

In this manner, the German homeland will make a decisive contribution to the destruction of our enemy's every hope of once again staving off total and final defeat.

The purpose of the gigantic new labour service is to make use of all the hugely rich resources which the army, fighting under the leadership of Adolf Hitler, has achieved and consolidated to such an overwhelmingly great extent, in order to strengthen the Army and feed the homeland. The raw materials and fertility of the conquered territories, and their manpower resources, must be perfectly and conscientiously utilized for the benefit of Germany and our allies through the labour service.

Despite the fact that most able-bodied German people have already put their strength to work for the war economy in a manner worthy of the highest recognition, considerable additional reserves must still be found and made available under all circumstances.

The decisive measure to implement this is the uniformly regulated and controlled labour service of the nation at war.

To achieve this goal, the following principles must be stated and carried out:

A. All important manufacturing programmes running at the present time must under no circumstances be disrupted, but rather must be further increased.

B. All orders of the Führer, the Reichsmarschall of the Greater German Reich, and the Minister for Munitions and Armaments must be obeyed as quickly as possible. The labour resources required for this purpose must be released and made available in Germany itself and in the occupied territories .

C. Equally urgent is the task of ensuring seed and harvest for the German farmers and all European areas under German control with the aim of achieving the highest yield. The agricultural workers required must be made available as quickly as possible.

D. A supply programme for the most indispensable commodities must be ensured for the German people.

Implementation of these principles for the labour service requires:

1. the cooperation of all forces of the Party, the economy, and the state under uniform leadership;

2. the best will of the German people;

3. the most extensive measures to ensure that all workers in service, men and women, place their highest trust in the justice of their treatment in terms of their personal fate and remuneration, as well as the best possible care for their health and housing in wartime;

4. the fastest and best possible solution to the question of service by women and youth.

If the objective set by the Führer is to be achieved, it can only be made possible through the simultaneous and earliest possible implementation of many different measures, all aiming at the same objective. Since, however, none of these measures may disrupt the others – rather, they must complement each other in a sensible way – it is absolutely necessary for all the agencies participating in this decisive task, in any manner – in the Reich, its territories and municipalities, in the Party, state, and economy – to proceed according to uniform guidelines.

Thus, the labour service of the nation will make an extraordinary contribution to the earliest possible victorious conclusion of the war. It will also require the final effort of the German people in the homeland. It is for these German people – for their maintenance, their freedom, their happiness, and for the betterment of their nourishment and the maintenance of their lives – that this war is being fought.

Basic Principles:

I. In the districts, the task of the NSDAP district leaders will consist of propaganda, in the enlightenment of the German people with regard to the necessity for the labour service, and for the implementation of major steps providing for the youth and women set to work, while taking care of the conditions in camps and lodgings.

They must also ensure the closest and most comradely cooperation of all participating institutions.

II. The principal duty of the General Plenipotentiary – in fact, the sole precondition for the success of his task – is to ensure the unreserved cooperation and harmony of all superior agencies –

especially the agencies of the Army, whose scope of responsibility extends to the present assignment.

III. The agreement of all Reich Leaders of the Party, its organizations, particularly, the cooperation of the German Labour Front and the installations of the economy, is equally indispensable.

IV. The General Plenipotentiary for the Labour Service will therefore – using the smallest possible personal staff of fellow workers of his choice – make exclusive use of the available Party, state and economic agencies, and guarantee the quickest success of their measures through the good will and cooperation of all.

V. The General Plenipotentiary for the Labour Service has therefore set all district leaders of the Greater German Reich to work as his plenipotentiaries in the German districts of the NSDAP with the approval of the Führer and in harmony with the Reichsmarschall of the Greater German Reich and the leadership of the Party Chancellery.

VI. The Plenipotentiary for the Labour Service will make use of the responsible agencies of the Party in their districts. The leaders of the highest offices of the state and economy responsible for their districts will consult and instruct the district leaders with regard to all important questions of the labour service.

The following will be especially important for this purpose:
– the President of the Agricultural Labour Office;
– the Labour Trustees;
– the State Agricultural Leaders;
– the District Economic Advisers;
– the District Leader of the German Labour Front;
– the Leaders of the District Women's Organizations;
– the Regional Leaders of the Hitler Youth;
– the superior representatives of the Interior and General Administration or Office for the Agricultural Economy.

(If the region of an Agricultural Labour Office consists of several districts, and if there is no Agricultural Labour Office in the district capital, then the President of the Agricultural Labour Office must make his closest and hardest-working employees available to the district leaders involved so as to ensure constant instruction of the district leaders on all measures relating to the labour service in that district.)

VII. The principal and most important task of the district leaders of the NSDAP in their capacity as plenipotentiaries in their districts is, therefore, to ensure the best possible harmony of all the agencies in their district in participation in the labour service. The strictest care must be taken, however, to ensure that the superior officers of the party or agencies of the NSDAP, as well as its organizations, branches, and related associations, neither take over functions for which only the authorities of the state, the Army, or institutions of the economy are responsible or may assume responsibility; nor may they arbitrarily interfere in the course of agency matters for which they are not responsible, according to the best will of the Führer.

But if we succeed, with the assistance of the Party in all districts, areas, and municipalities, in convincing all German workers, both the workers of the intellect and the workers of the hand, of the great significance of the labour service in deciding the war; if we succeed in caring for and in strengthening all German men, women, and youth, doing their duty in the labour service under extraordinarily difficult conditions, in the best possible way, with regard to their physical and spiritual powers of endurance; if we furthermore succeed, with the cooperation of the Party, in utilizing the service of prisoners of war and civilian workers, both men and women, of foreign blood, but without harm to our people – yes, even to the greatest benefit of the war effort and the food industry, then the most difficult part of the task of the labour service will have been solved.

The Task and Its Solution

(In accordance with the requirements of secrecy, the following contains no statements in terms of figures. I nevertheless ask you to believe that this is the greatest labour problem of all times, especially in terms of numbers.)

A. The task:

1. The war situation has necessitated the call-up of new soldiers into all sections of the Army in huge numbers.

This means:

a) taking workers out of all commercial enterprises, above all, great numbers of technical workers from armaments factories which are of the utmost importance to the war effort;

b) taking workers out of the military food industry, although they are indispensable precisely at the present time.

2. The military situation, however, also requires the implementation of armaments programmes which have been hugely expanded and improved by the Führer in comparison to the previous situation.

3. The commodities most necessary to the German people must also continue to be produced in the necessary quantities.

4. German housewives, particularly agricultural housewives, must, especially as mothers, suffer no harm to their health as a result of the war; they must therefore be relieved, insofar as possible, in whatever way.

B. The solution:

1. All technical workers called up for military service from industries important to the war effort must be replaced immediately and absolutely so as to avoid interruptions or drops in the production of equipment of importance to the war effort.

All labour service authorities are therefore responsible for taking account of these conditions in every case.

The most suitable manpower must therefore be taken out of reserve, from industries which have been shut down and are less important to the war effort, as well as from agricultural industries which have also been shut down, and be allocated to industries where the manpower has been called up for military service, eight weeks before they are drafted, so that every conscripted technical worker can instruct and teach his replacement.

Similarly, all other workers released through closure actions and not being utilized in service as replacements for technical workers, must be made available to the armaments industries without delay, especially for work on the night shift.

2. Male and female workers who have, for example, been released through destruction or damage to their companies by enemy air raids, must be equally quickly retransferred and set to work in the armaments industry.

3. The challenges in armaments and food now require, however, the importation of foreign manpower as an urgent necessity, in addition to the total utilization of all German manpower.

I have therefore immediately tripled the transport programme which I found in taking over my job.

The main bulk of that transport was brought forward in time to the months of May/June, so that the introduction of foreign workers from the occupied territories will still be effective for increased production under all circumstances with regard to coming Army operations, as well as for agricultural work in the sector of the German food economy.

All prisoners of war who are already in Germany, in either the Western or Eastern territories, must also be imported for German armaments and agriculture without exception, insofar as this has not yet occurred; their production must be brought to the highest conceivable levels.

It must be emphasized that huge numbers of foreign workers must nevertheless still be brought into the Reich. The largest reservoir for this purpose is the occupied territories in the East.

It is therefore indispensable that full use be made of the existing human reserves available in the conquered territories. If we do not succeed in winning over the required manpower on a voluntary basis, then steps must be immediately taken to go over to levies or compulsory manpower call-ups.

In addition to already-available prisoners of war who are still in the occupied territories, it is also particularly necessary to mobilize male and female civilian and technical workers from the Soviet territories for the German labour service, from the age of 15 upwards.

According to the available possibilities, on the other hand, a quarter of the total requirements in terms of foreign workers can be imported from the occupied European territories to the west of Germany.

The importation of manpower from sympathetic or even neutral countries will only satisfy a fraction of the total needs. These workers will be principally technical and special workers.

4. To provide German housewives with a perceptible amelioration of their burdens, particularly for mothers with many children, as well as German agricultural wives, who are already overburdened with responsibilities, and to avoid further endangering their health, the Führer has also ordered me to bring approximately 4 to 500,000 selected healthy, strong girls into the Reich from the occupied territories.

5. It is also planned to ensure early service by German youth, in the order of school years, together with men and women teachers, on the basis of an agreement with the Reich Youth Leaders and the responsible superior Reich authorities. The necessary orders and implementation instructions have already been issued.

6. Labour service by German women is of very great importance.

After learning the basic view of the Führer and that of the Reichsmarschall of the Greater German Reich, and having very conscientiously reviewed this very difficult problem in great detail on the basis of my own most meticulous investigations and reports, I must basically dispense with compulsory service for German women and girls by the State for the German war and food economy.

Even though I myself first believed – and with me, quite the greater proportion of the leaders in the Party and women's organizations on certain grounds – that it would be necessary to introduce compulsory service for women, I must now, however, and so should all responsible men and women of the Party, state, and economy, give way, with the greatest respect as well as the deepest gratitude, before the wisdom of our Führer Adolf Hitler, whose greatest concern is for the health of German women and girls, and, at the same time, for the present and future mothers of our people.

I need not recall here all the reasons that have been decisive in making my decision. I ask you, however, to believe me, as an old and fanatical National Socialist district leader, when I say that, precisely in the last analysis, the decision could not have been otherwise.

We all completely agreed that this decision apparently, however, entails a very great injustice and hardship with regard to the millions of women who are [already] working under very difficult conditions in war service in the armaments and food economy every day, but we also agree upon this: that one does not improve an evil by generalizing it to the utmost consequence, and conjuring it up onto everybody.

The only way to eliminate the present hardships and injustices is to win the war; then we will able to take all German women and girls out of all professions which we then consider to be unfeminine and harmful to the health of our women, dangerous to the birth rate of our people, harmful to family life, and to the life of our people.

It must be further considered that it makes, in fact, a huge difference whether a woman or a girl has already been accustomed to a certain job in a factory or in agriculture from an early age, and whether she has already endured this work or not.

In addition to physical harm, however, German women and girls must therefore also continue to be protected from harm to their emotional life and spirit under all circumstances, according to the will of the Führer.

This condition of the Führer could hardly be fulfilled through mass compulsion and mass service. German women cannot be compared to German soldiers in this regard without further consideration. There are inborn differences between men and women which are determined by race and by nature.

We could not take responsibility before the innumerable men of our people, doing duty at the front as brave soldiers, and particularly before the fallen, for the damage to the entire life of our people which threatens to arise here in the context of women's service.

All the many millions of women, however, who are truly and conscientiously doing worthwhile work within the German planned economy and especially now in the war, deserve the best care and security conceivable. They deserve the greatest thanks of our nation, just as much as our soldiers and workers. They must be treated in the best manner possible by the Labour Offices and authorities; the most generous possible account must be taken of their economic and health requirements. Both the Führer and the Reichsmarschall of the Greater German Reich place the greatest value on this. It would be totally wrong to use threats, or inflict penalties on women, or even take them to court, for example, for staying home from work prior to maternity leave because of physical complaints related to pregnancy; this has, unfortunately, already occurred. Nevertheless, it will and must be possible to maintain the indispensable working discipline.

7. A last, but not inconsiderable reserve consists of increasing the possible individual industrial production per German worker. It will be the principal task of the Party and the German Labour Front to attain such increases in production. There is no doubt that the German worker, both skilled and unskilled, wherever he may be employed, can nevertheless do his best, even under the most difficult conditions of today's food situation.

This will be an expression of the overwhelming gratitude of German workers in the homeland with regard to the soldiers at the front, who have endured the most fearful suffering, hardships, and deprivation during this hard winter, and nevertheless remained victorious over the enemy.

In this regard, the cooperation of Party, state, and economy remains reserved, therefore, to take care that the industrial health services, and understanding cooperation on the part of the social security services and doctors of industrial medicine, allow us to lower the sick rate by 1%. This was possible in the district of Thuringia. For the whole Reich, such a general improvement in the sick rate would mean 200,000 additional workers.

Severe measures must obviously be taken against loafing vermin, since loafers cannot be permitted to shirk their duties in this fateful fight for our people at the cost of the decent and hardworking.

Under points B. 1-7, I have attempted to describe the exterior solution of the task of the German labour service under the present war situation.

It is obvious that the possibilities indicated in these points must all be entirely exhausted. The rejection of general compulsory service for all women and girls in no way means, however, that I have at all abandoned my intention to make able-bodied women and girls available for suitable service, wherever they can be used to the benefit our war economy, without violating the basic principles of the Führer.

This will be carried out in the closest cooperation with the agencies of the Party, the state, the army, and the economy involved for this purpose.

The labour service programme established in points 1-7 means quite the most gigantic labour service ever implemented by any people, indeed in history.

Adolf Hitler has, however, revealed to us, through the concept of National Socialism, that numbers are not the decisive factor in the life of a people. In addition to the huge numbers of people set to work, there is the productive capacity. This productive capacity is, in turn, dependent, not just on the calories which I make available to them in the form of food, but also upon the inner attitude, the will, as well as the life of the mind and the emotions of the people who have been set to work.

In addition to the huge organizational problems which must be solved in the labour service in this war, there are also, therefore, the questions of food, housing, education, propaganda, and social care.

Social Care for German Workers Men and Women

There must be no doubt in the mind of any German person and National Socialist that the working German person, when he is correctly led, and given political and ideological guidance, in his conscientiousness at work, in his readiness to take the greatest efforts upon himself, in his ability and his performance, towers high over all the other workers on earth.

The district leaders of Adolf Hitler in the districts of the NSDAP entrusted to them, must therefore guarantee that – with the help of all the installations and organizations of the Party in the now decisive stage of the war – they will give the German working people the best political and ideological guidance which has ever existed in the history of human labour and in times of war.

As the Plenipotentiary for the Labour Service, I am certain that all steps will be taken in this regard by the Party, both outside and inside industry, through the utilization of all means of propaganda and education, through waves of collections, and through industrial appeals, to maintain the proper attitude and morale of the German worker, in keeping with the dignity of the homeland with regard to the front, in this hour which is to decide our fate, and which is also the sole precondition for meeting this huge challenge and winning the war.

It will be my constant concern to see that the labour service authorities, as well as all industrial leaders, support the Party, and particularly the German Labour Front, which has a decisive and great task, in every way.

Even when workers, men and women, are set to work in armaments factories in their own localities, and can sleep and eat in their own homes and sleep with their family, they must be cared for in the most meticulous way. I will mention only: ensuring the coal and potato supply, and considering the approach routes to and from work.

Lack of spring vegetables and other hardships of wartime, which get on people's nerves and harm our people's health, must thereby be equalized, so that all decent people and women may therefore derive all the more strength from realizing the National Socialist principles of the racial community, of social justice, and the necessity for common sacrifices, and faith and trust in the Führer.

The challenge will be, however, much more difficult when it involves caring for those millions of workers, both men and women, rendering services which they are not accustomed to, far from their own homes. This is a necessity of war.

Such service can neither be restricted, nor can the related hardships be eliminated.

Everything must be done for these racial comrades, both men and women, to make their lives more enjoyable and their work easier, insofar as possible. All these German people must be supported so as to be housed in decently furnished quarters under equally decent conditions insofar as possible, to permit them to enjoy comradeship in their leisure time, through the Party and through the Labour Front, and to receive their coupons and so on, at the correct time.

In this regard in particular, the "Politeness" Action of Reichsleiter Dr. Goebbels must be binding on all labour offices and all economic and food offices to the highest degree.

Wherever German working people, whether men or women, are housed in camps, these camps must represent perfect examples of German cleanliness, order, and health care.

German industries and the German economy must spare no sacrifice to make life tolerable for all those racial comrades, both men and women, who are housed in camps far from their own homes and families, on the basis of compulsory service. Just as in the German Army, the German soldier, in his company, considers perfect order with regard to both his outer needs and his character as a German soldier to be a matter of course, in a manner which raises him above the soldiers of all other peoples in his military qualities, this must also be possible for the working German people, in a manner suitably adapted to the labour service.

Care for working German people in the armaments industries, in the war economy and the camps, must therefore be fundamentally guaranteed by German labour front to the most perfect degree.

The more widespread utilization of women and girls outside their localities and away from their families must basically proceed according to the model of the women's labour service with regard to housing and care.

Prisoners of War and Foreign Workers

The utilization without exception of all prisoners of war, as well as the importation of huge numbers of new foreign civilian workers, both men and women, has become an indisputable necessity in meeting the challenges of the labour service in this war.

[THE FOLLOWING SENTENCE WAS TAKEN OUT OF CONTEXT AT NUREMBERG TO PROVE GERMAN INHUMANITY AND CRUELTY.]

All these people must be fed, housed, and treated so as to produce the greatest possible output with the greatest possible economy of industrial effort.

[WHILE THE FOLLOWING PARAGRAPHS WERE SIMPLY IGNORED.]

For the Germans, it always has been a matter of course to treat a defeated enemy – even when he has been our cruellest and most irreconcilable enemy – without any cruelty or cheap trickery, to treat him correctly and humanely, especially when we expect useful production from him.

As long as the German armaments industry did not urgently require it, the importation of both Soviet prisoners of war, as well as civilian workers, both men and women, from the Soviet territories, was to be dispensed with under all circumstances. But that is no longer possible now. The manpower of these peoples must be utilized to the greatest extent.

I have therefore, as my first step, regulated the nourishment, housing, and treatment of these foreign working people with the responsible superior authorities of the Reich, and with the approval of the Führer and the Reichsmarschall of the Greater German Reich, so that optimal labour production may be demanded from them, and can also be obtained from them.

Please remember, in so doing, that even a machine can only produce what I make available to it with in terms of fuel, lubricant, and maintenance. How many more requirements must be taken into consideration with a human being, even if he is of a primitive type and race, compared to a machine.

I could not take responsibility before the German people for the importation of huge numbers of such people into Germany if, instead of bringing forth highly necessary and useful production, they one day become the heaviest burden or even become hazardous to the health of the German people, due to failings in nourishment, housing, and treatment.

The most meticulous principles of German cleanliness, order, and hygiene must therefore apply in the Russian camps as well.

Only in this way will it be possible, without all false sentimentality, to ensure the highest benefits from this service as well, in terms of armaments for the fighting front and for the military food economy.

The necessary instructions for the nourishment, housing, and treatment of people from the East have already been issued to the responsible authorities of the police, war economy, and agricultural offices; in addition, I am now requesting the districts of the NSDAP to support me to the utmost in this matter, to avoid everything which may result in harm to the German people from this service.

Members of racially related peoples and [German-]allied and friendly nations working in Germany should be treated and cared for with particular care.

We must avoid everything which could make the stay and the work of foreign men and women doing service in Germany more difficult, or even cause unnecessary suffering, under the restrictions caused by the conditions and hardships of war. We are greatly dependent upon their good will and their manpower.

It is therefore in keeping with the laws of reason to make their stay and their work in Germany as tolerable as possible, without compromising ourselves.

This must, for example, be realized by making concessions to them with regard to their national or racial habits in food, housing, use of their leisure afternoons, etc., insofar as conditions permit, taking the situation of our own people into account.

It is entirely possible that, if the authorities of the labour service, the general and interior administration, Party, and labour front, cooperate closely in the service of foreign men and women workers, with complete understanding and in close cooperation, in addition to the huge benefits which this mass service of millions of prisoners of war and foreign civilian workers may bring forth for the German war effort and the agricultural economy, just as great an advantage may accrue to the propaganda of the National Socialist Greater German Reich and its prestige in the world.

Contrariwise, if the cooperation of all forces is not ensured, and if these problems are not eliminated by all authorities in the most meticulous detail, the greatest harm may result for our war economy.

I therefore ask you, in conclusion, to pay exacting attention to the following principles:

1. All technical matters or procedures relating to the administration of the labour service are the exclusive responsibility and competence of the General Plenipotentiary for the Labour Service, the agricultural offices, and labour offices.

2. All matters and tasks of propaganda, education, observation of political effects, and care, are the responsibility of:

a) outside industry: the Party;

b) inside commercial industry: the German Labour Front, the agricultural industries, the Office for Agricultural Policy.

3. The supply of food coupons, clothing ration cards, financial equalization and support, are the exclusive competence of the authorities or institutions responsible for the economy.

I ask the district leaders of the NSDAP, as my plenipotentiaries, to ensure harmonious methods of procedure, the best conceivable mutual agreement, and the most complete mutual information.

4. Meeting the challenges of military production is so important to the war effort that no consideration may be given even to the most important local or regional interests, or the most prominent challenges of the peace. Anyone who violates this must take the responsibility upon himself if German soldiers, in the struggle to decide the fate of the life of our people should lack weapons or munitions, synthetic gasoline or rubber, vehicles or airplanes.

I would, therefore, most sincerely as well as most emphatically like to make it a duty for all German men and women wishing to cooperate decisively in the labour service, to take the most heartfelt account of all these necessities, decisions, and measures, according to the old National Socialist principle:

Nothing for ourselves, everything for the Führer and his work, that is, for the future of our people!

Fritz Sauckel

* * *

Note: Under the 4th Hague Convention, the Germans were entitled to utilize lower-ranking prisoners of war and resistance members for their labour, and to conscript civilian labour "for the needs of the army of occupation"; what the latter actually means in practice is somewhat unclear. In view of the scope of Allied war crimes and atrocities, it seems frivolous to argue the matter. *De minimis non curat lex.*

THE MYTH OF
"A THOUSAND YEARS WILL PASS"

INTRODUCTION

I think we have all heard the following quotation from defendant Hans Frank at Nuremberg with relation to the alleged "extermination of the Jews" (a.k.a. the so-called "Hoaxoco$t").

"A thousand years will pass and still this guilt of Germany will not have been erased."

The "thousand-year" period referred to has already expired, according to the final statement of this same person, and thus no longer applies.

THIS IS WHAT FRANK SAID
ON DIRECT EXAMINATION

(Nuremberg Trial Transcript, 18 April 46, XII-13)

DR. SEIDL: Did you ever participate in the annihilation of Jews?

FRANK: I say "yes;" and the reason why I say "yes" is because, having lived through the 5 months of this trial, and particularly after having heard the testimony of the witness Hoess [!!!], my conscience does not allow me to throw the responsibility solely on these minor people. I myself have never installed an extermination camp for Jews, or promoted the existence of such camps; but if Adolf Hitler personally has laid that dreadful responsibility on his people, then it is mine too, for we have fought against Jewry for years; and we have indulged in the most horrible utterances – my own diary bears witness against me.

Therefore, it is no more than my duty to answer your question in this connection with "yes." A thousand years will pass and still this guilt of Germany will not have been erased.

Rudolf Hoess, victim of merciless British and American torture for the purpose of extracting false statements, Nuremberg.

THIS IS WHAT FRANK SAID FOUR MONTHS LATER IN HIS FINAL STATEMENT TO THE COURT

(FINAL STATEMENT, HANS FRANK 31 August 1946, *IMT* XXII, 383-385)

Adolf Hitler, the chief defendant, left no final statement to the German people and the world. Amid the deepest distress of his people he found no comforting word. He became silent and did not discharge his office as a leader, but went down into darkness, a suicide. Was it stubbornness, despair, or spite against God and man? Perhaps as though he thought: "If I must perish, then let the German people fall into the abyss also." Who will ever know?

We – and if I now use the term "we," then I mean myself and those National Socialists who will agree with me in this confession, and not those fellow-defendants on whose behalf I am not entitled to speak – we do not wish to abandon the German nation to its fate in the same way without a word; we do not wish to say simply, "Now you will just have to see how you can get along with this collapse which we have left you." Even now, perhaps as never before, we still bear a tremendous spiritual responsibility.

At the beginning of our way we did not suspect that our turning away from God could have such disastrous deadly consequences and that we would necessarily become more and more deeply involved in guilt. At that time we could not have known that so much loyalty and willingness to sacrifice on the part of the German people could have been so badly directed by us.

Thus, by turning away from God, we were overthrown and had to perish. It was not because of technical deficiencies and unfortunate circumstances alone that we lost the war, nor was it misfortune and treason. Above all, God pronounced and executed judgment on Hitler and the system which we served with minds far from God. Therefore, may our people, too, be called back from the road on which Hitler – and we with him – have led them.

I beg of our people not to continue in this direction, be it even a single step; because Hitler's road was the way without God, the way of turning from Christ, and, in the last analysis, the way of political foolishness, the way of disaster, and the way of death. His path became more and more that of a frightful adventurer without conscience or honesty, as I know today at the end of this Trial.

We call upon the German people, whose rulers we were, to return from this road which, according to the law and justice of God, had to lead us and our system into disaster and which will lead everyone into disaster who tries to walk on it, or continue on it, everywhere in the whole world.

Over the graves of the millions of dead of this frightful Second World War this state trial was conducted, lasting for many months, as a central, legal epilogue, and the spirits passed accusingly through this room.

I am grateful that I was given the opportunity to prepare a defense and justification against the accusations raised against me.

In this connection I am thinking of all the victims of the violence and horror of the dreadful events of war. Millions had to perish unquestioned and unheard. I surrendered my war diary, containing my statements and activities, in the hour when I lost my liberty. If I was really ever severe, then it was above all toward myself, at this moment when my actions in the war were made public.

I do not wish to leave any hidden guilt which I have not accounted for behind me in this world. I assumed responsibility on the witness stand for all those things for which I must answer. I have also acknowledged that degree of guilt which attaches to me as a champion of Adolf Hitler, his movement, and his Reich.

I have nothing to add to the words of my defense counsel.

There is still one statement of mine which I must rectify. On the witness stand I said that a thousand years would not suffice to erase the guilt brought upon our people because of Hitler's conduct in this war. Every possible guilt incurred by our nation has already been completely wiped out today, not only by the conduct of our war-time enemies towards our nation and its soldiers, which has been carefully kept out of this Trial, but also by the tremendous mass crimes of the most frightful sort which – as I have now learned – have been and still are being committed against Germans by Russians, Poles, and Czechs, especially in East Prussia, Silesia, Pomerania, and Sudetenland. Who shall ever judge these crimes against the German people?

I end my final statement in the sure hope that from all the horrors of the war and all the threatening developments which are already appearing everywhere, a peace may perhaps still arise in whose blessings even our nation may be able to participate. But it is God's eternal justice in which I hope our people will be secure and to which alone I trustfully submit.

FINAL COMMENT BY CARLOS W. PORTER

Back to the drawing board for the purveyors of eternal and sole German guilt. The Germans are no longer guilty of anything – if indeed they ever were – and are free to go about their business. Case dismissed.

I wonder what Frank would have said if he had realized that he had been hoodwinked by statements extracted under torture?

Plus ça change, plus la même chose.

INDEX

Documents 2430-PS, 120, 162
Documents PS-2542, 36
Dudak, Rudolf, 143, 145

E

Edeiken, 3, 71–76, 78, 80, 87, 92, 100, 102, 105
Enemy soldiers, 109, 111–12, 114
Euthanasia, 32–33
Evidence IPS document, 152–54
Extermination, 13, 15, 28, 31, 36, 40

F

Fourth Hague Convention, 75, 78–80, 89–90, 180
Fourth Hague Convention on Land Warfare, 73, 75–76
Führer, 14, 21–23, 208–12, 214–16, 218–19, 221

G

Gas chamber, 4, 35–36, 39, 41, 120, 141, 150, 159, 162, 171, 191–97
Gas vans, 35, 39
Geneva Conventions, 68, 74–75, 78–79, 96, 106, 110, 119
Geneva Prisoner of War Convention, 74–76, 79, 102, 180
German concentration camps, 9–10, 142, 146
German foreign policy, 7–8
German Labour Front, 211, 216, 218–19, 221

H

Hague Conventions, 67–68, 71–75, 78–80, 90, 92, 100, 106, 110, 222
Hague IV, 72–74, 76, 78, 84, 90
Hearsay
admissibility of, 119, 132
admissible, 120
written, 69
Hess, Rudolf, 72, 83, 98, 101
Hitler, 19, 24, 33, 65, 82–83, 225

Human flesh, 154, 169–70

Human skin, 4, 159, 198, 200

I

IMT, 5–6, 9–10, 16, 18–20, 77, 224

IMTFE (International Military Tribunal for the Far East), 132, 168–69, 171, 187

International Military Tribunal for the Far East. *See* IMTFE

J

Japan, 4, 75–76, 89, 103–4, 133, 168, 180, 188, 202–6

Japanese, 67–68, 74, 76, 101–2, 121–22, 126, 131, 154–55, 164, 168–69, 174–75, 178–80, 183–84, 186, 204–5

Japanese Atrocities, 4, 183, 186–87

Jewish Question, 19, 36, 39, 61, 63

Jews, 6, 10, 12, 15, 19, 29–31, 40, 48, 58–65, 139, 144, 194, 198–200, 223

JUSTICE JACKSON, 23–24

K

Kaltenbrunner, 16–18

L

Laws and customs of war, 66, 68, 78, 80–81, 93

LOGAN, 123, 125–32

M

Manstein, 5, 10–11, 13–16

Mauthausen, 36, 143, 145

Mukden, 4, 187–89

MYTH of JAPANESE ATROCITIES, 4, 183, 187

N

Neutrality, 67, 86, 103–4, 108, 134, 138

Non-combatants, 86, 107, 116–17

NSDAP, 211–12, 217, 220–21

Nuremberg, 36, 40, 44, 46, 72, 76, 79, 134,

www.ingramcontent.com/pod-product-compliance
Lightning Source LLC
Chambersburg PA
CBHW031951080426
42735CB00007B/349